AUCTION ACTION!

A SURVIVAL COMPANION FOR ANY AUCTION GOER

RALPH ROBERTS

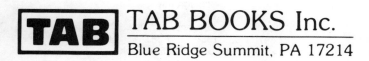

TAB BOOKS Inc.

Blue Ridge Summit, PA 17214

Notices

CompuServe is a registered trademark of CompuServe Information Services.
Delphi is a trademark of General Videotex Corporation.
FinalWord II is a trademark of Mark of the Unicorn.
Fisher-Price is a registered trademark of Fisher-Price Toys.
IBM is a registered trademark of International Business Machines, Inc.
Jacuzzi is a registered trademark of Jacuzzi Whirlpool Bath, Inc.
Source is a service mark of Source Telecomputing Corporation, a subsidiary
of The Reader's Digest Association.

FIRST EDITION
FIRST PRINTING

Copyright © 1986 by TAB BOOKS Inc.
Printed in the United States of America

Library of Congress Cataloging in Publication Data

Roberts, Ralph.
Auction action!

Bibliography: p.
Includes index.
1. Auctions.   I. Title.
HF5476.R63   1986   381′.1   86-14450
ISBN 0-8306-2752-9 (pbk.)

Contents

Acknowledgments   vi

Introduction   vii

Section I   General Information   1

1   Auction Action   3

The Joy and Magic of Auctions—Entertainment and Practical Values—Why Auctions?—Before All That

2   History of Auctions   13

The Roman Empire: Going Once, Going Twice . . . Sold!—England Makes a Bid for Auction Supremacy—The Auction Comes to America—Auctioning in the 19th Century—Antiauction Movement—Auctions Become Respectable—Back to the Present

3   How Auctions Work   24

How To Find an Auction—Going to Auction—Your Greatest Enemy—Preview Period—Tools of the Trade—Deciding on Your Bid—Getting a Bidder's Number—Restrictions—Bidding Process—Conclusion

4   Bidding Strategies   35

Bidding Signals—Attracting Attention—Opening Bid—Bid, Bid, Who's Got the Bid?—Multiple-Piece Lots—Bidding Tactics—The Right Time to Bid—Absentee Bids—Getting Started—Summing Up

5 Chicanery and Legal Aspects   **44**

Checking Out a New Auction—Getting the Best of a Dishonest Auctioneer—Avoid Bidding Against Yourself—Substitutions—Dealers Do It Too!—What's Your Recourse?

6 Knowledge: Your Most Potent Weapon   **54**

Books—Price Guides—Publications—Dealers and Museums—Antiques Enter the Space Age—Conclusion

7 Comfort for the Serious Bidder   **61**

Sitting Pretty—Bumbershoots and Other Mythical Creatures—Nectar of the Gods, It Ain't—Feast Fit for a King—Packing Materials—In Case of a Tie Bid—Friends—Conclusion

8 Good Morning, Colonel!   **67**

Call Me Colonel—Why Be an Auctioneer?—Getting Promoted to Colonel—Learning the Profession—What Do I Learn?—Summation

9 Selling Instead of Buying   **73**

Knowing the Market—The Right Auction House—Estate Sales—Fund-Raisers—Concluding Thoughts

Section II   Specific Auctions   **81**

10 Antiques and Collectibles   **83**

Furniture—Rugs and Other Orientalia—Glassware, Art Pottery, China—Folk Art—Other Areas—Provenance—Auction Report and Interviews with Experts—Conclusion

11 The Art of Buying Art   **95**

La Creme de la Creme—Importance of the Catalog—Dropping on Down the Scale—Summary

12 Autographs and Manuscripts   **101**

Interview with George Sanders—Conclusion

13 Getting It In Gear: Auto Auctions   **108**

Classic Automobile Auctions—Practical Car Auctions—Car Auction Dealerships—Turning off the Ignition

14 Bankruptcy/Going-Out-of-Business Auctions   **113**

Good Buys for You—Types of Forced Sales—Farm Sales—Summing Up

15 Commodity Auctions   **118**

Tobacco Auctions: The Ultimate Entertainment—Conclusion

16 Welcome to the Future: Computer Network Auctions   **121**

On-Line Auction—Conclusion

17 Estate Auctions   **126**

On-Site Insight—Good Buys at Estate Sales—Turn-of-the-Century Cabin Auctioned—Rain Fails to Dampen Auction—Conclusion

18 Government Surplus   **132**

General Services Administration—Department of Defense Auctions—Other Government Auctions—Conclusion

19 Livestock Auctions   **136**

Why Attend a Livestock Auction?—Buying and Selling Livestock—Horses—Rounding Up

20 Real Estate Auctions   **139**

Why Auction Real Estate?—Services of a Real Estate Auctioneer—Conclusion

21 Retail Auctions   **142**

Appendix A   Sources   **144**

Appendix B   Recommended Reading   **147**

Index   **148**

Acknowledgments

The author gratefully acknowledges all those who helped in the preparation of this book, with special thanks to:

My mother, who provided office space, coffee, and put up with the sometimes irascibility of a writer at work.

Phil Burrows, editor of *Carolina Antique News*, who made me a contributing editor and actually pays me to attend auctions.

To some other of my favorite editors: Tom Hoepf, *Antique Week/Tri-State Trader*; Nancy Adams, *Antiques Dealer*; Bill Haglund, *Collector's Journal*; Ginny Thompkins, *Joel Sater's Antiques & Auction News*; and Michael Jacobi, *Yesteryear*.

To Robert Bunn, at 86, the dean of Southern auctioneers.

To the many other auctioneers who patiently answered my multitude of questions and especially to Robert Brunk, Angus Davis, Harold DeBruhl, Bill Hagan, Terry and Sherry Hester, Jerry King, Cameron Long, Lee Long, Johnny Penland, Jerry Sluder, and Thad Woods. I salute you, Colonels!

To Bryan Eggers and the Delphi on-line Antiques Special Interest Group for bringing antiques and collectibles into the Space Age.

For Kim Tabor and Leslie Wenger, who believe in me.

And to my trusty Compaq computer, which held up under it all.

Introduction

You would be hard put to find a town or city anywhere in the United States and Canada that doesn't have numerous auctions throughout the year. Pick up the local newspaper; chances are at least one auction is scheduled for this very week within easy driving distance from your home. More likely there will be a whole string of listings.

Antiques, land and other real property, bankruptcy (alas, lots of those these days), retail goods, dealer sales, government surplus, automobile, industrial tool liquidation, art, livestock, commodities, estate auctions—all attract millions of happy auction goers each year.

You may be one of these fine people, or someone who just wants to find out more about auctions. This method of selling, which is thousands of years old, has a mystique, a liveliness about it that is absolutely addictive. Auctions are fun to attend. They can also be profitable if you have the basic knowledge to take advantage of the bargains and the foresight to avoid the pitfalls.

This, then, is meant to be a helpful and informative book for you, the auction goer. To be a bit less than modest here for a moment (since hiding one's light under a bushel doesn't sell books), my experience has made me particularly suited to do a book of this type. Having written on a regular basis in the last several years for most of the major collectibles-oriented publications, auctions have been of considerable interest and importance to me.

Additionally, as contributing editor for *Carolina Antique News*, my auction coverages have often been featured on the front page, having become a regular and popular feature. I have been getting more fan letters from these auction reports than from my fiction in national magazines—which perhaps says something about my fiction (no, please don't agree so fast now).

As to the other types of auctions in this book, it seems like I've been preparing to write such a helpful study of auctions all my life. Government surplus, livestock (born and raised on a farm), commodities, estate, antique, wholesale, retail—I've been to many auctions in all these categories over the years.

All this aside, I really wanted to do this particular book, feeling it will be helpful to a great number of people. Auctions can be costly if the basic rules mentioned previously are not observed. Knowledge is your most potent tool at an auction, and we will look at the various ways of successfully analyzing and bidding in auction situations. The various terms and their meaning will be covered, as will the such things as the auctioneer's liability in the case of misrepresented or defective merchandise.

This book is structured to appeal to several levels of auction goers. The novice will find within these pages how to pick worthwhile auctions, how to sign in and get a number, how to bid, the way payment is made, what the often-used term *as is* really means, and much more. The immediate auction goer will find information on bidding strategies, how to use the preview period to best advantage, how advance and absentee bids work, and much more. For the advanced bidder, there will be money-saving information on how to detect fakes and reproductions, how to research authenticity before and during an auction, how to tell if an auctioneer is pulling bids *off the wall* (illegal in most states) or bidding for himself (legal, for example, in South Carolina), and much, much more.

What's more, I'll do my level best to make all this information fun to read. So, why waste time? On with the book!

Section One:

General Information

PUBLIC AUCTION

Pu...

AN EXCITING SIX DA...

Davis Auction Service is pleased to announce they have an
auction the contents of a three story building full of fine an...
that has been in storage for eight years along with person...

Auction will be held in seven (7) sessions as follows:

Tuesday, January 21, at 7:00 p.m.
Wednesday, January 22, at 7:00 p.m.
Thursday, January 23, at 7:00 p.m.

Auction will be held at Main Street & Coffee Street
are as follows:

Furniture
Teak & Ivory Coromundel Screens (3)
Marble Top Tables & Wash Stands
16 Dining Tables in Oak, Walnut, Etc.
Desks, All Sorts of Buffetts
China Closets, Console Tables
Court Cupboard, Heavily Carved
Carved Bookcases
3 Pump Organs (1 ...
Chi...

Gilbert J. Hollifield Auction & Realty Co.
Hwy. 70 W. - P.O. Box 939
Marion, N. C. 28752

ABSOLUTE AUCTI...
April 5, 1986

PUBLIC ESTATE
AUCTION

Saturday, April 12, 1986
10:00 a.m.

Estate of the late Mr. Robert J. MConaty
12 Conway Drive, Greenville, S.C.
Conway Drive is behind Hidden Lake Apartments
off Pleasantburg Drive, Rt. 291

Auction Will Be Held Absolute At The Above Conway Address
TERMS: Cash or Good Check
PREVIEW: Friday, April 11th from 12:00 p.m. till 5:00 p.m.

CHINA, GLASS DECORATIVE & COLLECTIBLE ITEMS: Royal Doulton Toby & Oliver
Twist Mug, 4 Planters Peanut 75th Anniversary Jars, 2 Large Size Beswick Tobys, Delft
Planter, Signed Hawkes Etched Glass with Sterling Lid, Sterling Compote, Sterling
Flatware, Lots of Costume Jewelry, Musical Figurines, Venetian Glass Pieces, Majolica
Cat, Paperweights, Ruby Pinch Bottle & Stopper, Black Iron Fire Insurance Marker, Seth
Thomas Steeple Chime Clock, Service for 12 and Serving Pieces Noritake China,
Assorted Pen Knives, Lenox Swans, Nut Dishes and Vase and Leaf Server, Group of
Miscellaneous Foreign Coins.

PICTURES AND LAMPS: "Common Wild Duck" Framed Print: Curier/Ives "Clipper-
ship" Sweepstakes Print, Black/White Framed Theatre Poster, String Art Framed
Piece, Limited Edition Signed Print R.J. McDonald #887 of 1776, Pr. Duck Decoy
Prints, Several Wall Barometers, Many Other Oils and Prints, Brass Electric Oil Lamp,
Pr. China Based Table Lamps, Brass Double Student Lamp, Brass Floor Lamp, Brass
Double Student Floor Lamp, Pr. Satin Glass Lamps, Other Lamps.

FURNITURE: Pine Two Door Cabinet, Rush Bottom Pegged Ladder Back Chair,
Handmade Large Round Table with Lazy Susan, Upholstered Lounge Chairs, Small
Desk and Chair, Library Table, Maple Entrance Hall Cupboard/Table, Pr. Oak End
Tables, Oak Coffee Table, Rocker Recliner, Tweed 3 Cushion Sleep Sofa and Matching
Chair, Birch Student Desk and Chair, Tweed 2 Cushion Sleep Sofa, Maple Captains
Chair, 6 Drawer Cherry Chest, Twin 7 Drawer Cherry Dressers with Mirrors, Bedside
Tables, Double Bed, Metal Office Desk, Wooden Desk, Painted Chest of Drawers and
Small Table.

OTHER MISCELLANEOUS: Quasar Microwave, Old Perfection Oil Heater, Morse
Portable Sewing Machine, Bell and Howell Floor Model TV, Stereo AM/FM, Admiral
Stereo in Maple Cabinet with Freestanding Speaker, Fireplace Tools, Portable Motorola
TV, 12" Penncrest TV, Fisher Stereo/Radio Record Player, Sylvania Portable TV,
Projector, Screen, Tripods, Minolta Camera and Accessories, Air Rifle, Binoculars,
Many Pots, Pans, Kitchen Accessories, Linen, etc.

Many Telephones, Calculators, File Cabinets, Typewriter, and Miscellaneous Office
Equipment.

AUCTION

Unreserved Auction

Personal property from five local estates,
private collections, and other consignments
Saturday, March 22, 1986, 10 A.M.
Preview Friday, March 21, 7-9 p.m., 2 hours prior to sale
Asheville Country Day School,
1345 Hendersonville Rd., Asheville, North Carolina

Partial Listing

Furniture and accessories: Federal (Southern) 2 drawer
server with scroll cut skirt, pair 19th century William and
Mary style wing chairs, French Art Deco armoire, English
Hepplewhite chest, 6 drawer chest with overmantle, pair Louis XVI style loveseats,
mahogany breakfront, pair Louis XVI style loveseats,
butler tray on stand, 5 drawer walnut chest with marble
top, English Art Deco dining room suite, drop leaf
Sheraton style dining table, set 6 shield back chairs, carved oak sideboards, 18th century style bedroom suite with
queen size bed, lingerie chest, chest of drawers, stand,
drop leaf dining table, 6 chairs, Chippendale style camel
back sofa, Queen Anne style leather wing chair, French
style bookcase, 2 stack lighted bookcase, early Bible box, 3
drawer sewing stand, many other chests and tables,
rosewood barometer, early 19th century rosewood melo-
dion, copper lavabo (dolphin), brass spy glasses, compass,
nautical protractor, nautical sign, brass accessories including candlestands, fender, sconce, over 20 clocks including wooden works (unrestored) by Seth Thomas,
Thomas Barnes, O. Hopkins, 8 day mantle clocks, many
paintings and prints including works signed R. H. Collins,
C. P. Dietsch, W. McClean, B. de Blois, R. Nippress, W.
T. Richards, W. Towne, M. ...

Glass, porcelain, and related: Large Stuben vase, 106 pieces
(service for 12) English china, Limoges tea service, custard
set, 33 piece set pattern glass (pleat and panel), Venetian
glass, Cambridge, figurines, stemware, Art glass vase, Art
Deco compote, cut glass, much more.

Silver gold, and related: $5, $10, $20 gold pieces, fine cameo
tiara with fitted case owned by Gen. Johnson Pettigrew,
Sterling holloware including 3 piece tea service, bowl,
basket, dresser pieces, water pitcher, purses, over 200
pieces Sterling flatware including 47 piece set in fitted
case, 14K Tiffany earrings, 14K, 18K rings, stickpin, gold
thimble, Sterling cigar cutter, misc. jewelry, ornate plated
ware, Kirk Repousse berry spoon, much more.

Other: 18th century style upholstered chairs, child's pull
wagon, down comforters, Planisphere (1871), frames,
chandaliers, meerschaum pipe, lamps, mirrors of many
styles, child's Chippendale style slant front desk, marble
bench, tribal artifacts (Africa, New Guinea) weapons,
...ield, drum, early Coleman lantern, old telephone, post
...rds, fans, daguerreotypes, set 5 ice cream chairs, boxes
...ens, books including art and antiques, leather bound
...oks, penny slot machine, furniture of all descriptions,
...terprise Coffee grinder, much more.

...ms of Sale: Cash or approved check. Buyers unknown
... to us, must present proof of credit. All items sold by
... program without reserve.

... Plan for a full day. Over 500 lots will be sold. Food
...available. Preview will not open before 7:00 p.m. Delivery
... service available.

...tions: 2.5 miles South of Intersection of I-40 and
...25 south on U.S. 25 South (Hendersonville Rd.)

Auction Schedule
...4 Asheville Country Day School
...l 30 year private collection antiques (contents of home)
... Johnson City, Tenn.

...vices, Inc.
...s
...na 28787

...54-6846
...nd Tennessee

LEE LONG
REAL ESTATE AND AUCTION COMPANY
Candler, North Carolina 28715

ESTATE
AUCTION

Saturday, October 5, 1985 at 10AM
(preview: Friday, October 4th 3-6 pm)

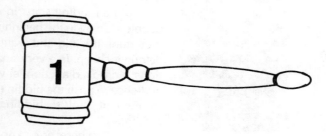

Auction Action

Auctions have been around for thousands of years. You cannot name an object people wear, drink, eat, covet, enjoy, live in, admire, love, need, or use which has not been sold at auction at some time or another. Even people themselves, for century upon century, went up on the block.

From sparkling little stones to towering, larger-than-life statues, from common grass-roofed huts to mighty empires, the auctioneer's hammer has marked winning bids on them all. From mundane chamber pots to the most exquisite egg-shell-thin porcelain art vases worth tens of thousands, from ratty and torn old comic books at mere pennies apiece to the Guttenberg Bible for millions of dollars, all these and more have gone to the highest bidder. Today, the auction marketplace is even more vigorous and popular than ever.

You can buy it all at auction: a house to live in, antiques to decorate it, a refrigerator and stove to provide a means of keeping and cooking the produce bought at another auction, even a truck to get it all home in. Carpets, lamps, chairs, tables, cameras, stereos, a lawn mower, a birdcage and a bird to put in it, bundles of old newspapers for the bird's convenience, a goat to replace the lawn mower that quit working, the list goes on and on. You can buy anything at auction if you look long enough.

What's more, you can, with the knowledge provided in this book and a little perseverance on your part, save lot of money by shopping in this manner. Except on that lawn mower, of course—that was a mistake. Just don't hang out the laundry close to the goat. Which brings up something else that will help you survive auctions: a sense of humor.

You really are able to get some fantastic bargains at auctions. On the other hand, you can also pay three times retail for something that K-Mart has on special just down the road, or you can buy a piece of junk, like the hypothetical lawn mower just discussed. Knowledge is even more important than money in attending auctions. Make sure the pockets of your brain are stuffed with it. Then you will be ready to pounce on those wondrous finds that everyone else thinks are mere junk.

Fig. 1-1. Colonel Thad Woods of Waynesville, North Carolina holds forth at his weekly country auction.

The sense of humor is important for many reasons. Auctioneers normally move hundreds of lots through an auction, spending just a few seconds on each. Even an extremely knowledgeable gavel wielder cannot possibly know the facts about every item. So he will fall back on jargon and canned sayings, especially in small-town auction houses, which are the most fun—and potentially the most profitable to you.

It might go something like this some night during one of these weekly auctions. Let's say you're at an antiques sale and a bookcase comes up on the block. The auctioneer is already so hoarse he can barely talk after a long night of moving pieces as fast as he can knock them down "sold." He's already broken two gavels doing this.

"She's a good one, she is folks. Old as the hills. Oak, I think it's oak. Better not let this one get away. It is oak, ain't it, Marve?"

Now ol' Marve is the auctioneer's assistant who works days as the town drunk and Friday nights at the auction house. He takes considerable pride in his daytime profession, but could care less about all this old junk. He probably can't even spell *antiques* and he and his buddy are in a strain

anyway, holding the heavy bookcase up where the bidders can see it. He just wants to get shut of it.

"Yeah, yeah it's oak," Marve grunts.

"Knew it!" says the auctioneer, as if Marve is some kind of internationally recognized expert from one of the big prestigious auction houses in New York, like Christie's or Sotheby's. "Old too, ain't it Marve."

"Yeah," Marve mumbles, "real old. Old as the hills."

So the bidding starts in earnest, with a lot of people bidding in the beginning stages just because they think it is old and want to take a chance on getting it cheap. In a very small percentage of auctions, a crooked auctioneer will have a shill in the audience to push the bidding up more. Regardless, excitement builds, bidding engendering more bidding.

Here's where prior knowledge is important, too. In the preview period you've examined the bookcase. Let's say you found it to be just a common wooden one maybe 15 years old, and that the only relationship to oak it bears is that they both come from trees. In this event, you can just sit on your hands and chortle merrily as the bidding rages and a $20 bookcase sells for $75 or $100 (and this happens all the time).

On the other hand, suppose that during the preview period you examine the bookcase and discover that it is oak. What's more, on one side is the famous incised orb and cross trademark of the Roycrofters. Armed with prior knowledge, you know that the Roycroft shops turned out some of the most collectible pieces in the mission oak style around the turn of the century.

When the bidding starts, you wait a bit then join in. You let them push you to $75 before finally winning it. Everybody turns around to see what idiot bought a $20 bookcase for $75. You have the grace to look slightly embarrassed and abashed.

"It's real old," Marve assures you as he helps to get it in the back of your station wagon, with you fervently hoping there are no open flames around to set off his breath.

The antiques dealer who gives you $500 for

it the next day also thinks you're an idiot. After all, you just gave him or her a beautiful example of Roycroft that he is sure will bring $800 retail, if he can just find the right collector.

Sometimes it pays to be thought an idiot.

Knowledge, that's the key. Knowledge and a sense of humor will carry you triumphantly (or at least enjoyably) through auction after auction.

More about all this soon, but first—why are auctions so much fun? Many people go week after week and just sit on their hands, never even bidding, much less buying anything. It can't be for the coffee, auction coffee is notorious. Why do they go? Why do I go?

THE JOY AND MAGIC OF AUCTIONS

The auction is not only one of the oldest methods of buying and selling in the world, it is also the most fun. As I said in the Introduction, this method of selling, has a mystique, a liveliness about it that is absolutely addictive.

Many components go into making up the wonder and the mystique of the auction, not the least of which is the thrill of the hunt. The very survival of our ancestors depended totally upon hunting and gathering food. The man who chased down and killed the biggest, juiciest saber-toothed rabbit, or the woman who found and dug up the tenderest, heftiest edible root were the most admired and a shoo-in to be mayor of the home cave.

Way down deep in all of us, there still exists the *hunting* instinct, clamoring to be let out and run rampant. There are many ways that the modern civilized person deals with these deep yearnings. Some still take to the woods, fields, and rivers for hunting and fishing. Why else would a grown man pay several hundred dollars for equipment and spend freezing hours in the wilds merely to bag one scrawny little brown rabbit if there wasn't some inner compulsion forcing him to do it? Why would someone float a loan (pun, as always, intended) for a $6,000 bass boat in order to land a 3-pound anemic fish if there wasn't something inside crying out for him to do so?

Many a wife has asked exactly these questions, but I am not making fun of people who hunt and fish. They do it because it feels right, because it fulfills this strong need within them, because it's fun.

Most of us, whether we realize it or not, channel this hunting and gathering instinct into other areas. The housewife who spends hours shopping, who clips coupons and stalks through the grocery store in search of the elusive spotted-tailed bargain, is a gatherer/hunter *par excellence*. The man who goes all over town harassing hardware clerks almost beyond endurance just to get the best buy on a gallon of paint to do the basement family room is a hunter. Nod respectfully to him; he just bagged a Sherwin-Williams.

Fig. 1-2. A cane-bottomed and -backed rocking chair goes up on the auction block. Such furniture items, commonplace to previous generations, are now in demand by collectors and decorators, fetching high prices.

Fig. 1-3. Cameron Long (next to the pillar with his hand up) and his father Lee (seated next to him and facing forward) are a father-and-son auctioneer team that is very successful.

We all, whether we admit it or not, have this hunting instinct. One reason auctions and other endeavors such as flea markets and junk stores are so popular is that they provide an outlet for our expression of this internal compulsion.

The thrill of the chase is wondrous once it is backed with a little knowledge. Finding a $350 Rookwood vase in with the junk pottery and getting it for a $4 bid, or paying $2 for a box lot of books because you know it contains a $4,000 first edition of Edgar Rice Burroughs' *A Princess of Mars*—this is the game that we auction goers stalk by the dim light of the auctioneer's chant.

To be sure, such windfalls are the exception rather than the rule, but they happen often enough to keep us happily casting about for the spoor of such juicy, mouth-watering game. Whether we realize it or not, this hunting instinct is perhaps the strongest reason that many of us become so firmly hooked on attending auctions of all types, but there are others as well.

Competition no doubt grew out of the hunting urge, it being the desire to bag the biggest game, to be admired by our fellow cave dwellers—er,—that is, neighbors—as astute and

competent. Competition is by no means bad. It spurs us on to excellence, to greater heights, to the achievement of things we once thought impossible.

This competitive playing of the auction game—and, indeed, auctions can be both a spectator sport and one in which you can carry the ball to the cheers of onlookers—should never be taken too seriously (as many do where the almighty dollar is involved). Instead, armed with knowledge, you can while away many pleasant hours frequenting auction sales of all types.

Yes, you can and will make money if you do your homework, regardless of what is being auctioned off. Yet, look upon profit as much as a means of keeping score as anything else.

Regardless of whether you play the game just to rack up a pleasing score for your own amusement or to make money, competition will always be a major component of the sport. In most cases, competition will be friendly—auction goers are among the nicest, most mature people in the world, at least until the bidding starts. Seriously, auction folk are nice, warm, outgoing human beings.

There are a good many reasons for this, some of which has to do with the self-discipline and humorous attitude that it takes for success in this field. Also much knowledge will be bandied about in authoritative tones during the *previews* (the chance you get to look over the merchandise before the auction starts). As an aside, hearsay during previews is not the most reliable source of information. In the case of antiques especially, get your knowledge from books, the many fine periodicals in the field, museums, and experts at seminars. Do not take someone's word at an auction, no matter how well intentioned he might be.

Knowledge is a theme you will find recurring frequently in this book. The appreciation for knowledge is absolutely the single most important gift I can impart to you within these pages. Remember, though, this book is only a starting point, an introduction to auctions and the techniques and strategies for being successful in them. Follow up my words with more specialized writings into the type of auction that you want to pursue.

Back on the track now of the joy and magic of attending auctions. *Companionship* is the third reason that auctions are so wonderful. Competition with strangers is not all that much fun—it pales after a while—but competition with our friends is a different story. Friendly competition, that is.

People band together for a variety of reasons, but a common interest is usually the strongest. In my work as a writer I cross a lot of boundaries that other people may not even realize are there. It has always struck me as amazing how incredibly similar various groups are. Such widely diverse happenings as an amateur radio "hamfest," a science fiction fandom convention, a Western film festival, a religious retreat, and the various types of auctions all follow the same general rules. Understand these rules and you can easily find your way around and understand what's going on. It's uncanny—like there's some universal rule governing all the situations.

Those who collect stamps, coins, autographs, vintage automobiles, antiques, comics, or whatever all make acquaintance of and form friendships with persons of like interest. Name any of thousands of such hobbies, professions, avocations, jobs, religions, etc. and you will find groups of friends banded together with the same unifying factor. In essence people all join for the same reason; companionship. It's just that the excuses for doing so are all different. I've always found this occurrence a bit awesome and wonderful.

This fundamental reason for gathering together applies as strongly to auctions as to any other pursuit. People who enjoy the same pursuits enjoy the company of like persons. As you start to attend auctions regularly, you will begin to notice familiar faces, recognizing other fervent auction goers like yourself. You'll strike up conversations with these excellent fellow enthusiasts and, before you know it, they will be expecting you to buy them a cup of coffee (who ever said there was no price on friendship?)

It is wonderful, the joy and verve that human

Fig. 1-4. A Rookwood vase by Elizabeth Barret Jensen, art deco design from 1929 with a mat finish is worth about $600.

Fig. 1-5. The ability to recognize unique items when they come up at auction is important. This tiny chest of drawers is not a toy but a nineteenth-century salesman's sample.

tion world. Sitting starch-stiff at a Christie's auction and watching a dapper English dandy suavely twitch his bids on an original Rembrandt in hundred thousand dollar increments is almost as much fun as cheering on gentleman in overalls at a country antiques auction as he, red-faced and puffing, defends his honor and his way of life by outlasting a Yankee dealer to take a nineteenth-century flat iron for $45. The fact that the dealer was canny enough to drop out when the price passed a reasonable retail level, of course, has not one whit to do with honor.

As an aside, pride and the type of honor just described has no place in a logical auction strategy. During the course of this book I'll go into this facet in much detail. The British gent might be bidding in $100K increments, but you can bet your crumpets he knows to the pound sterling how high to go. The man in the country auction simply let himself be outsmarted, and the loss came out of his pocket.

Seeing stories like these unfold make auctions tremendous fun. Part of the attraction at an auction, or any human excuse for grouping together, is to stand around and talk about those who aren't there and those who are out of earshot. We like to to watch people and what they do. It's entertaining.

To this, at an auction, we can add the mystique of the moment. Any auction is a happening. The big, fancy ones in New York have a restrained elegance about them, but you can sense the underlying excitement, the tenseness of the major players as they civilly jockey for position. The lift of an eyebrow, the muted clearing of a throat, the brief flash of a Mona Lisa smile—all take on great significance to the observer, if not to the participants themselves.

Country auctions, by and far my favorite, have much more of a carnival, a festive air about them. You expect the sound of steam organs and the smell of cotton candy and roasted peanuts—and at some, you get them. Regular weekly auctions are the tops of these because they also have a regular cast of characters.

The setting for this grandest of shows, the gen-

relationships add to any endeavor. Having friends who enjoy auctions just as much as you makes going to auctions all the more exciting. You'll have somebody to sit next to, to punch in the ribs and whisper things like, "You see that idiot pay $75 for a $20 bookcase?"

So there we have three major reasons to attend auctions: gratification of the hunting instinct, the urge to compete, and companionship. Are there others? You bet and we'll cover many of them during the course of this book, but these are the majors. They are nothing to be ashamed of, and you don't even have to understand them to enjoy auctions, yet, they are why you do.

Enough of profundities now and on with more easily comprehended incentives to make the auction scene your scene.

ENTERTAINMENT AND PRACTICAL VALUES

Auctions are entertaining in many ways. The first and foremost—as is true in every field of human endeavor—is the people themselves. We never seen to tire of watching ourselves, and an auction offers plenty of opportunity for people-watching.

This is true from the top to bottom of the auc-

uine weekly country auction, is usually some nondescript building in a poorer section of town, or a free-standing, low-rent edifice out in the boondocks somewhere. Auctioneers on this level are not getting rich; they have to keep their overheads down.

Come Friday or Saturday evening, these decrepit structures take on a new life. Like the old high school gym on Prom Night that is transported from the realm of smelly sweat socks to an enchanted fairyland of colored bunting swaying in dimly lit golden-glowing wonder, courtesy of Mrs. Smith's art class, the auction site is transformed. This is the time when you first get to meet Bozo.

You know Bozo is at the auction because, in positioning his car to best advantage in case he wants to leave early, he has blocked off about six other spaces. These six spaces are, naturally, the only ones left by this time. So you have to park a hundred yards down the road and walk up. Bozo greets you at the door, slaps you on the back, and says how great it is to see you again. You take him over to the concession stand and buy him a cup of coffee. Auction coffee being notoriously horrible, this is a fitting revenge.

The spirit of the moment is upon you, though, and you leave Bozo manfully choking down his coffee and head for the merchandise display. The hum of dozens of conversations are in your ears as you ford away through excited humanity to the front (or back, or side) of the auction house.

This is where the marvel of a country auction really intensifies. For there, stacked against the wall, laid out haphazardly on rickety tables, or bravely standing on their own are the wonders of the universe. Objects of magic and beauty, raiments of light and implements of unknown purpose, treasure of the ages and the recovered hoards of ancient miser kings. Junk! Wondrous, lovely, delightful, fantastic junk!

Thank the Great One in the Sky that this is so, that country auctions are filled with junk, with the castoffs and leavings of every generation from *now* back to *then,* from artifacts snatched only yesterday out of a city sanitary landfill to genuine eighteenth-century folk art. Thank the Great One, for this is your joy and your financial salvation.

Which brings us from entertainment to practi-

Fig. 1-6. This selection of pewter items was offered at a recent auction, with several pieces bringing in excess of $100 each.

Fig. 1-7. Auctions can be good places to pick up Roseville. This "Dutch" tankard sold for $45 in a North Carolina auction. A set of three Roseville "Mostique" vases brought just $70; a "Donatello" bowl, $30; and a "Bridge" pitcher with a small crack went for $30. All were good prices, allowing the buyers room to make a nice profit.

cal values for a moment. Why is there so much junk in country auctions? It's because most people who attend come to be entertained and don't bother to read the many fine books and periodicals that impart flood tides of information in the antiques and collectibles fields.

Also, to be fair, what is junk to you and me might truly be a wonder to behold for someone else. Take Bozo, for example. Bozo has the largest collection of Elvis portraits painted on black velvet in his whole end of the state. If one comes up on the block (and down South it surely will), don't try to bid against Bozo. He'll either outlast you or

drop out when an unreasonable level is reached, leaving you holding the bag... er... painting.

Knowledge, knowledge, knowledge. Say that word to yourself over and over. Roll it around your tongue and taste it. Delicious, satisfying, savory knowledge. That's what you need at an auction, especially these fascinating country auctions.

There are gems in with the dreck, gold down in the dirt, buried treasure and hidden wealth, but you must be able to recognize it when you stumble across it. A good starting point, if you are unfamiliar with antiques and collectibles, is Emyl Jenkins' excellent book, *Why You're Richer Than You Think* (Rawson, Wade/1982). Jenkins is a professional antiques appraiser and a well-known writer in the collectibles field. Her book concerns the many valuable items that most folk consider to be just worthless trash.

"Throw out those ugly old plates, Herbert, I got these great, new, yellow plastic ones on sale at K-Mart." Herbert dutifully does this and someone scrounges them out of the dump (the unbroken ones at least) and takes them to Mad Dog Ivan's Auction House. Mad Dog doesn't know (or much care) what they are either. You, of course, recognize vintage Blue Willow and get 14 plates for a $1 each.

You gloat quietly, knowing these beautiful plates book out at over $20 apiece. Herbert and his wife are the real losers, eating their hash off modern gaudy abortions instead of the elegant Blue Willow that was once prized by nobility. They lose the soul, the magic, the sense of being one with history that antiques provide—accepting instead lifeless substitutes stamped out on some arrogant machine the week before in the hundreds of thousands.

Herbert, by the way, is Bozo's father-in-law and Bozo knows where the plates came from (being the one that dug them out of the landfill in the first place) and tells you what an idiot you are to have paid a buck each for that trash. You give him all the respect he deserves—none—and continue to carefully wrap your prizes in old newspaper for the gentle, loving trip home.

In the antiques and collectibles field, it pays

to have at least one current price guide available, maybe even carry it in your car where you can slip out and consult it during the preview period. There are several good ones; among the best in a general guide are Schroeder's, Warman's, and Kovel's. They are readily available at most bookstores. If you specialize, say in glassware or primitive furniture, there are more comprehensive guides in those areas.

Knowledge, then, may be said to consist of three phases. You must first realize that what might superficially appear to be junk is indeed valuable. Next—through reading articles and books, examining authenticated examples in shops and museums, and becoming thoroughly familiar with the areas you choose to specialize in (for none of us can ever know it all, alas)—you enable yourself to recognize the valuable, separating the wheat from the chaff. Thirdly, you must know the current market value, using this data to formulate your bidding strategy.

Because, let's be realistic, other people can read also. If you're not the only one to joyfully realize that a dusty old vase is an authentic Roseville, then a spirited contest can ensue during the actual auction. If you have troubled to check out market value, you know this fine example of art pottery made in Zanesville, Ohio, is worth $300. It stands to reason that paying more than that for it is not in your best interest, so drop out at $275 or $290. The person you're bidding against will probably get it for $350 or so.

The reason he will pay more is that your initial contest has drawn others bravely into the fray. They don't know why such a, to them, grungy old pot is worth so much, but the fact that you and someone else seem to think so is enough, like waving a red flag to Ferdinand the Bull. If Bozo has money in his pockets, he might even outlast your competitor, the other knowledgeable bidder, and take the piece for $375 or $400.

On the other hand, Bozo might not be totally a bozo. If he should pay more than current market value and treat the piece as an investment, holding onto it for 10 or 15 years, then he might turn a tidy profit.

Roseville pieces seem to fall within this category of "good investment." Collector interest (the true determining factor in market value for any class of items)—has remained strong albeit fluctuating, for Roseville art pottery. We now seem to be coming out of a waning period into one of increasing activity. So you might want to familiarize yourself with Roseville's many patterns and marks. In pottery and glass, marks are the maker's and/or artists names and/or symbols and are usually located on the piece's bottom. Pick the item up and turn it over—there could be treasure buried there!

Generally, however, current market value is the safest indicator to go by. Here you must learn to exert discipline over yourself. Once the level of bidding passes that line, you stop and sit on your hands. This sounds awfully simple, but it takes practice when you are caught up in the liveliness of an auction in progress.

Let's sum up this discussion here of the entertainment and practical values of auctions. Essentially, *any* auction is a happening, a lively gathering of people, a place where the very atmosphere seems electrically charged. Auctions are interesting, entertaining, exciting. Even if you never bid, the fascination can keep you entranced literally for hours.

Yet there also exists the practical side of auctions. You can make money. With a little effort on your part to become knowledgeable in the areas covered within a particular type of auction, you can easily profit on a regular and consistent basis. Again, if you are willing to invest in yourself, auctions are the best method of buying and selling yet devised.

Auctions, quite simply, are loads of fun and you can make money. As the saying goes in my part of the country, "it's purely flat out the doggone most fun you can have with your clothes on."

TYPES OF AUCTIONS

What precisely is an auction? An *auction* is an event featuring the rapid selling of items based on competitive bids from a varying sized group of individuals, normally in person but sometimes also via written communication or telephone. This technique lends itself very well to moving large accumulations of merchandise that are too cumbersome for one store to handle or, as in the case of real estate or livestock, are too big or messy to have inside. (If you have ever visited a farm, you will quickly comprehend the incredible wisdom of the latter).

Large collections amassed over a person's lifetime, estates consisting of a complete house and furnishings, bankruptcy sales where all the inventory and fixtures in a business must go, 54 Tennessee walking horses, or a 100-acre piece of property broken down into 1-acre lots—these are some of the things that really work well for the seller when they are auctioned off. The reason is simple logic.

Auctions excel at selling things fast! Take the bankruptcy auction as an example. A business that goes under will still have many hundred of items left on the premises: unsold stock (after all, one of the reasons it failed), shelving, file cabinets, office desks, cash registers, typewriters, handtrucks, tools, a myriad of things. Since the firm is bankrupt, obviously it is unable to continue paying the rent to house this stuff. The owner of the building will also want it cleared out so that he can rent it to someone else.

Compound this situation with creditors anxious to recoup at least part of the money left owing them, not to mention the IRS hanging around to make sure it gets a heaping helping, and you have a good many reasons why the sale must be fast. An auction is the answer. An auction company is engaged, brochures are made up and mailed out, and advertisements are placed in various newspapers and periodicals.

People arrive for the preview period—the day before, an hour or two prior to the auction, or both—and prowl around the building, checking the tagged items against the descriptions on the brochures. They make cryptic notes to themselves on what they want to bid on and how high they will go.

The auction starts up and zips along with the auctioneer devoting only 30 to 60 seconds to each piece, assistants and bidders striving bravely to keep up. By four or five in the afternoon, the building is cleared and all items are sold and awaiting pickup. That's how fast an auction can be. On the other hand, trying to have a going-out-of-business sale might take days, weeks, or even months, with buyers and gawkers trickling in haphazardly.

In less logical moments, you sometimes must wonder if auctioneers don't practice wizardry the way crowds materialize for auctions and the thousands of dollars that change hands in such short intervals of time. Magic, it's got to be magic—the nice wondrous white magic like the Good Witch of the West produced for Dorothy and Toto.

Several categories of merchandise, by a combination of traditional usage and the kind of practical expediency just mentioned, are more likely to be sold at auctions than others. These are the general types that we will cover in Section II of this book. Each individual type of auction has its own advantages and pitfalls, as well as the general ones common to all auctions.

Some of you will want to specialize in one type of auction or another. However, we'll cover all of the major categories of sales in which the auctioneer chants, the gavel falls, and a successful bidder antes up and takes possession of his buy. In the case of mail or telephone auctions, the gavel might be figurative, but the closing of the bids is the same no matter how effected. If the auctioneer calls your number, you bought it!

BEFORE ALL THAT

Before we get to all that good stuff, we have some preliminary information to get out of the way. Chapter 2 concerns the history of auctions and, while not all that necessary from a practical standpoint, will give you an insight into, and an appreciation for, auction traditions and usages. Chapters 3 through 9 do cover the practical and important things you'll need to know for any sort of auction and they'll speak for themselves. So, without further ado, let's forge steadily onward into the wondrous world of auctions!

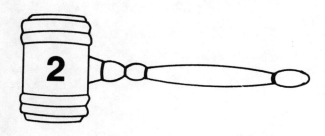

History of Auctions

An auction, of course, is a proceeding at which people are invited to compete for the purchase of merchandise or other objects by successful offers of increasing sums. They have been around literally from the dawn of recorded history, and the advantages of this method of buying and selling were as obvious to early cultures as they are to us today.

Herodotus, the ancient Greek historian, described a custom that prevailed in Babylonian villages in which maidens were disposed of in an annual auction that married them to the highest bidder.[1] Because the Babylonians took much of their social customs and mores from preceding cultures such as Ur, its allied city states, and the Sumerians before that, it is safe to say that the institution of the auction predates the civilization of Babylonia by well over 1,000 years, which would make it at least around 3,000 to 7,000 years old!

Although little documentation exists on these auctions in the Fertile Crescent, there is much more information available on those the Romans held

a few hundred years later.

The *Guinness Book of World Records* claims incorrectly that the largest auction ever held occurred in Anchorage, Alaska, on September 11, 1969 for 450,858 acres of the oil-bearing North Slope. Also mentioned is the all-time-high single bid of $72,277,133 made by the Amerada Hess-Getty Oil consortium for an oil lease on just 2,560 acres (that's $28,233 per acre).

Yet these pale in significance, proportionally, to what the Romans did. They sold the entire known civilized world at auction!

THE ROMAN EMPIRE:
GOING ONCE, GOING TWICE . . . SOLD!

The auction mode of selling was first used by the Roman legions for the disposal of military spoils of war among soldiers grouped behind a spear thrust into the ground. Because of this symbol, such sales came to be called *auctio sub hasta*, meaning "under the spear," the basis from which the word *auction* originated. The sign of the spear was af-

[1]Book i. 196

Fig. 2-1. It is the job of auction assistants to display lots being bid on and to help the auctioneer recognize everyone bidding.

terward put up at all sorts of auctions, and the name remained long after the signal was no longer in use.

At auctions in Rome, for which the permission of a magistrate was always needed, a spear was fixed in the forum by a crier who proclaimed the articles to be sold and furnished a catalog on tablets. Later, sales were proclaimed by the blowing of trumpets. Bids at these auctions were made by holding up the fingers or sometimes by winking.

A number of historians have detailed these Roman auctions, and they were very close in format and operation to those we are familiar with today. In fact, the Romans, being as fond of government regulation as any long-established civil service, had a number of rules concerning auctions in the body of law that governed civilians, the *Corpus Juris Civilis*. While by no means clearly enunciated, these rules do show that auctions were used widely as a means of both public and private transactions.

There are some interesting stories associated with these early auctions. James Bough in his book *Auction!* relates a tale about the emperor Caligula (A.D. 12-41), who became quite mad soon after assuming the mantle of power. He thought he was a god and named his horse to a top post in the imperial service. However, Caligula was not so crazy as to be unable to recognize the advantages of the auction for raising money in a hurry, as he once needed to do to cover his debts.

He put family furniture and ornaments, worth about $5 million in today's money, on the auction block —in Roman times, an actual block of stone—for quick sale. A certain Apponius went to the auction and, no doubt lulled by too much wine and the droning of the auctioneer's voice, dozed off, his head nodding back and forth. The auctioneer took this nodding to be a signal of bidding. Poor Apponius awoke to find himself the new owner of Caligula's goods, and this is no doubt where the concept originated that you have to be careful of your movements at an auction. (Which by the way, is not so at any reputable auction.

14

There are distinct methods of bidding and no decent auctioneer is going to mistake your scratching your nose as a legitimate bid unless you are secretive and have arranged beforehand with him to have this gesture so interpreted.)

Caligula was soon offed by his own troops, who were fed up with his insane excesses. About a century and a half later (A.D. 193 to be precise), the emperor Pertinax suffered a similar demise due to the sudden intersection of a Praetorian guard's sword with his neck, the resultant decapitation leaving the empire to be disposed of by the elite members of Pertinax's own traitorous bodyguards. They elected to do so by auction, wanting quick disposal and a good return—again, something that an auction is admirably suited to accomplish.

Having decided that they could not get enough for what they now held by private contract, the Praetorians mounted their ramparts and declared to all and sundry that the empire was for sale to the highest bidder. Only two dared approach the foot of the fortifications and enter into competition: Sulpicianus and Julian, also called Didius by some writers, his full name being Didius Julianus.[2] Julian successfully outbid his rival and took the imperial toga for the sum of 6,250 drachmas per soldier involved (perhaps between $2,000 and $3,000 in modern currency per man). He was then crowned emperor.

To be sure, this high-handed action by the Praetorians was not exactly cheered by the general populace, nor by the armies in the field. The legion stamped hastily and angrily back to Rome and began knocking heads together. The Praetorian Guard quickly deserted Julian (but kept his money) and General Severus took over, having Julian decapitated in his turn, and the head paraded through the streets impaled on a spear to be mocked and spat upon. Poor Julian is no doubt the most unlucky successful bidder in history, but he did have his delicious moment of glory. Imagine what a feeling it must have been to win the entire civilized world at auction!

---

[2]Gibbon, vol. i, ch. v.

ENGLAND MAKES A BID FOR AUCTION SUPREMACY

No one appears to be sure whether the Romans brought the auction to the British Isles, or whether it merely evolved out of simple logic as to the advantages of buying and selling in this manner. What is certain is that England has utilized auctions to a greater extent and for longer than most other countries, with these traditions carrying over into the now independent countries first colonized by the English: the United States, Canada, New Zealand, Australia, South Africa, even India to some extent. The goods typically sold at British auctions over the centuries have included real estate, art, furniture, and household goods.

In England, the manner in which auctions are conducted has varied over the years, but a common one was to set up an inch of lighted candle.

Fig. 2-2. Popular Southern auctioneer Cameron Long displays this piece from a large sale of Americana he and his father recently presided over. The auction was a very good one, presenting a large selection of primitives from the estate of a well-known collector.

Fig. 2-3. This primitive chair brought over $400 at auction.

The person making the highest bid before the wick fell was declared the winner. The minimum price at which the owner was willing to part with his property was sometimes put under the candlestick, called a *dumb bidding*. In the north of England it was the practice not to let others know your bid, called *candlestick bidding*. There was also the *Dutch auction* in which the items were offered at a certain price and then successively lower ones until a bidder finally agreed to accept the merchandise.

Other picturesque methods of conducting bidding were used as well, including accepting bids until a sandglass ran out or a running boy reached his goal. (How those kids must have hated the big auctions with hundreds of lots!)

A fascinating tradition was sometimes practiced by females (one would assume of somewhat loose reputation, although the writer[3] doesn't say so). The lady would not speak during the sale but would give each person a glass of brandy the moment he bid. The purchaser of her wares received the last glass in a private room. It is a little surprising that a practice so well calculated to warm up competition should have become obsolete.

When Charles I imitated the Roman emperors by losing his own head in 1643, his collection of paintings was sold at auction. In fact, the sale was extremely successful, glutting the fine art market for over almost a century afterward. The fabulous group of masterpieces amassed by the Stuart family over the generations brought, according to historians, the highest prices since Roman times.

By act of William III (1698), the auction was prescribed as the method of selling goods imported from the East Indies. Henry VII had earlier issued, and Charles I had confirmed, a charter regulating the practice of auctioning by confining it to an officer called an *outroper*. All other persons were prohibited from selling goods or merchandise by public claim or outcry. Thus arose the first auctioneering licenses.

These strong auction traditions in England resulted in the rise of the great auction houses of Christie's and Sotheby's, which are still, in both their London and New York branches, the very tip of the auction world. The auction scene in the British Isles has always been, and still is, strong. As an example, even back in 1908 there were 6,639 licensed auctioneers in England, 760 in Scotland, and 839 in Ireland.

However, things were happening across the Great Salt Pond as well. The auction was alive and quite well in the New World.

THE AUCTION COMES TO AMERICA

The early colonists brought the auction tradition with them to America. It was an especially effective way for supply ship captains from England and Holland to quickly dispose of their cargoes. Over-

---

[3]*New American Cyclopedia*, 1858.

16

head costs of storing, displaying, and selling were kept at a minimum. These same reasons also apply to the continued, modern practice of auctioning off such commodities as livestock, cotton, wool, and tobacco, as well as the liquidation of property to quickly settle estates and bankruptcies.

As happened in Europe, colonial authorities put in effect regulations to control the conduct of auctions, thus intending to eliminate abuse and fraud. It is through an application to hold an auction in New Amsterdam (now New York) in 1662 that the earliest recorded auction in the colonies is known. Details of other seventeenth-century auctions are more sketchy, although there were many of them. Newspaper accounts, printed broadsides, and auction catalogs all provide bountiful data on numerous eighteenth-century swings of the auctioneer's gavel.

The literature on early American auctions is extensive. Two comprehensive lists covering the period in detail (when taken together, list all known American auction catalogs at the time of the lists' publication. These, published by the New York Library and available in many reference libraries today, are George Leslie McKay's *American Book Auction Catalogues (1713-1934)* and Harold Lancour's *American Art Auction Catalogues (1785-1942)*.

Taken as a complementary set, these two works list nearly 20,000 auctions. There were, no doubt, many auctions not listed in these works since there was little incentive for anyone to retain an auction list after the event itself, thus resulting in many being lost forever. Also, a goodly portion of early auctions, like those wondrous country auctions of today, did not bother to issue catalogs at all.

The earliest American auction catalog extant is that provided by Ebenezer Pemberton for a sale of books at the Brown Coffee House in Boston on July 2, 1717. In fact, for most of the eighteenth century, Boston was the most important auction center in all the colonies, including those that were to become the Dominion of Canada.

Auctioneers of this early era were specialists who would conduct a sale for a set fee or a prestated percentage of the proceeds. As the colonies became stronger economically, auctioneers prospered as well. Gradually, the more prominent auctioneers in Boston, Philadelphia, and New York gained enough prestige and business success to establish firms with their own auction rooms and to hold frequent sales. By the time America had become an independent nation and the nineteenth century had arrived, auctions and auctioneers were a well-established part of the national fabric.

Philadelphia, for example, was home to several men important in the history of the Ameri-

Fig. 2-4. Collecting Americana furniture can be interesting. The use for which this nineteenth-century Pennsylvania-made commode was intended is pretty obvious. Pieces like this fall within the $200 and up range, so don't sneer when you come across one.

Fig. 2-5. This Pullman blanket was used on railway passenger trains in the early part of this century. Such items are in demand by collectors of railroad- and train-related pieces. This one is worth about $60.

can auction. Thomas Birch started a firm in 1845 that continued until 1890. Other notable auctioneers in Philadelphia included Stan V. Henkels—who began auctioning in 1882, running his own rooms from 1913 to 1934—M. Thomas in 1823, and T.B. Freeman in 1826.

Boston's strong position in colonial times was continued by such auctioneers as Joseph Leonard in 1842, Charles F. Libby in 1878, and Lewis J. Bird in 1882—all founding firms that lasted until after World War I.

New York was also working its way up to the preeminent place it holds today on the American auction scene. The great ones of the nineteenth and early twentieth centuries were: P.L. Mills (1816), Thomas Bangs (1837), E.H. Ludlow (1840), Robert Sommerville (1862), James P. Silo (1900), and John Anderson (1900)—all starting auction houses that endured many years.

From the middle of the nineteenth century until the beginning of the Great Depression in 1929

was a golden age for auctions (and it seems as if we are entering one again). During that period, many major art and antiques sales set new records for prices realized in various categories. Art and antique collections, and occasionally the expensive Fifth Avenue mansions that contained them, sold in the millions of dollars. As often happens today, some of the very happy owners sold their holdings for three or four times what they had paid for them.

It was the nineteenth-century auctioneer who forged this market and made it all possible.

AUCTIONING IN THE 19TH CENTURY

A fascinating insight into the way auctions both worked and were viewed is offered by *The New American Cyclopedia*, edited in 1858 by George Ripley and Charles A. Dana. This beautiful leather-bound set, by the way, I got from an auctioneer for the lowly sum of $15—one of my minor triumphs. As an aside (and since a minor dose of erudition never hurt any of us), this set is important because both Ripley and Dana were significant in nineteenth-century letters. In 1841 Ripley founded the famous Brook Farm in Roxbury, Massachusetts—an attempt at cooperative communal living, where such famous men as Dana, Nathaniel Hawthorne, and John Sullivan Dwight lived. Hawthorne based his *Blithedale Romance* on experiences there. In 1846, the community proved unable to support itself and was abandoned.

What does all this have to do with nineteenth-century auctions? First, the books were bought from an auctioneer; second, I had the knowledge to recognize they were more than just another set of old encyclopedias because of this association; and thirdly, here we have the highly respected figures of George Ripley and Charles Dana writing about auctions (or at least editing the article), which adds considerable weight to it and definitely enhances its credibility from a scholarly viewpoint.

Regardless, following is a condensed and edited version of their article on auctions. In fact, once you've read the chapters on the way auctions work today and have attended a few, you might want to come back and read this article again to contrast today's auctions with yesterday's. I believe you will find more similarities than anything, and hence the significance of including the article in this book. The continuity of auction traditions is amazing.

In modern times (i.e., the 1850s) sales at public auctions are as common as private sales, and directed in most cases by the law, where it interposes between the owner of property and the purchaser—its object being the protection of those who necessarily put the disposition of their estate in the hands of a trustee, as bankrupts or the members of a municipal corporation.

The red flag is the ordinary sign of the trade, and the auctioneer, with his hammer, his boisterous "going, going, gone," his humorous appeals to the company, is often a very original character. No prejudice appears to exist against him or his business now; but from 1817 to 1831 there was a strong antiauction feeling in this country, particularly in New York and upon the part of importers and jobbing merchants. Auctions were charged with furnishing facilities for concealment, smuggling, and perjury, and with being injurious to the growth and prosperity of cities, and it was vainly attempted to induce Congress to pass a law imposing such a duty upon them as would amount to prohibition.

The auctioneer is the seller's agent, and as such has a special property in the goods and a lien upon them or upon the purchase money, where he is authorized to receive it for his commission, the auction duty, and the charges of the sale. If he exceeds his authority or refuses to give the name of his principal, he renders himself personally liable. In sales of real estate he is usually authorized to receive the deposit, but not the residue of the purchase money. He often receives this deposit as a sort of stake holder, to be paid over if a good title is made. It is his duty to do his best to possess skill, to pursue the regular course of business, and to comply with all legal instructions.

The conditions of sale and the plans and conditions of property, particularly if real estate, should be accurately made known beforehand. If printed or written, they control the oral statements of the auctioneer, for in the words of Lord Ellenborough, "men cannot tell what contracts they enter into, if the conditions of sale are to be controlled by the babble of the auction room."

Slight inaccuracies of description do not, but substantial ones do, void the sale. A bid at an auction may be retracted before the hammer is down, and, in cases where a written entry is required to complete the sale, before that is made. For a bid is only an offer which does not bind either party until assented to. Fraud upon either side voids the sale.

The employment of bidders by the owner is or is not illegal, according as circumstances tend to show bad or good faith. To employ them in order to prevent a sacrifice by buying in the property, is, except where the sale is advertised as being "without reserve," allowable. But it is a fraud to use them for the purpose of enhancing the price through a fictitious competition. On the other hand, the sale is void if the bidder prevails upon others to desist from bidding by appeals to their sympathy or false representations.

Mock auctions live by the disregarding of these rules. The only *bona fide* bidders at them are persons unacquainted with the ways of the city, to whom, therefore, articles are knocked down at once. A sentence from the *Penny Cyclopedia* precisely applies to this country, particularly in New York: "In many large towns, persons make a trade of holding auctions of inferior and ill-made goods; barkers are generally placed by them at the door inviting strangers to enter and puffers are always employed who bid more for the articles than they are worth, and thus entice the unwary. Ineffectual attempts have been made to put a stop to these practices."

THE ANTIAUCTION MOVEMENT

The public bias against auctions that Ripley and Dana mentioned actually continued for somewhat longer, not really dying off until the latter part of the nineteenth century. Wesley Towner in his excellent book, *The Elegant Auctioneers* (Hill & Wang, New York, 1970), is a good source for more detailed information on this situation.

Towner gives a fascinating example of the type of auctioneer who, well into the late 1860s and 1870s, engendered this sometimes quite justified and organized public bias. Colonel J.P. Gutelius was in the auction business a little later than the 1870s, but is still typical of the auctioneers of that period. As an aside, let me hasten to point out that "colonel" is a traditionally honorary title awarded or assumed by auctioneers. This tradition continues today most strongly in the South and Midwest.

A lot of Gutelius' shenanigans were self-recorded in his own book, *High Lights on Auctioneering*. Whether or not honestly felt, he poured religion into his auctions like syrup on pancakes.

He claimed to have been the wickedest man in Oklahoma before his conversion and said that he was "for twenty-two years without Christ and ten in the service of the Master."

This ploy, again whether heartfelt or not, worked quite well for him for many years in the evangelical spirit of those times in the Midwest. Gutelius claimed to have been converted one rainy night by a comet appearing through a black umbrella. After that he combined soul-saving and auctioneering. If the bidding was slow, he would roll his eyes heavenward and say something like "O, Lord, if I could only turn this sale into a revival!"

Evidently he sometimes did, claiming in his book to have won almost 2,000 souls to Christ. However, he also bragged that he could sell things at auction that were absolutely unsalable otherwise. He sold oil paintings, rusted farm machinery, blind horses, and other less-than-first-rate offerings—all somewhat at odds with his professed religious beliefs.

Gutelius also had definite ideas about promoting his auctions. The best method, he averred, was to be kind to mothers, love children, and entertain the multitude. He made sure, in addition to the religion, that there was plenty of other excitement also. Such inducements as a free lunch and a Wild West show with six cowboys and an outlaw horse reputed to have killed a number of men were regularly used to attract sizable crowds. They got the show they came for, too.

He would stand on the back of a wagon draped with a red blanket, wearing a red shirt and cowboy hat, and using a bell for a hammer. His performances were grand happenings. He would do things like sing a hymn at the top of his voice while a crippled horse was led to the block, and would get a good price for the horse. He sometimes hired two black men to stand behind him and shout "O Holy City!" for background effect while he was auctioning. It must have been an incredible happening, but respectable, professional, and totally honest it was not.

Still, it would have been wonderful to stand there in the awestruck crowd and listen to him chant, waving his arms, casting his eyes to heaven, sweat dripping from the end of his nose in the hot summer sun.

"Thirika, makita five, makita five . . . O let's take the glory road, folks! I got the five, makita six . . . Six! Thank you, Lord, for the blessings of the day. The six . . . and the seven . . . and the lady makes it eight! Thank you mother. I'll ask Him to give you a double portion of grace . . . Nine . . . nine . . . There's the nine! I'll put you down on my prayer list, brother . . . Now let's hear the forty! O come angel band and bear me to my home! Makita fortika, Lord! . . ."

At least Gutelius gave entertainment value for the money he so easily squeezed out of the attendees at his auctions. Again, though, you tend to somewhat doubt the veracity of his religious beliefs by some of the advice he offered in his book, which was aimed at people wanting to become auctioneers. "Put in a few real ones," he writes, "so nobody can say you're only selling the cheap ones."

Those contemporary fellow auctioneers of Gutelius, especially the ones in the big cities, were no more bound by ethics than he was, so the antiauction movement is no real surprise. For 75 years, from 1800 to 1875, many memorials, petitions, and reports were written condemning auctions as "academies of trick and chicanery."

Among the strongest of the groups organized to combat auctions was the New York Anti-auction Committee, publisher of a torrent of pamphlets and brochures on "this painful subject." The standard themes of these pamphlets were "death, dissipation and bankruptcy," all of which were said to be part and parcel of "the ruinous tendency of auctioneering."

Here's a quote from one of the pamphlets (which, ironically, bring quite decent prices at auctions today).

". . . that the evils which afflict commerce and palsy enterprise have been produced not by the downfall of Napoleon's empire, but by thirty-six auctioneers residing in the city of New York. Their zeal has ripened into crime, their genius into profligacy, shedding luster upon error. Speculation, deprived of its accustomed opportunities for ad-

venture, now shows itself in sales at auction, which are fashionable machines of polite and licensed swindling, producing all the pernicious effects of gambling . . ."

The New York Anti-auction Committee and like groups might have eventually triumphed, except that auctions became respectable, with powerful people finding it in vogue to attend them. Because of this, the auction prospered and higher-level auctioneers became as well thought of as doctors and lawyers (well, at least doctors).

AUCTIONS BECOME RESPECTABLE

From 1865 on, while the South lay licking its wounds in silence, the North, and most especially New York City, was becoming more and more the auction center of the country. This trend was especially pronounced in the field of fine art, even daubings assumed to be such. If there was lack of taste and artistic erudition in some quarters, there was no lack of money.

Many northerners became rich during the Civil War and in the time immediately following. Persons like the Vanderbilts, whose fortune was already firmly established by the railroad monopolies of old Commodore Vanderbilt, got richer, and a good many lesser robber barons established and added to their fortunes. In a day of practically nonexistent governmental regulation and no income tax, there was little impediment to the ruthless in business. The halls of business abounded with watered stocks and outright humbug of all sorts. Merchant princes and captains of industry were spending gigantic sums on mansions to flaunt their successes and were furnishing these lordly residences in lavish, if oft tasteless, style.

Towner, in *The Elegant Auctioneers*, also describes how the lesser moguls imitated the greater: how the best came to New York to acquire the trappings of their dizzying new monetary heights and how all the smaller sharks swam in their wake, slavishly mimicking the leaders to whatever extent their often-bulging purses allowed.

In the decades from 1865 to the Great Depression in 1929, with lapses for such minor inconveniences as the First World War, art collecting provided the proof that a man had arrived, that he could indeed afford this ultimate luxury (whether he really could or not). Collecting became all the rage among both old money and new. Works of art became highly sought after, being bought and sold at ever-rising prices as demand regenerated and increased.

A young auctioneer named Thomas Kirby, inspired by this "upsurge of negotiable culture," moved from Philadelphia to New York in 1876. It was his intention, which came to be well realized, to sell art. His training for the job as an auctioneer was respectable, having served 13 years with Moses Thomas, an old Quaker who had been auctioning for over 50 years. However, the firm that Kirby had been crying sales for specialized in the traditional selling of books, farm implements, and real estate. Kirby, with an instinct for more expensive items and with the glittering example of the 1876 Centennial behind him, was convinced that he was wasting his time on these more common items.

The move did not produce the immediate results Kirby had dreamed of, so he struggled along in New York, hawking the same kind of less-than-elegant wares he had in Philadelphia, until 1881. It was then that Kirby took over the American Art Gallery on Madison Square in New York (later, home to Madison Square Garden). This proved the perfect time to do it. By 1883 New York was in the midst of an unprecedented cultural upsurge. The Metropolitan Opera opened in October. Tiffany & Company, the now-famous jewelers, received recognition that was previously unheard of for American craftsmen by being appointed jewelers to Queen Victoria, the czar of Russia, the sultan of Turkey, and numerous other royal clients. Even the Brooklyn Bridge was opened to traffic that year.

However, there was a condition attached to Kirby's new position: he must henceforth and forever give up his crass occupation of auctioneer. Luckily for both Kirby and the American Art Association (which later became part of the famous Park-Bernet Galleries auction firm), this stipulation did not last long.

The buying of fine art by the Vanderbilts, the Rockefellers, the Goulds, the Huntingtons, the Whitneys, and all those with money who wanted to be like them had increased. The demand was so great for European art that, responding to such a wide open and mostly gullible market, forgers had a glorious field day. Into this situation stepped Kirby and his American Art Association, pointing out vigorously that no European painter had more than two hands, hence many of the numerous works attributed to them had to be forgeries. People flocked to the gallery, but American art was still not selling that well. Then came the financial panic of 1885.

George I. Seney, president of the Metropolitan Bank, was one of those caught in the crunch, having just lost his fortune, and a good deal of the bank's, by speculating on railroad shares. He turned over his mansion in Brooklyn and 285 fine paintings to a creditors' committee and suggested that the American Art Association be allowed to sell it at auction.

The others associated with the gallery were aghast at the thought, but Thomas Kirby was delighted. This is what he had been waiting for all his life. With the highly respectable Samuel P. Avery named as "manager" of the auction (auctioneers were, after all, still considered to be seedy characters by most), Kirby sailed ahead with preparations for the auction.

A catalog was printed, and since many of Seney's paintings were European, the signs warning that imported artworks were probably forgeries disappeared from the gallery's walls. An admission fee of $1 was advertised in order "to keep the riffraff out." Because of the large crowd expected on the three days of the auction, a large concert hall was rented to hold the actual auction in, although the gallery itself was used for the preview period.

Getting ready for the auction was not all that easy, however. Many art dealers and auctioneers who considered themselves more "respectable" than Kirby objected vigorously. The creditors' committee itself got cold feet. After all, there was a financial panic on, they pointed out to Kirby; surely no one would bid decent prices. However, Kirby would have none of this, retorting that human nature being what it was, people would indeed pay good prices for the paintings just because it was a distress sale, a principle often proved down through the century and more of strong auctioneering activity that has followed this historical and pivotal sale. He also asserted that the titans of Wall Street and other moguls would attend.

On Auction Day, Kirby's predictions proved correct: the house was packed with big-money people; all seats were filled; and individuals were actually standing in the aisles. Kirby, elegantly arrayed in tails and wing collar, took his place behind the pedestal where the orchestra conductor normally stood and began leading his own kind of symphonic ensemble, the audience. By the time item number 9 came up—a painting of a priest fishing, by some long-forgotten artist—the crowd was warm and excited. A winning bid of $1,200 took it—and $1,200 was big money in 1885.

Kirby, of course, tearfully declared that it was worth twice the amount, and the crowd ate it up. The tempo quickened. The magic and liveliness that is the hallmark of the auction had now invaded the hearts of the rich and famous. Auctions were suddenly respectable again, the antiauction forces fading into the woodwork of the highly polished paneling of that concert hall as Kirby made the most of a glorious occasion.

On the third night, exhausted and with a hoarse voice, Kirby reached his true triumphant peak of the auction, selling a painting called *Evening In The Hamlet* for $18,500! Nor were the final results any less pleasing. When all the sales were added up, the total was $405,821—very big money in 1885. Kirby, fully vindicated, had now achieved instant respect. The New York *Sun*, long edited by Charles K. Dana (quoted earlier in this chapter), was enthusiastic about the auction in its April 3, 1885, issue, saying it was "the largest, the best managed, and the most interesting sale that has been known in New York . . ."

Kirby went on to even more fame and fortune as one of America's leading auctioneers, and the door that he had so emphatically kicked down afforded entrance into the game for many of the other greats in the field and made New York into the auction capital that it is today. If you want to find out what happened next for Thomas Kirby and the others, again I heartily recommend Wesley Towner's *The Elegant Auctioneers*, which goes into far more detail than we have room for here.

BACK TO THE PRESENT

Okay, now we've seen where the auction's been. It's time now to get back to the present. The following chapters detail the practical aspects of attending auctions, forming bidding strategies, making money, and having fun!

So, without further ado, what am I bid for Chapter Three? . . . Going once, going twice . . . Sold to the nice person holding this book!

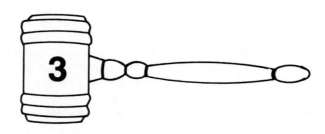

How Auctions Work

Regardless of the type of auctions you elect to specialize in—antiques, real estate, commodity, or any of the other specific types covered in Section Two—certain basic rules apply. In this chapter, we will discuss how you go about finding an auction, registering to bid, competing for items, and paying for the ones you win.

HOW TO FIND AN AUCTION

This situation will sound like a Catch-22, but the best way to find an auction is to attend one. People are very important to auctioneers; the more who come, the higher his received bids and the greater his potential profit. When you sign up to get a bidder number, usually you will also be asked for your address so you can be put on the auctioneer's mailing list. You will then get brochures in the mail describing all of that auctioneer's forthcoming sales.

Also, most auctioneers cooperate with others in the business by providing a table near the entrance with stacks of free flyers advertising other auctions. You can attend those that appeal to you and get on other mailing lists. In addition, the mailing lists will be sold to other auctioneers, and your mailbox will soon budge with invitations to auctions. Then you can delightedly pick and choose the ones that appeal to you.

The quickest way to find an auction (or three or four) in your area is the classified section of the newspaper, usually under the heading "Auctions." However, don't have a heart attack if you can't find any such heading; there are as many formats of classified advertisement sections as there are newspapers in the United States and Canada. Luckily for me, most of the newspapers in my area have an "Auction" section, but in other cities I have found listings under such diverse headings as "Antiques," "Business Opportunities," "Merchandise Offerings," "Rummage Sales," and several others. Scan everything. A church- or lodge-sponsored auction, for example, could be under "Organizations."

Most auctions are held on the weekend; so check the Thursday paper. There will probably be

Fig. 3-1. Robert Brunk, former college professor turned auctioneer, has a less strident, more erudite style than most auctioneers. He currently holds the world record for a Thomas Wolfe book—getting $2600 for the Wolfe pamphlet, *Crisis In Industry*.

phone and start calling. You'll either get a long-winded enthusiastic sales pitch on why you'd be the greatest fool in the history of humanity to pass up the auctioneer's, or one of his friends' forthcoming Saturday night sale.

"You go on over to old Joe's sale now and tell him Colonel Hank says to treat you right, now heah?" If you call Joe three weeks later and he's not having a sale that week, he'll say, "You go on over to old Hank's sale now and tell him Colonel Joe says to treat you right, now heah?"

These techniques for finding auctions work as

several there, listing the times of the auction, the location, and also the times that the merchandise may be previewed. As we shall see later in this chapter, the preview period can be very important to you.

Many of these classified advertisements will include a listing, often quite lenghty, of items to be offered in the auction. However, don't ignore an auction just because you don't see whatever it is you are looking for. Space is limited and most auctions have several hundred *lots* (items or groups of items). The best thing to do is to at least attend the preview period. You might be able to preview three or four auctions in this manner, picking the one you want to attend and bid at.

Finding auctions is not all that hard, although some people persist in thinking it is. If all the previous methods fail, simply pick up your telephone book and look in the yellow pages under "Auctioneers." There will surely be several listed, along with their telephone numbers. Pick up the tele-

Fig. 3-2. Jack Kennedy wants no one to mistake his function of assigning bidder numbers at an auction sponsored by the Lions Club to raise money for an orphange. Just read the sign on his hat.

25

Fig. 3-3. Keeping track of winning bids on each item keeps two men busy at this auction. Each card has the lot number, the amount it sold for, and the bidder number. The winner redeems these cards by paying and claiming his merchandise.

well in your hometown as they do when you're out traveling. It's easy to find auctions, and you will be awed at how many there are—awed and pleased, once you become an avid auction goer, as I know you will. The bug bites deep and we all come to love it.

There is another way to find auctions, especially regular weekly or monthly auctions. When you are attending an auction, talk to the people there and, make friends. Soon you will be receiving enthusiastic recommendations that you attend this auction or that. "That old Colonel Hank, I wanna tell you, puts on one fine auction. You go right up there next week, now heah? I'll see you there."

Also—and this is important—you will learn from these contacts which auctions to avoid. There are saints, there are sinners, and then there's Bozo's third cousin on his father's side. The sinners and any auctioneer related to Bozo are the ones to stay away from.

Do talk to several people, though, about an auctioneer who has a bad reputation. An opinion from just one person could be merely a case of sour grapes, whereas a general consensus as to smoke rising means that a cheating blaze most likely crackles underneath. In my own area, reputations run this gamut. There is one auctioneer who, above all others, is said to be as honest as the day is long, while on the other end of the spectrum is the guy whom everybody tells stories about. Some must be true—there are so many and such a universal concurrence. How many I don't know because there is no way in Hades that I'll waste my time (and money) by going to that particular auction. You might find one or two like this in your immediate vicinity as well. Leave those for Bozo and all the little bozos. They're the ones who keep the crooks in business anyway.

Don't let this very small percentage of rotten auctioneers scare you away from the wonders, joys, and opportunities to make money that auctions offer. Use the techniques just described to search out and find auctions; the rewards are overwhelmingly worth it.

GOING TO AUCTION

Essentially, once you've located some auctions, you will find that they start much the same way year in and year out. A sale is advertised, a crowd assembles on the given day, and an auctioneer stands or sits behind a podium or table, or clips on a remote mike and wanders around waving his arms.

A good auction master, like a more conventional performer, will try to warm up the crowd. One of my favorite gavel wielders, Crazy Bill Hagan, uses one of the good old ploys. "How many people here," he'll ask, "are from more than 50 miles away?" A sprinkling of hands go up in the crowd. "How many from 25 miles?" Even more hands go up. "And how many are local?" Scores of hands wave in the air. "Good," says Crazy Bill, grinning. "That's the end of your short course in how to bid. Just keep those hands going up and down." A splattering of pleased laughter comes then and the auction is off and running.

An auction begins by the auctioneer announcing the name or number of an object or group of objects and asking for a bid. Someone in the audience speaks, or raises a hand, or waves a numbered card or paddle indicating acceptance. The auctioneer, whether of boisterous or restrained nature, is always mock-offended at the first bid. It is never enough for the grand and glorious merchandise he is offering. The more flamboyant will roll their eyes heavenward in supplication for being saddled with such a cheap audience. The more elegant ones will give their best impression of how the matron looked when the tradesman dared come to the front entrance.

Realize that an auction also is high theater. The auctioneer is a performer ranging from a Barrymore to a Bozo the Clown. (Yes, there are Bozos in the auction business as well. The fact that histrionics are so widely employed should not affect your judgment. Realize what they are, sit back and enjoy. Do not, under any circumstances, allow them to influence your bidding strategy or to sway you in any way because that is precisely why the auc-

Fig. 3-4. Auctioneer Doug Penland exhorts the crowd while selling a marble-topped washstand.

tioneer is up there hamming it to the max and bouncing around like the inmate of a nineteenth-century loony bin.

The magic and liveliness of the auction is a fact; it'll take over your soul and send blood singing through your veins in rousing three-quarter time. This is good. Enjoy, but don't let the psychosis of the moment wreck your logic, which is what happens in the great bidding contests where items sell for three, four, or five times their actual value.

These contests occur because two or more people decide they must have a particular lot, and they will be purely cotton-picking durned if they are going to allow any no-good so-and-so to take it away. Auctioneers eat this attitude up, posturing and prancing and waving the gavel like a drum

Fig. 3-5. Colonel Jerry Sluder works the crowd on a small item. A new auctioneer, this was Sluder's first auction in May, 1986. He gave a polished, smooth performance and shows much promise.

major his baton, pushing those bids ever higher.

Learn to realize when this is going on and sit on your hands. You will enjoy these contests immensely and it won't come out of your wallet or purse. We'll discuss how to plan out your bidding strategy shortly. Adhering to this strategy will allow you to profit at auctions while others tilt at windmills and dance to the auctioneer's tune.

The result of a series of bids on a lot is that finally the auctioneer will be unable to squeeze out another bid and will reluctantly point at the winner. "Sold, number 84. You stole them plates, just plain stole them." Auctioneers are never visibly satisfied, either. This makes some people sorry for them, resulting in higher bids on the next item. Others feel that the prices are low and bargains abound, so they pitch headlong into the waters as well, and the heck with rocks that might lurk under the surface.

Again, auctioneers are good at acting. The better ones can play your heart strings like Mother Maybelle Carter used to do "Wildwood Flower." That is an auctioneer's job: to get the most he can for his clients. It is his professional responsibility and there is nothing wrong with it. Your responsibility, and I emphasize it again, is to not be influenced by all this grand acting and to hew closely to the bidding strategy you mapped out beforehand.

YOUR GREATEST ENEMY

It is a game, an exciting game between you and the auctioneer. Concisely stated, you want a bargain and he wants the contents of your wallet, including that snapshot of Aunt Maude, which he will auction off to Bozo at the next auction.

However, you already know your greatest enemy at an auction, the one you really need protection from. Each morning, on arising, your enemy's face stares bleary-eyed back at you from the bathroom mirror. As that great philosopher, Pogo, once so succinctly put it, "We have met the enemy and he is us."

The auctioneer's job is to skillfully cajole you out of everything in your pockets down to your spare change, but you can hurt yourself far worse by not being prepared to withstand his wiles. Random buying, not inspecting the lots beforehand, exceeding your self-imposed bidding limit—all are pitfalls for the unwary and inexperienced auction goer, and they can so easily be avoided!

Not much help is going to be offered you by the auction firm if you make a mistake. If the auctioneer says, "She's oak I think," it means little. He says it because there has been a traditional passion for oak in antiques auctions for many years, and claiming a piece is oak marginally enhances interest and bidding. Auctions typically consist of hundreds of lots, and no company has the time or knowledge to authenticate every piece.

The auction has always been "let the buyer beware!" Yet, in that weakness also lies its strength. Yes, here comes that recurrent theme again: knowledge. Because of the volume of items in an auction, the auctioneer will often not realize what he really has; so you can gleefully let him push and shove you up to the $25 level for a $500 Tiffany vase or a $700 Mark Twain first edition.

It's up to you to gain that knowledge. Here's a quick aside as to Mark Twain. It was common practice in nineteenth-century publishing to include a facsimile of the author's signature in the book. Hold the page up to the light and look at it from the back. If the ink has soaked into the paper, it's a real autograph (and rejoice, you've got something); otherwise the signature was printed when the rest of the book was.

In general, those who know their fields of specialty and inspect the lots carefully during the auction preview period have nothing to fear. If you are a collector, attending a few auctions and perusing the price guides will give you a good grasp of the current going prices. Be sure to keep that price guide out in your car, too, since none of us can remember everything.

If you make a mistake at an auction, even if it was because the auctioneer mistakenly hyped a piece as something it wasn't, you have little recourse. You're stuck with it and the only guarantee is that if you break it, you get to keep all the pieces.

What this boils down to is that auctions are not really places to learn about the true value of pieces or how to authenticate them. This is homework that you should do before you attend the sale. Auctions are places to buy, not places to learn. They are chances for you to exploit and profit from your knowledge to best advantage, not to expect much in the way of reliable guidance. Oh, sure, Bozo will give you all kinds of hot tips and information by the heaping mouthload, but can you trust Bozo? The short answer is "no;" the long answer is "heck, no!"

THE PREVIEW PERIOD

The auction process, by custom and, depending on the state, by law, begins with a preauction showing. This preview period allows prospective buyers to closely examine the offers and to form opinions as to their relative worth. If you are considering attending an auction and find out that it

Fig. 3-6. Colonel Ronald D. Long auctioneering at a large antiques and fine art auction held in Columbia, South Carolina.

does not offer this preview period, make a 180-degree turn and practice jogging back out to the car. Do not return. Something is fishy.

The preauction inspection period varies. It might be for several days prior to the sale, just the day before, or as in the case of many country auctions, for an hour or so before bidding is scheduled to begin. Regardless, it is up to you to take full advantage of this time. If the auction is a goodly drive away, you might even want to call and make sure of the exact times of preview.

Nothing is more disgusting, or as potentially ruinous, than to arrive at an auction and to find out that the preview was the previous night and you will have to go in cold. It might be best not to go in at all if this is the case; you can flat lose some money in a hurry making snap judgments with no prior inspections.

Arrange to attend the preview period at its advertised time. Carefully scrutinize each item you're interested in. This doesn't mean just telling yourself, "My, that sure is pretty, I'd love to have that sucker in my living room." Instead, evaluate it carefully as to suitability, rareness, and condition. Decide then—after perhaps sneaking out to your car to consult one or more of your price guides—what is the highest reasonable price you will pay for the

Make yourself a note on this, being careful not to let Bozo see it. (He'll run around and tell everybody, and you'll play hob trying to get it at your price after that.)

Various fields of collectibles have danger areas that you should be aware of. Overall, condition is usually paramount. Damage, overcleaning and repainting, missing parts, substitutions, and restoration are all things that decrease the value of an object to a collector. While very old pieces will show a certain amount of wear and restoration, you must not allow yourself to be conned into paying the same for them as you would for a piece in mint or like-new condition.

TOOLS OF THE TRADE

There are certain tools that are handy to carry to an auction preview. Using them can save you a lot of money or, conversely, make you a lot, especially when you are dealing with antiques and collectibles. Obviously, the first is a pocket notebook to write your findings in. Make notes on the condition of the items you are interested in and the top bid you are willing to pay. This should be confidential information; otherwise the advantage of the knowledge that you are employing will be lost, especially if Bozo finds out.

Many veteran auction goers also carry a tape measure for checking dimensions. The needs for a tape measure are several. If you are going to buy a large piece of furniture, it is always good to know that it'll fit in your station wagon for the trip home and through the front door when you get there. Also, in the case of many items listed in the various price guides, dimensions are many times given, affording you a criterion to check against in determining a piece's authenticity.

The handiness of a tape measure was brought home to me at an antiques auction. It was a relaxed, informal country auction. While the lesser interesting smaller items were going, several of us were wandering among the larger pieces, rubbing hands across oak and checking finishes for mars or stains. Mark Wilson, an Asheville, North Carolina, antiques dealer and furniture restorer, was one of these. He quite kindly paused to give a

whispered impromptu lesson in fine antique furniture while the auction droned on behind us.

A Chippendale circular tilt-top table was the example, with Wilson ticking off the points that proved it was from the period, rather than a later reproduction. He mentioned the base, hefted it and talked about the weight, commented that the brass latch was of the correct type, and spoke about the finish as appearing authentic. However, the crowning proof—and here he pulled a tape measure from his pocket to conclude the lesson—was the amount of warp.

"You check warp," Wilson continued, "by measuring with the grain and then against it. A table this old will probably be 1/2 to 3/4 inch off round." He then performed the test and the table was found closer to a full inch off. "Must have been a very dry house," he said, grinning.

Wilson then stated his opinion that the table would go low because of some minor restoration work that would make buyers leery—the block that the tabletop rested on had obviously been replaced. The prediction proved correct, with $160 taking it.

Continuing with the recommended tools, a pocket flashlight is invaluable for peering into dark corners and underneath pieces. More about the authenticity of furniture, can be told by looking inside it than in any other manner. Usually a legitimate reproduction or even an out-and-out counterfeit piece will look fine on the outside, but telltale signs can be seen inside a drawer or under a bottom panel, or as you peer down at the back in the crack between it and the wall.

The reason is simple: it is much harder to fake unfinished wood than it is finished wood. Let an unscrupulous dealer or auctioneer slap some linseed oil and good-quality paste wax on the outside and hire Bozo to go after that sucker with an electric buffer, and you will swear by its appearance that it just came out of Versailles the week before and that the Sun King—old Louis XIV—is still wondering what happened to his favorite chest of drawers, or sideboard, or table. Once you look inside, though, where the wood is not finished, you can immediately tell it's a reproduction by the new wood. Also, pre-Revolution French craftsmen seldom used epoxyed-together plywood or chipboard.

Pieces are often forged by taking actual old furniture that is now just junk and making up what is purported to be a genuinely old and valuable antique. It's not, and you can detect this trick usually by quality of craftsmanship. Truly collectible eighteenth- and nineteenth-century pieces showed a very high level of craft, with joints painstakingly dovetailed and drawers that slip in and out with almost no hint of friction. If, on looking inside, you see that the piece is glued or nailed together and that parts are ill fitting, smile and walk on by, making a note in your little book to watch and see who the piece fools.

We'll go into more detail on detecting fakes and forgeries in the chapter on antiques auctions. Alas, forgeries are much more common than a lot of antiques experts will admit to in print.

Next in tools, a magnifying glass should be pretty much obvious, too. You can use it for reading hallmarks on silver, pewter, and pottery, and signatures on paintings, as well as more closely examining the joints and so forth just discussed.

One other item, for the more sophisticated china and pottery collector, is a small portable black light. These ultraviolet lights are readily available through such mail-order firms as Edmund Scientific or from many local electronics parts houses. Shining one of these on china, for example, will show up tiny cracks and skillful repairs invisible to the naked eye.

Almost all reputable auction houses expect knowledgeable buyers to perform this close scrutiny and usually have staff available to answer questions. They will also pull heavy furniture away from the wall for you to examine the back, hold things up so that you can measure them, or trundle things over into a better light for your perusal.

Auctioneers prefer this cooperation in the preview period to a dispute after the sale. This way he can say, "Wadda ya mean, it's fake? You had plenty of time to examine it at the preview." They are right, "buyer beware" is an understood and accepted fact. The only real protection, the only real recourse, is your knowledge. Taking the slight and enjoyable trouble to do your homework, to learn your field of specialty, brings rich rewards. Not doing so leaves you groping ineffectually in the dark.

I am not being discouraging here. The thing to understand is that so many people do not trouble to gain much knowledge that you can quite quickly gain a measurable advantage.

DECIDING ON YOUR BID

We've already discussed two ways of determining the current worth of a particular item: by attending auctions and noting the results for various categories and by checking the various price guides. You can extend your study of auction prices realized, in the antiques and collectibles field especially, by subscribing to the various regional newspapers specializing in such. These newspapers publish reports on auctions held in different areas and often list prices of what sundry pieces brought. In my own auction reports, I always include such prices, as do a number of other writers.

In Appendix A of this book are listed the names and addresses of several of these publications. Some of the ones I particularly like include *Antique Week/Tri-State Trader* for Illinois, Indiana, Ohio, and the surrounding states; *Carolina Antique News* in the mid-South; *Collectors Journal* in the midwest; *Maine Antique Digest* in New England; *Joel Sater's Antique News* in Pennsylvania; and *Yesteryear* up in Wisconsin. There are several other good ones as well. Some are weeklies, bringing you an incredible amount of timely information on antiques and auctions. Subscribing to several will pay off for you in knowledge you can exploit at your local auctions.

A third method is provided by some auctioneers themselves. Not all bother to supply a catalog of their auctions, but some do, and even go so far as to put down what they think an item might bring. This sort of data, naturally, should be taken with a large grain of salt; still it can be a good guide as to what level other bidders might be aiming at. If the suggested price is far lower than the guide's price, for example, you might have a good chance at it. However, if the suggested price is in excess of what you realize is the highest you should go, the bidding might start at such a high level that you are never in the hunt.

Recognize, however, that auction prices realized, and even the prices in the price guides, are only guidelines. They are not exact and, in setting the price you are willing to go for something at an auction, you might want to fudge a bit on the low side. Remember, as well, that if you plan on reselling the item, you need to get it lower than the price in the price guide so that a dealer can buy it cheaper than that from you—in other words leave him and you room to make a profit.

Also, as far as the auctioneer's suggested price goes, that doesn't mean the audience is going to concur, and he might be forced to drop back to a more reasonable level. So put down the right bid in your notebook and hope that you get it for less than that!

Let's take an example of how to price. You find and correctly identify a piece of Rookwood art pottery during a preview that, in surreptitiously checking your price guide, books out at $100 in value. For resale, you'd want to get it for about $40, since a dealer probably would not go higher than $60 or $70 for it, leaving him room to sell it to a retail customer at the $100 book price. You jot down something like "Rookwood, lot #101, $40!" in your notebook. If, during the bidding, you get it for that or less, fine; however, when the level goes above $40, you shrug and sit firmly on your hands, or you will get it for $80 and have to take a $10 or $20 loss on the resale.

Now, if you are a collector of Rookwood, buying it for your own joy and wonderment, setting the bid can be a little different. You can afford to put your bid price, assuming you really want the piece, at $90 or $100. Anything below $100 means that you got the vase wholesale, discounted off the retail price, and you can apply the savings to the next item you want.

There is, of course, a third area that falls in between resale to a dealer and buying for your own collection. That is, of course, if you are a dealer yourself—whether you have your own shop or sell at antique shows or flea markets. Should this be true, you can afford to go up to perhaps 60 percent or 70 percent of the retail value.

In any of these cases, however, getting it for less than your limit is the desired result. Be cool and don't show too much interest while you are bidding, or others will decide that you know something they don't (which is probably true if you've done your homework), and they will drive the price beyond your limit. A little subterfuge is a hallowed tradition on the auction scene. Play your cards, as the old cliche goes, close to your vest.

Whatever you decide the piece is worth, write down that amount and stick to it. Do not let yourself get caught up in the fervor of bidding fever and pay more than the item is worth just to satisfy your ego in beating someone else for it. That is the quick way to ruin, even if auctioneers do gaze at you with mooncalf eyes whenever you walk into the room. And why not? If you are so stupid as to make them rich, they are naturally going to love you for it.

This auction fever, by the way, is not just my opinion; it's a documented psychological phenomenon in which bidders lose their heads and slug it out via bids for something, pushing it sometimes far above its true market value. Do this a few times and auctioneers will definitely start sending you flowers and candy. However, a little self-control and setting your bid beforehand and sticking to it like the best glue you can get is a sure cure for this disease.

GETTING A BIDDER'S NUMBER

When you arrive at the auction site on the day of the sale, you are required—assuming you want to be able to bid, (watching is usually free and downright entertaining!)—to register and are then assigned a bidder number to identify you. To get this number, you must usually supply your name, address, and some form of credit. Until you've been attending an auctioneer's events for some time, it is usually hard to get them to accept a personal check. A growing number of auction firms now accept the major credit cards, but cash still remains the desired method of transaction. A few auctioneers will insist that first-timers put down a deposit to ensure that they will actually pay for the items they win.

Once your credit is established, you are given a bidder number, often in the form of a card or some sort of paddle with your number displayed prominently on it. When you win a bidding contest, you are expected to hold the number up where the auctioneer can read it. He'll say "sold, number 84, thankee now," which will cause his bookkeeping crew to enter your number against the tag for that article. At the end of the auction or whenever you elect to leave, you go over to the checkout stand and they pull all the tickets you won. You pay the total and load your goodies into the back of your station wagon, truck, van, moped, or whatever, and ride off happily into the sunset.

RESTRICTIONS

Now, this is a good time to talk about another limit you must be aware of: much you can afford to spend. If your check is not acceptable and you only have $100 in your pocket, obviously your limit is $100 less however much you need for gas to get home. Spend more than this, and the auction people are rightly going to be ill with you because, by winning those bids, you are legally obligated to pay for your purchases. You cannot back out after the fact, and there is seldom such a thing as a return for refund allowed at auctions. This is simply not the way they work.

There are usually other restrictions on you as well; these are called *conditions of sale*. They are set forth in the printed material given you, are on a sign on the auction house wall, or are announced by the auctioneer prior to the start of the sale. Heed these well—they, too, can save you money. Among these conditions of sale will be whether there are any reserves attached to the bidding.

Auctions with Reserve

State auction laws vary rather widely. For example, some may allow the seller to make his own rules before the sale. He might specify that no bids will be accepted below a certain figure. As a result, auctions differ widely in their methods of operation. Usually, however, they can be divided into two basic classes: auctions with reserve and auctions without reserve.

Auctions with reserve have traditionally been the most common type, although this appears to be lessening to some extent. Unless an announcement is made to the contrary, you can pretty well assume that an auction is with reserve. Under this system, the seller or the auctioneer reserves the right to withhold the item from sale if he feels the price is too low. In operation, the auctioneer calls the bids until the highest one is received. At that time a determination is made as to whether that bid is to be accepted or not. In such an auction, your sweet victory can be snatched away in mere seconds and there is nothing you can do about it except grin and hope for better on the next piece in your bidding strategy notebook.

If, however, the bid is acceptable, the auctioneer pounds his gavel or otherwise indicates a sale, and the offer is confirmed. In this case, it means that you have now entered into a binding contract with the auction firm to pick up and pay for that piece before you leave.

Auctions without Reserve

An auction advertised in the conditions of sale as being *without reserve* means that the seller is committed to sell to the highest bidder, although provisions might be made in which a minimum acceptable figure is attached to various pieces. In this case the highest bid, or the highest bid above the minimum figure, is a binding contract on both parties. The items cannot be withdrawn from the sale, nor can you—once your bid has been acknowledged as being the winning one—refuse to take the piece.

BIDDING PROCESS

The actual process of bidding is usually very easy to follow. The auctioneer starts the ball rolling by asking for an offer. "What am I bid for this fine example of early American craftsmanship," he might say, holding up a piece of folk art. "How about

$50? Do I hear $50? $50 now," starting to get into his chant. Someone might flip up a card or wave a hand to get the bidding rolling, or everybody might just smirk, forcing him to come back with a lower offer.

Once started, bidding moves in regular increments determined by the second bid. "I see $50. Asking $55, $55, $55, asking $55 . . . " Another bidder languidly flips up his card (or paddle or hand), and the auctioneer happily jumps up to the next level. "I got $55. Looking for $60, $60, $60 now . . ."

If bidding is hot and heavy, the auctioneer might bump the increment up to $10 or, if it's slow, lower it to $2.50 or $1. Whatever happens, though, following along is easy. Just keep track of your limit and don't get sucked above it when you are bidding.

Should you mistakenly find yourself bidding on the wrong lot, either drop out immediately by not giving any more bids, or—if you are the current high bidder—yell out something like "Not my bid!" to let the auctioneer know you're out so he can drop back to the next highest bidder. Do not let him knock the item down to you or you will be expected to pay for it.

It's really not complicated; you just need to keep your head about you and not get flustered. There are horror stories around of bidders who accidentally scratched their nose and wound up buying a hideous stuffed moose or something, but these are just that—stories. Most auctioneers do not want to sell something to you that you don't want because they must then go through the hassle of collecting from an unwilling buyer. So they really make it easy for you.

The stories that also circulate about the elaborate bidding signals of twitching eyebrows, or pushing eyeglasses up and down one's nose, or standing up in a certain manner are not applicable to the level of auctions that you and I attend. These are for the big international houses, where bids involving millions of dollars are taking place. Such arcane strategy is not only not necessary in most auction houses, but would most likely not even be recognized by the auctioneer. Just raise your hand or flip your card or bat your paddle around. That's all there is to it. Simple enough, huh?

CONCLUSION

All auctions follow the basic rules we have discussed in this chapter. You can use this information to at least understand what's going on at any type of auction. However, we are really just getting started good. Let's move on, honing our auction skills even more. Next comes more detail information on the legal aspects of the auction.

So, what am I bid for Chapter Four? Chapter Four? Chapter Four? . . . Ah, I got a good reader, got a good reader... sold to the good reader! (Psst, that's you! You've won! You got it! Hold up your bidder card so I can get the number, and go pick up your chapter. Thankee, thankee.)

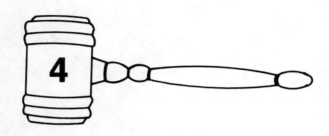

Bidding Strategies

Most auctioneers do not want to sell something to you that you don't want because they must then go through the hassle of collecting from an unwilling buyer. So they really make it easy for you. If an auctioneer thinks you are scratching your nose, he will say something like, "Whatcha doing back there, Charlie? Scratching yer nose or bidding?" You will then be forced to say "Scratching," which will get a great laugh from the crowd and embarrassment for you—but at least you don't get stuck with no dadblame stuffed moose.

BIDDING SIGNALS

The straightforward signals are almost always the best. Flip that number card up, wave the catalog, fan the air with the paddle, wobble your upraised hand back and forth—do something obvious! Once you are in the bidding and the auctioneer keeps glancing back to you, then a slight nod of the head might suffice to inform him that you are still in the race, or a sideways shake will let him know that

you are dropping out of contention on this particular lot.

On the other hand, it's safer to be blatant about it. There's nothing so frustrating as thinking you're winning something at a really great price only to hear another bidder's number called as the winner. The fact you thought the auctioneer was looking at you during the bidding doesn't count for beans after the sale is *knocked down* or sold, to some other number. Make it easy for him. There's a sea of faces out there from the podium, and even an experienced auctioneer will miss a timid signal now and then.

Those stories about elaborate bidding systems usually concern bidders who for one reason or another wanted to remain anonymous. These people have sometimes gone to ridiculous lengths to invent systems and try to explain them to the auctioneer, from such simple things as "whenever I'm standing, I'm bidding" (you wonder what gets bought should a sudden trip to the restroom be in order), to precise and varied positioning of eyeglasses on the nose, to crazy things that would have

Fig. 4-1. In a large crowd it pays to be obvious with your bidding, like the person holding up her hand here.

delighted Rube Goldberg into designing a machine to duplicate them.

Charles Hamilton, in his book *Auction Madness*, covers the New York auction scene. He relates some fascinating information about bidding schemes, which is synopsized here just for general interest. Again it is unlikely that you will run into these schemes in the normal levels of auctions found in most parts of the United States and Canada. Only in the big-money auctions do some dealers feel the need to be secretive and try to outwit their foes—a bit silly, but money does that to people.

These methods include such zaniness as crossing your legs to bid and uncrossing them to stop bidding, or moving your eyeglasses up to the forehead or down to the tip of the nose to show bidding and replacing them over your eyes to stop. Some have been known to bid by unbuttoning the top button of their coat and closing it to cease. A favorite method of some big dealers is to pretend to be reading the auction catalog to indicate bid-

ding and closing it to show that they are no longer in. Yet more methods are to stare into the auctioneer's eyes while you want to be in the bidding and avert your gaze to end. Or scratch a prearranged portion of your anatomy—preferably something socially acceptable, I suppose, like your ear, nose, or head. In ancient Rome and by at least one modern dealer, bidding is shown by winking at the auctioneer.

Yes, these and the others that Hamilton describes are all amusing, but—even with prior arrangement with the auctioneer—you are unnecessarily complicating the auction process by trying to use something on this order. First of all, most auctioneers on a level lower than the giddy heights that Charles Hamilton is privileged to tread simply won't allow themselves to be bothered by such foolishness. If they do agree, chances are that in the heat of the auction they forget completely about your cryptic signals and those of the 14 other people who were crazy enough to try the same thing, or worse, mix them up and suddenly you find yourself buying things you hadn't even bid on, just like the horror stories. Leave well enough alone. Bid in a conventional, clear-cut manner.

ATTRACTING ATTENTION

Beginners to auction-going often worry about how to get the auctioneer to notice them. They fear that their bids will be missed or ignored. Well, forget it, my friend; auctioneers want all the bidders they can possibly attract on each and every lot. He is going to be looking for your movement out there in the audience—hoping and praying for it, as a matter of fact. You are going to be encouraged to bid soon and often.

In a large crowd, however, it is hard for the auctioneer to keep track of everyone, which is why many of them use helpers, called *spotters*, to help him spot bidders.

"Yo, Colonel Bob, thar's one!" they might shout, or more likely just yell out some single word and point at you. As long as you are bidding, they will watch you and make sure that the auctioneer

doesn't miss any of your bids.

If you do feel you are being ignored, you can shout out your bid. "Forty-five!" However, this practice will often get you more recognition than you might want, with everybody turning around in their seats to see who's bidding.

One situation (really a matter of the auctioneer's style) in which you think you are being ignored but aren't is when the auctioneer is focusing on just two bidders, pairing them off against each other. He's running your response in there as well, but flogging two people he thinks might go to the top. If one of these drops out, he'll pick another focal point, maybe even you! Don't let this fluster you in any manner—just stick to your bidding plan and do not be goaded into going over your limit.

OPENING BID

An experienced auctioneer can usually gauge his crowd well enough to accurately determine what the opening, or bottommost, bid for an item should

Fig. 4-2. The auctioneer's assistants—the row of people standing and facing the crowd—help the auctioneer spot all the bids and also hold up the items being bid on so that everyone can see them.

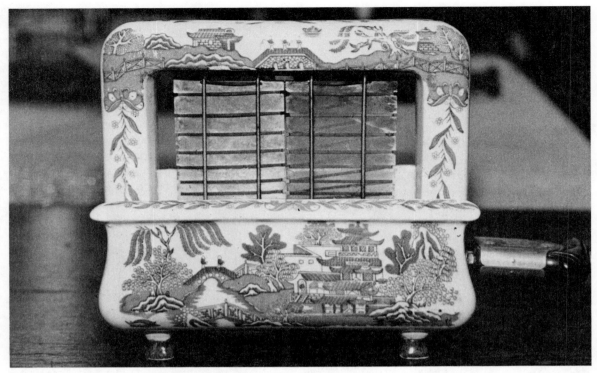

Fig. 4-3. Unique items are usually good buys. This unusual Blue Willow toaster, circa the 1920s, is worth more than $150 retail, yet someone got it at auction for much less just because the person recognized it for what it was.

be. However, if the bidding doesn't take off from there, he'll adroitly slide downward in price until he gets a response.

"Here's a nice chest of drawers," he'll say. "She's oak and she's a beauty. Do I hear $300 for this Fi-ne piece? . . . No, how about $200? $200 will steal 'er away . . . $100, do I have a hundred dollar bill? . . . $50, I need a $50 bill . . ." At this point somebody's hand jerks up. "I got $50, looking for $75. Do I hear $75?" Bingo, up goes another hand and the bidding is off and running. The chest of drawers might very well wind up selling for more than $300, but no canny group of bidders is going to let an auctioneer start them that high, unless, of course, our infamous buddy, Bozo, is there. He'll jump at the first bid like a bull to an electric cattle prod. Auctioneers just flat love bozos.

Some auctioneers have set policies on opening bids in order to get the bidding moving fast and not waste time. With hundreds of lots to move, spending more than a minute or so on any one item will kill your schedule very quickly. So they will start by asking perhaps 10 percent of the high estimate of what the piece will bring, or 2/3 of the low estimate, or some other prearranged figure. Others merely rely on their intuition, shooting from the lip according to the dictates of the moment. If they happen to miss, then they will go sliding down until something clicks.

Still, however, you should realize that *significant pieces*—those that the auctioneer believes will bring a high price—are usually puffed beforehand so that a higher opening bid can be asked for and will stick. Puffing takes many forms, from an erudite descriptive paragraph in the catalog, to the auctioneer grabbing you by the arm as you enter the preview period and dragging you over in front of the piece, let's say a nice oak table.

"Lookit here, would ya, Mr. Roberts. This

here's a genuine Roycrofter. Lookit that Orb and Cross." I dutifully bend over and gaze at the trademark. Sure enough it is Roycroft. For once, he knows what he has. "Gonna go for $600 if it goes for a dime," he whispers so confidentially that only the nearest 40 or 50 people can hear.

That's puffing. His $300 opening bid, in this case, could very well stick. First of all, the table probably is worth more than that, and secondly this sort of puffing affects even people who have no idea of the significance of Elbert Hubbard, the Roycroft Shops, and East Aurora, New York, or why one of these pieces from the turn-of-the-century Arts and Crafts movement era really can be worth $600 and more. It's enough for them to think they're onto something. They'll run the bidding up quite nicely, pleasing the auctioneer immensely.

As for me, because of this ballyhoo, my bidding limit will be passed in the early going and I'll have no chance at the table, which would have been as grand to have as mission oak is. Oh well, the point here is that you learn to recognize puffery and do not let it affect the way you set your bidding limit. If your limit is $250 and the bidding starts at $300, smile and sit that one out. There'll be better bargains along later in that auction or the next.

On the other side of the coin, sometimes there is simply no interest in an offering at any price. In that case, the auctioneer, once he has slid down to a level he considers ridiculous, will withdraw the item from sale. This situation will happen even in an open or no reserves auction. There is nothing unethical about this procedure. No one can be expected to give merchandise away, not with operating costs and other expenses as high as they are today.

BID, BID, WHO'S GOT THE BID?

Auctions are often enough heated, fast-moving af-

Fig. 4-4. Colonel Jerry Sluder's auction assistant holds up two pieces of Pisgah pottery, which were taken at bargain prices because the buyer had done his homework and knew what they were and what their value was.

fairs. It's easy enough for you to get confused, to lose concentration and not be sure of who actually has the bid. Auctioneers, especially as the bidding nears its climax, will take pains to let people know where they are seeing bids.

"I got $40 by the post . . . I got $50 down front . . . $60 over on the side . . . $70, we're looking for a $70 bill, $70 . . . Yes, I see you, sir. I got $70, looking for $80 . . ."

However, if you are still confused, it's perfectly okay to ask "My bid?" or to signal your query in some other manner, perhaps by a perplexed expression. The auctioneer or his spotter will reply something like "Yours at $60" or "Against you," meaning your bid has been raised and you'll have to bid again to get back into the fray.

In the case of two hands going up at once, it is usually the policy of the auction firm or house to let the auctioneer decide which bid to accept. Sometimes this policy is to accept the tie bid nearest the auctioneer—it does pay to come early and be as close to the front as possible. Should this happen on the final or winning bid, the auctioneer will sometimes stage a runoff, allowing only the two tied bidders to participate.

If a late bid comes in, after the auctioneer has knocked down, it is too late, even if the bid is higher than the winning one. Bidding is not really that hard to keep track of, but it does move fast and you have to be on the ball so you do not miss anything.

MULTIPLE-PIECE LOTS

In auction parlance, a lot can be either a single item or a group of items. You should realize, in setting your bidding limits, exactly how this works or you could get a very nasty and expensive surprise.

Basically, to keep the auction moving faster, the auctioneer will quite often group smaller items together. In estate auctions, which have to sell literally everything in the house, odds and ends of junk will be tossed into cardboard boxes and sold as a *box lot*. When you bid, it is on everything in the box. During the preview period you should make careful note in your little book as to the exact numbers of which box lots you are interested in; other-

wise you can find yourself buying one that not only doesn't have the item which caught your eye, but that does saddle you with a heavy load of worthless crud.

A more symmetrical example, *group lots* are the ones containing such items as silverware, plates, or six dining room chairs. These lots might be sold in one of two ways. The auctioneer will typically announce them either as "six chairs, one price takes them all," or "six chairs, six times your money."

The former, of course, you can handle as you would a one-piece lot: Just recognize that if you win, at least three chairs will have to be tied on top of your station wagon—unless, of course, you have made other arrangements for delivery, which some auction houses offer. The latter example, however, is where the nasty surprise can happen. *Six times your money* means just that. It means that if your winning bid for the chairs is $50, you owe not $50 but $300, or $50 times six chairs. You can't weasel out by just taking one, either; you made a binding contract to buy all six by tendering the winning bid.

Therefore, during the preview period, assuming you are interested in the dining room chairs, you need to put down two bidding limits—one per piece, and one for a total lot price. That way, no matter how the auctioneer sells them, you're ready for him. In this way, you will avoid confusion or trying to do hasty calculations while the auction is blasting along at full bore.

An honest auctioneer will make it crystal clear which way a group lot is being sold. He doesn't want you confused because you might not bid, and he wants your bid—you are doing him a favor by bidding.

BIDDING TACTICS

The famous Confederate cavalry general, Nathan Bedford Forrest, is attributed as having said, when asked the secret of his victories, that you should "Git thar fustest with the mostest men." Since Forrest was a wealthy Tennessee cotton plantation owner, it is assumed by historians that he actually phrased this advice in considerably better English.

I mention this quotation merely to point out that while this may be indeed excellent for whipping Yankees on the battlefield, it will get your pocketbook or wallet slaughtered at an auction.

Only Bozo leaps in unheeding if the auctioneer starts an item high, especially one that he's been puffing the heck out of beforehand. Instead you must not only set bidding limits, but also think a little about your overall bidding strategies.

There is a lot of manipulation occurring on the auction scene, and not only by auctioneers. A lot of people are playing the game, and you need to learn to recognize them. For example, someone who really covets an especially nice Philadelphia-made chest of drawers circa 1810 is not going to wander around during the preview period saying "Oh, my, what a wondrously marvelous chest of drawers. I'm going to bid my heart and soul for it." Rather this person will most likely not allow himself to be seen within 30 feet of the piece and can most likely be overheard saying things like, "See that chest of drawers over there? Worse out-and-out fake I ever saw." By this means he hopes to scare away a few bidders and get it cheaper for himself.

Here's where your knowledge comes in. If antique furniture is your field of interest, you should be able to form your own opinion as to the authenticity of the piece and recognize this guy's ploy as being just that. His bad-mouthing of a coveted piece is exactly the opposite of the auctioneer's (or his staff's) puffery. Sometimes the two opposing forces can get some pretty good arguments going. Ignore them both; rely on your knowledge.

There is consensus, however, among veteran auction goers as to the proper demeanor for a bidder: stonefaced inscrutability. Look at the crowd during your next auction. The ones sitting yawning and seemingly bored out of their gourds are probably the most canny of the bunch, and their concentration is really riveted on the auctioneer's tiniest twitch. They make "poker faces" seem like inane grins in comparison.

The idea behind this demeanor is the widely held opinion that any expressed enthusiasm will only serve to stimulate bidding and competition,

hence driving prices higher. The good side of this practice is that it keeps the auctioneer on his toes. He doesn't know whether the audience is with him or about to take a collective nap. That's why you see some of them running around waving their arms like an old-time revival preacher with an irate squirrel in his pants.

The general rule, then, is to be low keyed, to stay cool and calm on the outside (whether you are or not), and to hide your excitement as you zero in on that big kill.

THE RIGHT TIME TO BID

There are two schools of thought on when you should join in the bidding. Both theories are probably equally valid. You will no doubt want to have each in your repertoire, fitting one or the other to the specific situation.

The first theory goes that you should jump into the fray immediately—while, of course, bearing in mind the constraints we just covered of not appearing too eager or enthusiastic. The justification offered for earliness is that you are thus positioned to grab off those surprise bargains. These are lots, sometimes called *sleepers*, which, as a result of lack of interest, the auctioneer will knock down quickly—generally to the first or second bidder.

Continuing in this philosophy, it is also felt that by being aggressive and jumping in early, you keep the competition off balance, even sometimes scaring them off the lot. While this particular facet of the "in early with both feet" strategy might disconcert a few beginners, I wouldn't count on it swaying old-time bidders in the least. Still, there is much to be said for being positioned in such a manner. Again, your choice should be fitted to the particulars of the situation.

The second school of thought is the "hang back and see what develops method." It's obviously a more conservative approach, and is best on large-ticket items where the bidding will last for a longer time. Using this strategy, you merely watch carefully until the initial flurry of bidding wanes and many of the early goers have dropped out, then you pop like a ghost out of the woodwork, figuratively yelling "boo, y'all!"

The ideal execution of this ploy is to wait it out until the very last moment when one bidder has outlasted all the others and the auctioneer is just about ready to knock it down to him. Then, wham, there you are! The theory goes that this strategy will demoralize the bidder, who having lasted so long against a known opponent will bow out against this sudden, unexpected opposition. Sometimes it works, sometimes it doesn't. Remember, these are both just theories; each bidding situation is pretty unique unto itself. You must learn to be mentally flexible and exploit opportunities as they pop up.

One obvious benefit of the second school of thought is that you do remain essentially inconspicuous. If something goes over your limit, by waiting to put in a bid you haven't revealed either the limits of your pocketbook or what class of items has your interest. On the other hand, jumping in vigorously at the beginning does tend to cause people to notice you after awhile.

There is also a variant on the "hang back" school of bidding called the *shutout bid*. This is when you not only hang back until the last moment, but if your opponent persists in staying in, you suddenly and loudly double or triple the bid, disconcerting everybody, including the auctioneer. Heads will jerk around to gape wide-eyed at you. Bozo will probably even buy you a cup of coffee afterwards, especially if it works.

In my opinion, however, this is an exceptionally stupid tactic. So what if it works? All you've really done is to preclude any chance that you might have gotten the piece at a lesser price. What if your competitor calls your bluff and raises you, possibly doubling you and pushing you above your bidding limit? It's a no-win situation for sure.

ABSENTEE BIDS

The nice thing about auctions is that you don't have to even be there to bid, although it's far more effective if you are. Let's take a for instance. Say there are two, or even three, auctions coming off in your immediate area on the same day. One auction has a number of lots that have attracted your interest, and the other two have one or more as well. Obviously, you cannot be in three places at once. So how can you possibly bid on everything you want?

Almost all auction houses or firms will let you submit what's called an *order bid*, either in person or by mail; hence, you can (and many do) bid in auctions in the next state or a full continent away. The initial bidding strategy for order bids is the same as for an auction that you will attend; decide on your limit and write it down.

The way absentee bids should work is that someone in the employ of the auction house bids for you, going as high as necessary to get the piece and yet stay under your limit. However, the way it often does work is that if no one meets your absentee bid limit, you win the bid at that price. Bear this fact in mind when you decide on the amount of your limit.

However, order bids do enhance and expand your power to make a profit by enabling you to diversify yourself and work in several auctions in a shorter period of time than you could manage if you had to be physically present at each. Above all, knowledge counts here, especially if you are bidding by mail at auctions too far away for you to be at the preview. In such cases, you need to know exactly what you are bidding on, and perhaps lower your limits somewhat so that increased profits will counterbalance the occasional losers you get stuck with by not being able to check things out beforehand.

GETTING STARTED

Reading this book will give you a good background in how auctions work and what you can expect, but the only real way to learn anything well is to actually do it. Your final lessons in bidding must come on the floor of the auction house—a baptism under fire, so to speak.

My suggestion is that you attend an auction or two first, merely as a spectator. Don't bid just yet, but go through the motions as a sort of dress rehearsal to make you comfortable with the process. Attend the preview period, touch and fondle the merchandise, decide what you would like to have, slip out to your car and check your price guides. Come back inside, your notes now complete with bidding limits set on the pieces you'd like to have, and take a seat toward the back. (You want to be able to see the bidders as well as the auctioneer during this schooling experience.) When the auction starts, observe everything closely, making notes in your little book on points to remember.

As an observer, rather than someone who is caught up in the emotional high of being an actual participant, you can accustom yourself to the auction's flow of events completely free of charge. It'll be a grand show, too. Watch especially for the lots to come up that you set limits on and see how many of them you could have gotten if you had really been bidding.

Don't worry about missing something. One important lesson you should learn concerning your first auction is that another one will be along next week. Any item you want now will no doubt show up again soon, and that time you'll be ready to pounce on it with all the aplomb of the seasoned auction goer. Meanwhile, in this first sale, write down as many of the pieces as you can and the price they go for. Accumulate these prices realized and they will help you in setting your limits for future auctions.

At your second or third auction—or even at the first if reading this book has made you cocky and you want to dive right in—you can start bidding. Take it easy, though. Pick out three or four small, cheap items and put a moderately low limit on them. When they come up, bid your heart out, stopping abruptly upon reaching your limit. These items, if you lose, won't matter much, nor on winning cost you much. You also will learn by experience, suffering the agony of defeat and perhaps even the thrill of victory for mere pennies relative to what you will soon be confidently wagering.

SUMMING UP

Regardless of the type of auction, we all want one thing when we attend: merchandise at a respectable savings over what it would cost in a store or bought in some other retail manner. You can easily achieve this goal by following three general rules that you should adhere to with the consistency of premium glue.

First, use the preview period to maximum advantage by carefully examining the lots you are interested in, scrutinizing them not only in the light of your pocket flash but in the light of your knowledge, as well. Check them for hidden defects. Look for chicanery in repairs, refinishing, reproductions, broken or missing parts, and anything else that would decrease the item's value. (Remember in collectibles, especially, that condition is almost all important in determining the value of a piece.) Correlate the prices realized on similar pieces in your price guides and from your own accumulated auction results to find a price for it.

Taking all of this information into account, jot down a firm bidding limit for this piece. Something that you have to pay twice its worth for is no bargain whatsoever, and you have flat lost money by letting yourself be conned into buying it.

The last rule is the shortest and the most important: Stick to your limit. This is the single most significant bit of information I can impart to you. Hanging on firmly to this one precept could potentially save you many hundreds of times the cost of this book.

Now it's time to auction off the next chapter, this one on the legal aspects of auctions. You are buying a single chapter at one time your money. Let's go. What am I bid? . . . You there in front of the book, yes, I got your bid . . . Any other takers? . . . You got it, good reader! That's four in a row isn't it? You are coming along right nicely, indeed.

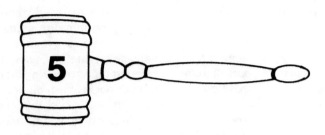

Chicanery
and Legal Aspects

This chapter covers not only the legal aspects—your rights at an auction and the recourse you have if you find yourself cheated—but also some ways to avoid having an unscrupulous auctioneer do you in. We discussed in the last chapter obligations to the auctioneer and the fact that a binding contract is executed when your bid is accepted as the winning one. In this chapter we'll delve into more detail, not only concerning your obligation to the auctioneer, but his to you.

Proportionally, there are only a few dishonest auctioneers. This profession—like law, medicine, politics (no kidding!), pharmaceutics, publishing, small business, and a hundred other occupations—will have it's share of bad apples. If there's an honest buck to be made in something, you can bet your best twist of chewing tobacco that some crook is around trying to bump the take up to three or four, and mine your teeth for the gold fillings as well.

In the auction game it's not always that immediately obvious that you are being cheated. A shady auctioneer has an arsenal of sneaky tricks that would make even the most corrupt politician seem tame by comparison.

CHECKING OUT A NEW AUCTION

It is hard, the first time you attend an auction by a certain auctioneer, to determine whether everything is on the up and up. First, you'll have to observe for a while to become accustomed to the auctioneer's style—there being minor variances in all of them, some positively unique. Also you probably won't know most of the people in the audience, and hence have no criteria to predict how they might react if they were to detect cheating. There are, however, several tip-offs that you should be aware of and apply to each new auction. These are, of course, not foolproof evidence of crookedness, but they are certainly indicators that it could be present.

Descriptions. If the auctioneer's descriptions of the lots greatly exaggerate their worth and significance, this can be a disturbing sign. Give him the benefit of the doubt if this happens only a few

Fig. 5-1. Blue Willow china has been popular for hundreds of years. Some pieces are worth hundreds of dollars; others, like this one (since Blue Willow is still being made), much less. Buying a $15 plate at auction for $30 is not good, getting a $30 gravy boat for $2 is a much better deal.

times—after all mistakes do occur and none of us can know everything. However, if gross overstatements are consistently applied to almost every offering, he is either ignorant as a two-month-old pumpkin or puffing the heck out of stuff—either way you need to watch him.

High Opening Bids. If high opening bids are commonly asked for and immediately received, again start to wonder—especially if these opening bids are not supported by other people and bidding is reopened at a drastically lower price with the lot eventually selling for a lower price than the initial bid. Such cases indicate the strong possibility of a fake bid.

Many Lots Passed. Any auctioneer will, for var-

ious legitimate reasons—such as not being able to meet a seller's reserve—remove lots occasionally from the auction. This situation is to be expected and accepted, but when this happens time after time, you can begin to suspect trickery. Either the auctioneer is trying to sell his personal inventory and doesn't want to take a loss on it, or he has done something such as borrowing the inventory from a retail store and is attempting to move it above the retail price. (This situation is not that uncommon, alas, in shady auction houses.)

Bidders are Not Always Identified. Usually an honest auctioneer will clearly announce the winner's bidder number or say that the piece was sold "to the order" of "Dr. Bob Cratchit over to

Fig. 5-2. This Civil War picture, circa 1863, of Union soldiers on the porch of a house in New Bern, North Carolina, brought $80 at auction because the photograph was authenticated.

Centerville," meaning the good doctor had a mail or telephone bid in and won the piece. If, however, the auctioneer you're watching often mumbles the number while pretending to be making a note or something, or if a high percentage of sales are knocked down as "sold to the order," without a name mentioned, you should also cast a jaundiced eye in the auctioneer's direction. On the other hand, if he takes great pains to very clearly enunciate the order bidder's name on a good many occasions, this is also cause for worry.

Let me give you an example that, to my chagrin, I found myself personally involved in. Back in the mid-seventies I had a retail stereo shop for several years and was also involved in buying inexpensive electronic items and wholesaling them to flea market dealers. One of these dealers promised me a real killing if I would load up a bunch of stuff and put it in a retail auction he knew of. "Bring along one of your expensive stereos," he added. "It'll sell."

I didn't believe the guy, but put a $500 set in the station wagon anyway. We got to the auction and my lots of cheap stuff sold moderately well—no big profit but enough to cover gas, my time, and the commission this turkey with me was getting. Then the stereo came up—I forget the brand now but remember it had two moderately nice Elector Voice speakers. It was truly worth $500 retail.

The bidding opened at $1000! I just about swallowed my tongue, sudden visions of profit dancing in my head. The bidding was that hot, but the unit closed out at $1500. I couldn't believe it and, as it turned out, shouldn't have. When the auction was over, we went to the office to collect our receipts, less the auctioneer's commission. "Be sure to pick up your stereo," the auctioneer said. The guy with me just grinned and winked. "Sure, no problem."

What happened was that a $500 stereo was totally out of place in that cheap retail auction. They just wanted to use it for glitter, to awe and astound the regulars (who probably knew better anyway). So the bids were fake, didn't mean a thing. Afterwards, I heard from several sources that this particular auction was more crooked than a dog's hind leg and I would be a real bozo if I ever went again. I never did.

One Bidder Wins Many Lots. If what seems to be an exceptionally large number of bids are won by one person, especially if he always jumps in on high starting bids, you are quite justified in beginning to suspect that he is a shill. The shill makes extra profit for the auctioneer—(for a cut of the proceeds)—by running items up as far as they will go. As often as not the price will go too far and he will be the "winner." Actually, in this case, no money changes hands and the lot goes right back into the next auction. It is on the sales where unknowing suckers are drawn into the competition and stuck with a piece of garbage at six times its true worth that the real money is raked in.

Remember, however, that one person winning a lot of bids is only an indicator, not ironclad proof. All of us, once we become heavy auction goers, will occasionally have a hot day, getting a lot of stuff at very good prices. There is a definite tendency (and something you should be aware of) that the more you buy, the more you are inclined to continue the roll by competing for other lots. Many auctioneers recognize this fact and will give big spenders a couple or three quick knock downs just to prime the pump, so to speak, and inveigle the

now-expansive gent or lady into overbidding on more expensive lots to follow.

If you do suspect a person of being a shill, you can further define your suspicion by watching the items he buys. Most people tend to specialize; if this cat has a go at an unbelievably diverse selection of categories, your suspicion should be taking root.

Excessive Advance Bids. If the auctioneer continually seems to be announcing that such and such a lot has an advance bid on it of $50, $100, or whatever amount—this meaning that someone has sent in a mail or telephone bid—and asks if anyone wants to beat it, you should be suspicious. If there really is an order bid, doing it this way is unfair to the bidder, as we discussed in the last chapter. However, if this situation occurs over and over, it is yet another indicator that something foul will stick to the bottom of your shoes if you don't watch your step around that particular auction house.

An Oddly Structured Estate. A common ploy of the dishonest auctioneer is to gather a bunch of things together and announce it as an estate sale. People will flock to these sales assuming there are—as is in the legitimate auctions of this type— bargains to be had. However, if you examine the offerings and find that it quite illogically consists only of desirable items, and usually one of each, then you can start to worry. A legitimate estate will

Fig. 5-3. At a recent North Carolina auction, this "Bridge" pitcher with a small crack went for $30. A set of three Roseville "Mostique" vases brought just $70; a "Dutch" tankard, $45; and a "Donatello" bowl, $30. All were moderately good buys.

Fig. 5-4. Collectible toys are popular at many auctions. This "Funny Andy" ferry boat was made around 1930.

consist of a jumbly hodgepodge of pieces. One-of-a-kind items usually mean that the auctioneer is conspiring with a dealer or importer and that the unsold items will be returned to a warehouse to await the next "estate" sale.

In my part of the country, considerate politicians in some of the smaller mountain counties have traditionally allowed the dead to continue to vote for decades, thoughtfully stuffing the ballot boxes so they won't have to get up out of the graveyard and do it themselves. Crooked auctioneers carry this time-hallowed practice a bit further, only instead of using real deceased people, like the politicians, they flat make them up and sell their estates over and over. It gives the imaginary dearly departed a bad name, it does!

Collections Are Too Consistent. The same type of tip-off as just discussed applies to large collections as well. Usually no collector will amass everything neatly within a narrow range of value—he'll have added a superlative example, worth more than the others, or some pieces barely worth spit. In other words, he'll have items differing in price over a fairly wide range. So if you see things are too close to be consistent with a normal collector's practice, it is logical to suspect that it was

the auctioneer who assembled the collection over a period of time—like maybe 15 minutes in an importer's showroom.

Unusual Furnishing in a House Sale. An auction of household furnishings is typically held on the site, i.e., in and around the house itself. During the preview period you can tramp up and down the stairs and peer into every nook and cranny. Estate sales are often held in this manner. If, upon attending one of these sales, you note that many of the furnishings do not seem to fit the house, you can also begin to have reservations about the auctioneer.

Tip-offs in this case include: furniture that is too big or too small for the room that it's in; paintings, bronzes, lamps, silver, crystal, and other collectibles that do not match what seems to be the general decor of the house; expensive oriental rugs that do not fit the rooms they are displayed in; and anything else that seems out of whack with the taste of the person who lived here.

Some seedy auctioneers make a career of doing such household sales, trucking in their own merchandise to tone up the place and make all the furnishings seem more valuable then they actually are. Often these "window dressings" will not really be sold in true competitive bidding, but knocked down to a shill and thus saved for the next house sale.

GETTING THE BEST
OF A DISHONEST AUCTIONEER

There is one more important thing to watch for, but first I'll tell you how to hoist a crooked auctioneer, squirming and screaming, on his own petard.

Even after your suspicions are pretty well confirmed that a particular auctioneer is indeed a right Bozo of a clown, it's not necessarily time to beat a hasty but dignified retreat. First of all, such a crook can be extremely entertaining. His blatant elaborations on fact, his constant contradiction of himself on technical matters, his posturings and pitiful attempts to evince erudition on an object that is totally out of his ken of comprehension, are wondrously hilarious indeed. Treasure and savor these moments. Store them up to tell wherever you

and other auction goers get together to talk shop.

Also, just because the guy is an out-and-out thief doesn't mean you still can't get some good buys off him. After all, in many cases he doesn't even realize what he has; he is so used to taking shortcuts in life that he does little or no research on his merchandise. Again, set your limit and strictly adhere to it. Plus, here, you will be laboring under the additional handicap of having to prove to the auctioneer that you will not be run up by one of his shills, or bite at a ridiculously high opening offer.

The problem the auctioneer has, especially if he is taking back a large number of lots or the shill is getting them, is that he needs to make some "real" sales to cover his overhead. Here's where you can move in and get some bargains. This guy is not going to let anything go very cheap, but if you know something he doesn't, you can whiffle it away before he has the least idea of what you're up to. And that will be the most delicious story of

Fig. 5-5. This Rookwood mug is authentic and by Tom Lunt, dated 1895. It is worth round $750.

Fig. 5-6. Country furniture like this nineteenth-century wardrobe was popular at antiques auctions—so much so that many copies are made and sold as authentic when they are really no older than last week. Learn to inspect closely before you commit yourself.

all to tell your auction cronies!

AVOIDING BIDDING AGAINST YOURSELF

One term that you will hear other bidders grousing about from time to time is *running up*, as in "that lousy sonuva %$@& ran me up!" This means that a less than honest auctioneer allegedly employed one of several tactics to get the bidder, even after he had actually won the bid, to pay more than he would have without the trickery. In other words, the auctioneer artificially kept the bidding going.

This bit of chicanery works by getting the bidder to bid against himself. A bidder who would have actually been quite willing to pay even more for his piece against some legitimate competitor

will become very upset when he suspects such underhanded tactics are being used on him. Letting an auctioneer do this to you is foolish, common, frustrating in the extreme, and almost impossible to avoid now and then. Sometimes this is an honest mistake on the auctioneer's or your part, but more often it is not.

If an auctioneer decides to run the bid on you, alas there's little you can do to stop him. Auctioneers have a vast grab bag of tricks perfected over the centuries to fall back on. These range from plants and shills in the audience, fraudulent reserves, fake order bids, and that hoary old device, the off-the-wall bid.

Off-the-wall bids are simply that—if no competitor ups your bid, the auctioneer simply pretends that one did, plucking it from thin air. In a large auction crowd, this is sometimes an effective technique since no one can see the entire audience. A crooked hammer-wielder, well versed in this trick, might get two or three more bids out of you in this manner before graciously knocking down the sale to you.

The lower-echelon crook, like the ones we just discussed, is pretty blatant about all this, sometimes attempting to run every single bid. The more sophisticated, however, reserves it for special large-ticket items or to use on customers he knows are easily influenced. Far more auctioneers than should give in to temptation and use the trick because it blends in so well with the normal flow of the auction that it is very hard for even the most astute bidder to catch.

A skillful auctioneer can usually gauge to within a very few dollars just how far he can push a particular customer. The less adept ones will finish a sale with a sizable number of unsold items, thus indicating they had been running bids and did not know when to stop.

Of course some auctioneers even have an answer when they overrun you. Let's say you suddenly realize you're being run up and craftily drop out just as the crook, gazing without focus toward the back of the room, manufactures a raise out of something, moonbeams maybe, and triumphantly brings it forward:

"$120, ah have $120, do ah heah $130 . . .?" He looks expectantly at you, but you just fold your arms and smile at him.

Well it won't work, he'll immediately look toward the back again, frown momentarily, and then say something like, "Oh, sorry, suh, I coulda sworn you raised your hand." Then he'll turn back to you, slam down his gavel, and say "Sold! Numbah 84! $110." And you have flat out, purely been had and there's really nothing you can do about it. The fall of the hammer is a binding contract and it's hard as blue blazes to prove you were being run.

Your real defense against such an auctioneer is word of mouth. If he persists in these and other dirty tricks, sooner or later people will begin cottoning to him and his attendance will dwindle. He might always be able to attract enough bozos and newcomers to stay in business, but it will be a seedy little auction house and not a significant factor in your local market. The only reason you would have to attend would be for entertainment and to hone your skills at detecting such tricks.

There are techniques you can use to stop running, or at least force him to tone it down with respect to you. One of these involves deliberately losing bids. Simply occasionally abruptly drop out while other people are still bidding, definitely doing so before you get close enough to winning where running could be employed against you. This, even in a totally honest auction, can be beneficial.

You don't want to become known as someone who is so out-and-out competitive that he will go to any heights to win a bid. Such people open themselves to all sorts of manipulations by unscrupulous and even honest auctioneers. Managing to lose an occasional lot in this way is a good investment toward the time when something goes up on the block that you really want. Because you will then have the reputation of being a pretty cool customer (forget the seething maelstrom that careens about inside you; they can't see that), no one—other bidders nor the auctioneer—will think to run the bid up on you.

An effective ploy to use when you are pretty well positive that the auctioneer is running you is to stand up, walk to the rear of the room, and turn to face him. This is the same as saying "All right, turkey, I know your game, let's see you try it now." Only the most stupid auctioneer in the world will persist in trying to run you after such a grand and forceful silent statement on your part.

It might surprise you to find how suddenly effective your bidding becomes. He may even give you a few early knock downs just to try to appease you, especially if you are a moderately good customer that he wants to keep.

The final maneuver, if he persists in running on you, is to quite openly stalk to the door and leave, of course redeeming any purchases you have already obligated yourself for. Even though the auctioneer has been cheating you, you are not relieved of that binding buyer contract generated by the fall of the gavel.

If the idiot persists, after all this, in running on you the next time you check him out, cross that auction house from your list and pass the word along to your friends. Hopefully, he will continue in his little tricks for a while and put himself out of business.

SUBSTITUTIONS

If an auction is "dirty," you can bet the tricks don't stop with the auctioneer's flimflam up behind the podium. A favorite one is the old substitution ploy. Here's how it works.

Let's say during the auction preview you come across a beautiful piece of art pottery: Weller, Roseville, Rookwood, or something equally as good. You sneak out to your car and check the price guide. Wow! $200. You set your limit at $150 and are luckily enough to get the vase for only $80, even after you know the bozo ran you up another $20. Still, it's a darn good buy and you are well pleased. That is, until you go to pay for and pick up your piece. The hunk of baked clay they give you has only a vague resemblance to the gorgeous creation you saw in the preview and bid on in the auction. It is worth, tops, $3. You rant and rave but it does you absolutely no good—it's their word against yours and no way you can prove a switch took place. A judge would just throw you both out of court as wasting his time.

To prevent this occurrence, most legitimate auction houses will have one of the assistants immediately deliver the smaller objects—the ones where physical switching might be possible—to where the bidder is sitting. If you buy pottery and glassware, you need to have some old newspapers and boxes with you so that they can be packed away.

Your defense in a crooked auction, once you win the bid, is to snap your fingers and motion the assistant to hand the piece over. If he is reluctant to do so, pop up and go get it. That is the only way you'll be able to forestall the possibility of a switch.

DEALERS DO IT TOO!

Just as a small percentage of auctioneers are crooked, so are a tiny portion of dealers, such as those who frequent antiques auctions. To begin with, most dealers, even the honest ones, will tend to discourage you from attending antiques auctions—being far more interested in selling you items at retail than seeing you down there competing toe to toe with them for choice pieces on an essentially wholesale level. A good dealer, however, will quickly get over this miff and even assist you by telling you where the better auctions are, and by buying some of your finds at auctions he didn't make it to. As you recall from Chapter 3, you need to set your limit so that you can sell the piece at a price which allows the dealer to add a reasonable retail markup.

However, not all dealers are so accommodating, nor forgiving. Some will refer to nontrade auction goers as "civilians" or "privates" and resent their presence. A few will go even further, instituting dirty tricks to stack the decks in their favor, cheating the other auction attendees and the auctioneer as well. Let me hasten to point out that this is not nearly as common as it used to be, bidders being more sophisticated these days, but it's still interesting.

The dealer trickery used is the ring or knock-out system to prevent private individuals from getting anything at less than retail price. This was used primarily in large auctions frequented mostly by the trade.

It worked like this: A group of dealers in a certain field would form a secret syndicate. They then made a pact not to bid against each other. When one member of this combine would bid, the others, no matter now much they wanted the piece, would refrain from bidding and running up the price. After the auction was over, these dealers would then hold a private auction among themselves, bidding on all the pieces they obtained.

If no one else wants a particular item, then that dealer pays for it and keeps it. However, if two or more are interested, they auction if off and the difference between what it sells for there and the artificially lowered public auction price is profit that goes into the syndicate's coffers—essentially stealing it from the legitimate seller by denying the realization of a proper price at the original auction.

Sometimes there were even rings within rings, with two or three dealers in cahoots against their fellow conspirators.

WHAT'S YOUR RECOURSE?

There are several ways in which you can be cheated at auction. Alas, there aren't really that many ways in which you can exact retribution. Crooked auctioneers, as pointed out earlier, have a tremendous grab bag of tricks perfected over the centuries. It's going to be very hard for you to try and explain it logically to some harried small claims court judge who just wishes both of you would go out behind the courthouse and slug it out, leaving him to his headache in peace.

Besides, a crooked auctioneer has had long experience with the law already. Most likely you won't have been the first to take umbrage at his shenanigans and try to pry what is rightfully yours out of his sticky fingered grasp. He'll also be an expert at skating around just on the very edge of the auction laws—assuming your state has them.

The best thing you can do, probably, is threaten to go to the newspapers or picket his auction house. Bad publicity resulting in loss of sales to him might possibly be the leverage you need to get the problem resolved. Otherwise, take your loss like a man (or woman) and make sure that all your friends and acquaintances know what happened. Eventually, maybe, the crook will have to go out of business.

Now it's on to the most important chapter in this book—the one on knowledge! So go ahead and bid for it, I promise not to run it up. Just indicate your bid by turning the page. I have a feeling you will get it.

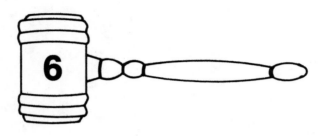

Knowledge: Your
Most Potent Weapon

Somewhere recently you've heard about knowledge, right? Like as a constant recursive theme throughout the first five chapters of this book. Well, guess what, old friend? This entire chapter also deals with, uh huh, knowledge.

This book is one I've felt someone should write for a long time. In over 20 years of going to auctions, it has often struck me how ill prepared many people are, including myself in the early years. In the past several years, I've been a heavy attendee of antiques auctions, covering them for the various antiques- and collectibles-oriented newspapers I write for regularly.

This general lack of knowledge has been brought home even stronger to me as I watch buyers make horrendous mistakes out of simple ignorance, or worse, lose some really good buys to others. As mentioned earlier, just a little knowledge can give you that racer's edge.

Don't panic now, nor immediately dismiss what I'm saying as being beyond your capabilities. It's not hard to obtain the basics you need in order to succeed at your favorite type of auction. You can easily and enjoyably prepare yourself in a number of ways.

All types of auctions require that you do some sort of homework. We will discuss various examples in the individual chapters on each type of auction, but here are some general examples.

For a real estate auction, you would need to check out zoning ordinances, if the deed has clear title, and find out if there are any restrictions on the property, like retention of mineral rights or no mobile homes allowed. For auto auctions, you should be familiar enough with cars to recognize such minor problems as the engine about ready to fall out and tires so thin that the air is showing through. In buying fine art, you need to know which painters are collectible and which are not, and a bunch of ways to detect blatant forgeries. Buying livestock requires specialized knowledge to make you outstanding in that field, and the same applies to commodities and all the other types of auctions. Antiques and collectibles, of course, are

Fig. 6-1. Is this piece of furniture a legitimate antique or just a reproduction? How do you tell? Knowing the answer to these and other questions often spells the difference between profit and loss when you are buying at auctions.

indisputably the area in which your knowledge can gain you the most consistent profits over the long term.

The realization that you need knowledge and the ways you can find it are the greatest gifts I can give you during the course of this book. So unwrap your present, here comes some tips on how to find and, yes apply, knowledge.

BOOKS

It is obvious that books are a great source of information, as you've indicated by buying this one. The tip on successful and profitable auction bidding is to specialize in just a few categories, reading everything you can find about those fields. Become an expert in furniture, art, glassware, antique jewelry, farm machinery, Chevrolet automobiles, whatever you like, and frequent the auctions that sell those items. You'll quickly find yourself recognizing the bargains, taking advantage of them, and enjoying the resulting profits that accrue to your bank account.

Trying to compete at auction without knowledge is akin to groping about in a large, dark room for the light switch while wearing boxing gloves,

having a lamp shade over your head, and clanking along with each foot firmly wedged in mop pails. Sure, you'll occasionally find the switch, but some Bozo will always wander along and turn it off on you again. Darkness slams back down then, like a portcullis in some ancient castle. Knowledge is all important.

This book is an overview. It is meant to get you off and running on the right path, but it is not the end of your quest. The fun and joy and money to be made loom wonderfully ahead of you during your auction-attending days. In these pages are the basics you need to properly stay on that path but— even if TAB were so kind as to publish 48 large volumes on this subject—there is simply not room to cover every topic in detail.

Once you decide on your fields of specialty— and you can always add or drop these as you go through the years—you should seek out books concerning these particular areas. Haunt bookstores with sections on antiques and collectibles, write this publisher (TAB BOOKS, P.O. Box 40, Blue

Fig. 6-2. Gilbert Hollifield is a successful North Carolina auctioneer who has held some very nice estate sales over the years, as well as a nationally significant antique toy auction.

Fig. 6-3. It takes some homework to be able to recognize and assign a bidding limit on a beautiful nineteenth-century clock such as this one.

Ridge Summit, PA 17214) and request the current catalog, write other companies who publish specialty books, become familiar with the offerings of your public library and those of the various colleges and universities in your area, most of which I've found will let nonstudents use their facilities for a small donation.

Become familiar with the recognized authors and experts in your particular field. In antiques, for example, there are a great many top-notch writers who are very good in a number of fields. Charles Hamilton is one. His book, *Auction Madness* is one of many that I read in researching this book. Hamilton is currently, without any doubt, the leading writer on the subject of collecting autographs and manuscripts, and a number of his books on this subject are now available.

The Kovels, Ralph and Terry, have been writing about antiques since the 1950s. Their column appears in scores of newspapers across the country, and many of their books are currently in print. They even offer a regular newsletter to subscribers who want the latest in the collectibles field.

There are many others as well—some very good people who are passionately interested in things you, too, find fascinating, and who already have done the hard work of searching out and compiling information from a myriad of sources for you. All you have to do is read their books, absorb the information (or at least know where to look it up when you need it), and apply that knowledge in your auction pursuits.

Are you cheap like me? Want to save money but still build an extensive reference library? Look in the "junk" bins at used book shops and scope out your local flea markets. It's amazing how many excellent reference books you can pick up for 50¢ to $1, just because the dealer thinks the book is

Fig. 6-4. At a recent North Carolina auction, this Roseville "Donatello" bowl sold for $30.

old and out of date. Remember, antiques don't go out of date, they already are! So a book about identifying Victorian lamps that was published in 1930 is just as current as one published today, and is considerably less expensive.

Also, many country auctions disdain books unless the books are old and have leather covers; so they typically sell them by the box lot. When you see a box lot containing antique reference books in such an auction, bid for them. They'll probably go for very little, and you can always try to trade off the unwanted books in the lot to a used book exchange for even more reference books. Using these techniques, you can quickly (as I have) amass a reference library of several hundred volumes for almost no outlay.

So obtain and read the books on the subjects in which you are interested. Take notes and correlate these with the items you run across at auction previews. You will be surprised and pleased at how fast this knowledge mounts up and how much more fun it makes prowling during preview periods.

PRICE GUIDES

The importance of price guides has already been stressed, but let's do it again. Price guides are just that: guides to what an object should bring at auction or be sold for in a retail store or other situation.

The opposite advice to what I gave you on books applies to price guides. Old ones are of little value because the worth of various collectibles fluctuates each year. A price guide several years out of date is good in helping you identify a particular piece, but it's pricing data is less than useless. You should periodically invest in a new one.

In the antiques/collectibles game, there are two that I especially find useful: Schoeder's and Kovel's. These are general books in that they have categories covering the most common items in all the important collecting fields. For in-depth coverage, of course, you need to find a guide that specializes in pottery, country furniture, or whatever your interest is.

Again, it is a good idea to have access to these price guides during the auction period, and prefer-

ably at some place where no bozo can see what you are looking up and run around blabbing out what pieces you plan to bid on. A good practice is to slip out to your car and check them out in privacy.

PUBLICATIONS

Every type of auction has specialty publications covering related fields in detail. Some of these are listed in Appendix A, and by asking people at various auctions, you can quickly zero in on the best ones for you to order.

Taking the antiques/collectibles field once more as an example, there are several publications at both the national and regional level. The big, slick, paper newsstand antiques magazines are nice, but it's the tabloids (newspaper format) that have the timely and specialized information you will find yourself devouring by the ream.

Regional antiques- and collectibles-oriented newspapers keep you up with auctions and auction prices realized in your own area. Subscribing to several will pay off for you in knowledge to exploit at your local auctions.

DEALERS AND MUSEUMS

Even a picture in a book or periodical comes nowhere near the real thing. Antiques shops and museums can be of great benefit in your endless quest for knowledge; so make the rounds of the ones in your locality, getting an idea in the shops of what retail prices run and looking at authenticated examples in museums.

Many dealers are fountains of useful knowledge, readily tapped if you are willing to do them favors in return. It will pay you to make friends with several. You will not only obtain data about who is an honest auctioneer and who is not, but also find out what fakes are passing through auctions and a lot of other good, solid intelligence (in the military sense) of what's happening in the local antiques/collectibles world.

ANTIQUES ENTER THE SPACE AGE

With the price of personal computers down to

where everyone can afford them, there is a new and exciting way to rapidly gain vast amounts of information in almost any area of antiques, as well as in real estate, commodities, and the other auction types. The computer network enables you to use your computer to tap into a vast network of huge, powerful mainframe computers and gigantic databases of information through your home telephone. The costs are very low, and a staggering amount of data can quickly be automatically searched for, retrieved, and recorded for printing out at your leisure.

Delphi, with over 40,000 members, is one of the largest of these networks specializing in private users like you and me. Bryan Eggers, the manager of the Antiques Special Interest Group on Delphi provided the following material explaining the service. I subscribe to Delphi, and recommend that if you have a computer, you seriously consider the benefits.

Delphi, an information service of General Videotex Corporation, now offers "Antiques & Collectibles," an international communications network, open to anyone who collects, sells, or trades rare and unusual items. Your personal computer becomes an international information center, allowing you to buy, sell, trade, locate, and discuss your favorite antiques and collectibles from the privacy of your own home.

You need very little to get started. Any personal computer and modem can be used, and it's a local call from most areas. Delphi is easy to use. The commands are simple and straightforward; they're in English. No computer expertise is required. Help is available through a toll-free customer service number: 1-800-544-4005.

Delphi's "Antiques & Collectibles" is the first and only worldwide communications system to unite all collectors and dealers. It can be accessed from anywhere in the United States, as well as from many other countries, including Canada, Japan, Europe, Australia, and several in South America.

As a member of this network, you'll be able to discuss antiques and collectibles with other collectors around the world. There is no better way to share information or search for antiques and col-lectibles in such a timely or efficient manner. This worldwide service greatly improves your chances of locating that elusive item and improves dealers' chances of locating you as a buyer.

With financial advisors now recommending antiques and collectibles as investments, pricing information must be as current as possible. Articles, announcements, appraisals, auction reports, and classified advertisements published in trade journals are often weeks or months old. Delphi's "Antiques and Collectibles" delivers the news instantly. If a piece sells for a record price at an auction, the information can be displayed there literally as fast as it can be typed.

The Forum section of the Delphi service is an electronic bulletin board that allows users to exchange public messages. You can read messages, add your own message, or reply to messages posted by other members. Members are encouraged to participate in these discussions, which might include techniques for locating, appraising, buying, selling, cleaning, restoring, displaying, insuring, and protecting valuable collections. Articles written by members can be permanently posted in databases for future reference. Dealers can also take advantage of a private Forum section reserved for discussing dealer-related business.

The conference mode allows any number of members to talk to each other "live," just as if they were having a club meeting in the same room. You can also send private electronic mail to any other user and it will be delivered instantly. Using a portable computer, you can even read mail and catch up on the latest news from your hotel room.

Delphi's "Antiques & Collectibles" offers the most sophisticated on-line Classified advertisement system available anywhere. Advertisements normally appear within 24 hours of being posted and remain visible for at least 30 days. Easy-to-use keyword searching capabilities let you instantly locate the advertisements you want to read. Current advertisement classifications include "General Information," "Advertising & Containers," "Amusement & Mechanical," "Apparel & Accessories," "Art," "Photo & Literary," "Clocks & Watches," "Firearms & Military," "Furniture,"

"Jewelry & Metalwork," "Miniatures," "Pottery," "Glass & China," "Stamps," "Coins & Stocks," "Toys & Dolls," "Vintage Vehicles" and "Miscellaneous Items."

Classified advertisements are free! You pay only the normal connect charges for the time you spend typing your advertisement. There is no limit to the number of advertisements that you can place, and no word, sentence, or length restrictions.

No individual can be an expert in all fields of collecting, but as a group, the people on Delphi represent a great wealth of knowledge and experience. As the network grows, the combined knowledge increases and even more opportunities are created for buying and selling your favorite antiques and collectibles.

"Antiques & Collectibles" is available through the Delphi Information Service, which charges a basic rate of $7.20 per hour during nonbusiness hours—6:00 P.M. to 7:00 A.M. your local time—on weekdays and all day Saturday, Sunday, and selected holidays. You can also access during business hours for $17.40 per hour. These rates are for the Mainland United States and Canada, via Tymnet or Uninet. Uninet or Tymnet network charges are included in the basic rate, but access from some international networks costs extra. Billing is assessed in 1-minute increments; if you use Delphi for 10 minutes you'll be billed for only 10 minutes. You can pay by credit card—Visa, MasterCard, or American Express—or by special-arrangement, direct billing. The rates just given apply to 300-, 1200- and 2400-baud modem access.

Even lower hourly rates are available by signing up for the Delphi Advantage Plan. With the Delphi Advantage, you are assured Delphi's lowest access rates, and access rates will never exceed the standard rates of 12 months earlier. With Advantage, you'll begin receiving the latest editions of Delphi Handbooks and Delphi Command Cards absolutely free. You also will receive, free of charge, the Delphi Oracle newsletter, which announces new services and enhancements to Delphi and provides you with helpful articles to let you get the most out of Delphi.

To gain the Delphi Advantage all you have to do is commit to using $24 worth of Delphi services per month. That use can be at any time—during either home time or office time. Delphi members who use credit card billing are eligible for the Advantage Plan, as are direct-bill customers who pay the $24 monthly fee in advance. The $24 charge, which is applied toward your usage, will be billed to your credit card on the monthly billing day. If at any time you wish to cancel your membership to Delphi Advantage, your membership will expire on the last day of the month.

By joining "Antiques & Collectibles" on Delphi, you can also access many other Delphi features, including travel services, airlines guides, on-line reference materials, business and financial information, brokerage services, national news and sports, weather reports, shopping services, appointment schedulers, computer groups, and newsletters, plus games and other entertainment features.

First think of a Delphi name. Your Delphi name is not your password; it identifies you to others for electronic mail, conferencing, and billing. It can be your initials, a nickname, or anything else you prefer. You may use up to 12 letters or digits, but no spaces or punctuation. You then register your Delphi name by dialing up Delphi with your personal computer and modem.

There are several ways to connect to Delphi, but most people call through the Uninet or Tymnet telephone networks. First, set your terminal program to 300 or 1200 baud (depending on the modem you have) and configure your terminal program for 8 bits, no parity, and 1 stop bit. If you have problems with these settings, call Delphi customer service for help.

Calling through Uninet. Call 1-800-821-5340 and ask the operator for the Uninet number in your area. Using the terminal program on your computer, call the appropriate number for your area. After your modem makes the connection, press < ENTER >, the period key (.) and < ENTER > again. At the "service:" prompt, type **Delphi** and < ENTER >.

Calling through Tymnet. Call 1-800-336-0149 and ask the operator for the Tymnet number for your area. Using the terminal program on your computer, call the appropriate number for your area. After your modem makes the connection, press the letter **A** no matter what appears on the screen. When *please log in:* appears, type **Delphi** and press <ENTER>.

Calling from Canada. Call Delphi customer service at 1-617-491-3393 for information.

Calling from Other Countries. Many countries have their own data networks that can connect to either Uninet or Tymnet. Check with the telephone authorities in your country for details on how to sign up for this service. Then, contact Delphi for further information.

At the *USERNAME:* prompt, type in the word **JOINANTIQUES** and press <ENTER>. At the *PASSWORD:* prompt, type **NEWUSER** and press <ENTER>. Have your MasterCard, Visa, or American Express card ready, because you'll be led through a series of questions so that Delphi can set up your account.

You'll then be asked to type your own personal Delphi name. Delphi is a friendly service; there are no numbers to remember. You'll be assigned a temporary password. Write it down in some secure place. You are not charged for this sign-up time.

Your account will be ready by 6:00 P.M. the following day. Once your account is opened, you'll be credited with an hour of free time (during nonprime time). When you connect with Del-phi the following day, use your chosen Delphi user name and your temporary password to access the system. At that point, you will then meet Max, who will help you match Delphi to your personal computer. Max will also help you change your temporary password into your own personal password. This is the password you will use for subsequent sessions. Never reveal your password to anyone! Again, there is no charge for the time you spend configuring your account. Your hour of free time starts after Max bids you goodbye.

You're now at the main Delphi menu. To join "Antiques & Collectibles," type **SHOP ANTIQUES**! See you on-line!

CONCLUSION

We've covered the main ways of obtaining usable and potentially profitable knowledge. Basically these are books, price guides, periodic publications, dealers, museums, and the exciting new medium of computer networking. There are, of course, other methods as well, such as using your own experience and tapping the knowledge of a long-time collector. Use all these avenues and more. Learn all you can because knowledge is, indeed, your most potent weapon in hewing a profit out of auctions.

Now, put up your feet and relax, because I've just accepted your order bid for the next chapter, the one (stretch, yawn) on comfort at auctions.

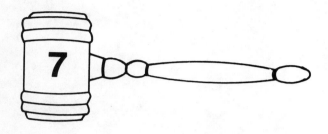

Comfort For
The Serious Bidder

If you're not properly prepared, auctions can seem to go on forever. The problem is that any auction with several hundred lots is going to take at least one day, maybe two, and if the pieces you want are scattered throughout, then you are going to be there for a good many hours. To stay competitive and alert, or just to enjoy the whole, magical happening better, you need to consider your creature comforts.

First off, dress sensibly and comfortably. Gentleman, forget about suits and ties; ladies chuck your high heels and wear slacks and flat-bottomed shoes. Auctions are not fashion shows. The auctioneer doesn't give a darn about how you look; he just wants you to keep those bids coming hot and heavy. You will find that most auction goers also dress casually (some to an extreme you have to see to believe), so you certainly won't be out of place.

If the auction is to be held out of doors—and you should always assume an estate auction will be—dress appropriately for the weather. During rainy weather, take an umbrella and a raincoat. In the wintertime, dress warmly enough to endure standing around outside for a few hours without freezing in place. Remember that estate auctions are often held, winter and summer, at the house of the dearly departed. Almost invariably, the auction itself takes place out in the yard because of lack of space in the house itself, although you are allowed in during the preview period.

Because such an auction has been advertised beforehand and people have come from great distances for it, auctioneers usually don't have the guts nor, truth be known, the inclination to call it merely because of weather. Your only choice when it rains is to huddle under an umbrella, and bravely continue bidding.

It is to your benefit to be comfortable at auctions; it is potentially profitable; and whoever said you had to rough it anyway? Let's take a look at some ways to make auction going even more enjoyable than it already is.

SITTING PRETTY

There are some things you might want to consider

Fig. 7-1. Expect to provide your own seating arrangements for an outdoor auction. "Sit-test" it, because you will be spending a lot of time there.

investing in—items that you will use again and again over the years. (You can probably buy them cheaply by attending an estate auction or three.) Not every auction will require such items, but they should be part of your auction kit, to be carried in the trunk of your car or in the back of the old station wagon.

The first and foremost of these is a good, comfortable, folding lawn chair. Although an auction house with regularly scheduled weekly or monthly auctions will most likely provide seating, it doesn't necessarily have enough seating for a larger than expected crowd. More importantly, on-site auctions for property or bankruptcy, and especially an estate sale at the house of the dearly departed most often have no chairs whatsoever. If you want to sit (and who doesn't during an 8-hour auction), you need to bring your own.

A folding chair is obviously the best for two reasons: it takes up less room in your car, and it's much easier to maneuver through the crowd when you see a spot open up down near the auctioneer or where the pieces are being paraded by the assistants.

Since you are going to be firmly ensconced in your chair for long periods of time, you might be wise to "sit-test" it for a few hours before you buy it. If it's during the summer, take your prospective chair, a good book about your area of interest, and a huge jug of iced lemonade out under the nearest shade tree. Should you want to test the chair during the winter, wait until summer.

For those auctions that do provide seating, you'll want to have your own cushion because, although you can sit in these auction-house seats, they are usually not the most comfortable in the world. After four or five hours, you'll begin to wish you had a cushion, so take one along as a permanent part of your auction kit.

In case you think I'm making too much of this, stand at an auction all day and see what nasty comments your feet have for you. Sit in an uncomfortable chair for the same length of time and hear what your . . . well, you get the idea.

Fig. 7-2. On-site estate auctions are often under severe time restraints, and buyers have come from many miles away; so an auctioneer can't call it because of inclement weather. Be prepared for rain, as this crowd was at an Angus Davis estate sale in Greenville, South Carolina.

BUMBERSHOOTS AND OTHER MYTHICAL CREATURES

A *bumbershoot* is not one of Dr. Seuss' fabulous creations, but rather British slang for *umbrella*. I've always wanted to use that word, and now I have.

For many years, as a young man, I thought it somewhat sissy to carry an umbrella. Should you also believe this statement, standing out in a cold, drenching rain at an auction a few times will cure you very quickly. Umbrellas are also useful to shade you from a merciless sun. Do exercise some courtesy, though, and stand to the side or back of the crowd so that no one's view is obstructed. Then you can gaze blissfully at them as their brains turn into chitlins and their skins blister cherry red.

So get yourself a good umbrella. Buy it at auction somewhere if at all possible; not only will you probably save money on it, but it just seems so right, somehow, to outfit your auction kit at auction.

Also, a good hat and something to cover your arms with on super sunny days are good choices if you sunburn easily or, in my case, have a very high and distinguished forehead (i.e., one that expanded by clearing out a lot of unnecessary hair all the way to the back of the head).

NECTAR OF THE GODS, IT AIN'T

Nectar is exactly what you will not get at an auction.

The quality of auction coffee varies widely, and you may not even like coffee, or need the nervousness the caffeine might engender. A good, large-capacity thermos is the answer. Fill it with your favorite beverage—cold for summer, warm for winter—and you can keep yourself refreshed without leaving your chair while others are standing in line at the concession stand, paying high prices, and missing out on the bidding. You can thus reap rewards from their human frailties (assuming you can keep the calls of nature down to a bare minimum).

A canteen of water is not a bad idea, either. Remember, the more you can do to stay in your place during the auction, and be comfortable while doing it, the greater your competitive advantage over those who did not have such foresight.

Many auctions, especially those of the country variety—and these are where the greatest potential for profit lies—do not sell lots in any particular order. You usually have no criteria to predict when the piece you want is going to come up on the block. Therefore, you *must* be there for as long as is possible. Anything you can do to help keep yourself in place is advantageous in the extreme.

FEAST FIT FOR A KING

Chili dogs, cardboard-tasting hamburgers, cellophane-wrapped sandwiches that taste more bland than the stuff they're wrapped in, candy bars, and those little bitty bags of potato chips that only have about three good mouthfulls in them—this is not stuff to impress the Galloping Gourmet. Okay, admittedly, I've wolfed down many a chili dog at these concession stands, but it is not really the thing to do. Most concession stands are run as a sec-

Fig. 7-3. Colonel Jerry King makes it easy for the bidders with a nice, well-lighted auction site and a good sound system. The hankerchief over the microphone is an old auctioneering trick: it acts as a wind screen.

ondary operation by the auctioneer, with whatever cheap help he can scare up. Gustatory delight rates down there somewhere with, "Now you keep most of them bugs outa there, Marvin. I don't want you making none of my customers sick like you did last time, now heah?"

If this isn't enough, consider also those long lines that beset the concession stand (assuming there is one in the first place, which is not so at on-site auctions like those of estates). What to do? You have to have food or you'll keel over about

3:30. How can you stoke up those old boilers?

You could go out to a restaurant, assuming that you know the area well enough to find one. You can imagine your luck in trying to hurry a harried waitress along with your food. "I gotta get back to the auction, there's this Hepplewhite-style dresser coming up that . . ."

"Can it," she'll say, "this is not my table," and sashay off, leaving you with yet another delay. While all this is transpiring, the auction continues full bore with you missing out on piece after piece. Auctions normally do not stop for lunch, rather a relief auctioneer will take over while the auctioneer grabs a chili dog or answers the various calls of nature. The gavel-pounding is nonstop.

The obvious answer to the food question is to "brown bag" it, to carry your own food. This way you not only get what you like, and of a known quality, but you can munch and crunch on it right there in your seat while not missing a thing.

Although the last bag you got your purchases in from the Blue Blazin' Lightning Fast In and Out convenience store is perfectly adequate, it might be wise to be just a trifle more elegant—wise, that is, in the sense of ease of use and permanence. Ever see a sack containing three peanut butter and jelly sandwiches and a banana after Bozo sat on it?

Lunch boxes are moderately common at various estate and junk auctions. Get yourself a good one and clean it up nicely. If, however, the one you pay just a buck or two for is a Gene Autry, Hopalong Cassidy, or Tom Corbett Space Cadet, don't be so crass as to not recognize what you have and carry your lunch in it. Look them up in the price guides; they are highly collectible.

A lunch box will protect your food and is easier to keep up with and handle than a paper bag. To supplement it, you might want an ice chest to keep in the car to store perishables and keep beverages cold. Again, you can get one of these at auctions—maintaining our theme on the rightness of outfitting your auction kit from auctions themselves.

PACKING MATERIALS

Most of my purchases at auctions are usually

smaller items, sometimes fragile, like collectible glassware. Once you win the bid on, say, a gorgeous rose-colored depression glass bowl, ol' Marve, the auctioneer's assistant, is most likely going to come traipsing down the aisle and shove the bowl at you with a muttered "here" and get on back up to the front to help with selling another lot.

As mentioned in Chapter 5, this practice is really to your benefit, but once the item is in your hands, its care and feeding is entirely up to you. If you break it, or if Bozo sits on it (he really is good at that), then your only guarantee is that you get to keep all the pieces. (In my area we call that the *Georgia guarantee*; in Georgia they probably call it the Alabama guarantee or something.)

Some auction houses provide packing materials in the form of empty grocery boxes, old newspapers, and the like, but most country auctions do not, leaving such details completely up to you. Part of your auction kit—assuming you buy small items— should be a couple of moderately large cardboard boxes with a bundle of old newspapers in the bottom, ready for use at those auctions that do not run to such amenities as civilized package fixings. The ability to transport your super buys home still in pristine shape obviously goes far toward helping you realize a profit on them.

Also, even if packing materials are supplied, it's better to have your own, rather than having to run around trying to scrounge enough when it's all probably in short supply anyway. Besides, anything that takes your concentration off the auction and pulls you away from your seat is to be avoided like the bubonic plague.

Even at those auctions that do not give you your merchandise until it is time to leave, you need to have your own packing material handy. At the end of the auction there will be a mad rush for the checkout and the stack of boxes and old newspapers. You will have it much better by merely being able to stroll out to your car, get your own boxes, and come back in to pack up your gleanings from the auction's fray.

Liquor stores are good sources of sturdy, reusable boxes. A carton designed to hold the not-inconsiderable weight of a dozen hefty, gurgling bottles of alcoholic potables will be more than sturdy enough to hold the your treasures you win at auction. What's more, they will probably have already been neatly razored open on three sides, leaving you the flap to easily and snugly close down over your purchases.

As to technique, be generous when you are packing something fragile, not only crinkling lots of newspaper around the item, but also making it a nice little nest to lay in, protected from its neighbor by walls of more wadded up newspaper. In choosing newspapers for packaging materials, chuck out all those thick, colorful, coated stocks that sales are advertised on; use just the soft, easily crinkled standard newsprint.

IN CASE OF A TIE BID

In one sense, there is no such thing as a *tie bid*. If two bidders have the same price and everyone else has dropped out, the auctioneer will engage in a runoff between these two people until one or the other throws in the towel. In the usage here, however, I am using a pun to help you better remember this additional suggested item to have in your permanent auction kit: a long hank of some good, old-fashioned clothesline (not the new plastic stuff that stretches when you try to use it). The reason for this need is simple: if you occasionally buy a piece of furniture too big to fit inside your car or station wagon, you can lash it on top and save considerable money on delivery charges—assuming such are even available at the auction.

A brief digression here to talk about vehicles for auction-hopping: my personal preference, after a good many years of attending auctions, is a station wagon. A van or truck, obviously, would let you haul the big stuff, and a car is more "acceptable." So a station wagon is a good compromise. You can maneuver it into tight parking spaces (the hallmark of auctions) as well as a car, and you can cram almost as much into it as you can into a van.

In addition to the clothesline, you should include an old carpet, quilt, or some other sort of padding to preclude scratching the paint on your car. Having a luggage rack on top does make everthing a lot easier—maybe you can get a good deal on one at an auction.

One more item to add is a large plastic sheet of some sort to provide a cover in case of inclement weather. One of those large, plastic ground sheets sold at camping stores is good for this need. Find a camping store going out of business and go to the bankruptcy auction. ''Sure,'' you are thinking, ''who's he kidding? That'll take forever.'' Not necessarily. A lot of other businesses stock large sheets; so it doesn't have to be a camping store per se.

FRIENDS

One part of your auction kit that you can't buy at auction is a friend. We've talked a lot about the importance of being in your seat every single moment so you do not miss the lots you want, especially in the generally unstructured atmosphere of a country auction. However, if there are two of you, the situation becomes easier.

The best team, assuming the marriage is a good one and you can get your spouse interested in auction going, is a husband-and-wife team. Seeing as how you convinced your spouse to marry you in the first place, such a minor favor as spending hours in a sweltering auction house just to buy a piece of dinky old glass should be a breeze, right?

If not your spouse, consider teaming up with one of your collector friends, preferably one interested in a different field than you. This way you can spell each other during the bidding. Also, those long trips to and from distant auctions will go more pleasantly with someone to talk to. However, do not attempt to throw your friend in the back with the rest of the permanent auction kit; he might take umbrage.

CONCLUSION

Being comfortable—which includes being prepared—at auctions is very much to your benefit, enjoyment, and potential raking in of profits. You should have a permanent auction kit, which you should keep in your vehicle.

In addition to the suggestions given in this chapter, you will no doubt come up with other necessities for your auction kit after you attend a few auctions. The items listed, of course, are in addition to the things you need for scrutinizing various lots at preview periods, which should also be considered part of your kit.

Just don't get carried away and have so much in your kit that you have no room for purchases in your car. Also, remember that part of the fun and rightness of assembling your permanent auction kit is in getting all of it at auction—the thrill of the hunt and all that.

Now, anyone want to bid on Chapter 8? Ah, I got hands all over the house, but the first was the kind reader down front here. Going once, going twice, sold to my favorite reader, you.

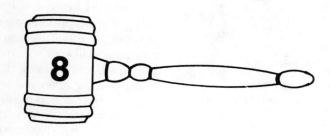

Good Morning, Colonel!

The classic impetus to entering a new career field is to look at an example of work in that field and say, "I can do it better." You might be so motivated while gazing up into the steely-eyed, fearless demeanor of the mighty gavel-wielder at a local auction house. "Look at that Bozo," you'll say to yourself, "my cat could do better than that!" The idea will suddenly dawn on you that, yes, you could be an auctioneer. Good morning, Colonel, suh!

CALL ME COLONEL

Unless you're a retired general or admiral, becoming an auctioneer is the fastest way to gain rank in a hurry. By traditional usage, an auctioneer is entitled to be called "Colonel," including the ladies. Many of them use the rank, especially in the South and Midwest.

This auctioneering title dates back to the time of the Civil War when contraband was required to be sold by an army officer of at least colonel's rank. Hence, whoever got stuck with the duty—

occasionally a very junior officer—received a sometimes temporary promotion to "colonel" to abide by the letter of the regulation. So in the eyes of the public, all auctioneers were "colonels." As such things have a habit of doing, the term stuck.

WHY BE AN AUCTIONEER?

Auctioneering can be a very rewarding profession, both in sense of accomplishment and in monetary recompense. Having an auctioneer's license, in those states that require it, means at the very least you can pick up considerable part-time income doing spot sales or working relief for established auction firms. Such pay typically is good—you can charge $20 an hour, $50 a day, or more, depending on the level of the auction and just how badly your professional services are needed.

Most people going into the auction field, however, are looking at it from a career viewpoint. There is, without question, the chance for big bucks. Take, for example, the dream that most antique collectors and dealers have of finding that

Fig. 8-1. Cameron Long—auctioning here in a rented National Guard Armory—brings a young man's vigor to the game, but you can be a colonel at any age.

can only be answered deep within your own soul. What does it take to be an auctioneer? The Mendenhall Auction School in High Point, North Carolina, has an excellent answer to that in the promotional booklet it sends to prospective students: "What makes a good auctioneer? It starts with desire. Knowledge, understanding, experience, ability to get along with people, willingness to work, knowing values, good voice and a good bid caller."

If you get along well with people and are not the least self-conscious standing up in front of a crowd doing silly flamboyant things, jerking your arms around like an old-time railroad semaphore gone mad, and dressing like Hoot Gibson only dreamed about, then you are going to make one doggone, fine, cotton-pickin' auctioneer.

Most of us, however, do not aspire to such high levels of P.T. Barnum-ism (to coin an especially appropriate phrase). That doesn't mean we can't be any less effective or professional an auctioneer. Styles vary widely; you can be wild, or elegant and snooty. (Wild or somewhere in the middle works much better than the stuck-up style.)

There are many reasons to become an auctioneer. It is a profession that is both more in demand and is being accorded more respect than was true in the past. A good, hard-working auctioneer should be able to easily make $30,000 or more per year. You often hear stories like that of the small-town bank president who became an auctioneer because the checks he cashed for the local "colonels" were larger than his salary as a bank president.

GETTING PROMOTED TO COLONEL

Like any other profession, auctioneering requires that you know at least something about techniques and procedures. The principles of auction bookkeeping, finding and securing the rights to sell items, advertising and merchandising, and more are also needed.

Additionally, because of abuses in the past, many states require that an auctioneer be licensed by a professional auction regulatory board. Therefore, to be an auctioneer in those states, you must

elusive rarity and selling it for a lot of profit. To a collector, this might happen once or twice in a lifetime, but for an auctioneer it happens more often because a lot of lucky people are coming to him with their finds to be auctioned off. Commissions of 10, 20, or 25 percent, or whatever you negotiate with the seller, can really mount up. Selling a $50,000 estate for a 20 percent commission means you could clear $10,000, less a few hundred for advertising and help, in just one day.

No capital investment is needed—you don't even have to have an office other than in one corner of your dining room—and you are most definitely your own boss. Besides, you get to wear a cowboy hat, boots, and a huge silver belt buckle that makes Bozo drool in sheer, green-eyed envy. On top of all this, people call you "Colonel."

Sounds good, huh? Too good? Well maybe, maybe not. Most auctioneers don't make that sort of killing right off, nor even if they do, is it done on a week-in, week-out basis. To be realistic, the auction business is like any other. It takes hard work, long hours, loads of dedication, and a good heaping helping of luck, not to mention good management skills.

When you get right down to it, the question as to whether you would make a good auctioneer

meet the requirements and pass some sort of examination. Fuller details, including addresses, are included in Appendix A, but according to an article in *The Auctioneer* magazine—the official publication of the National Auctioneers Association—the following require that auctioneers be licensed: Alabama, California, Connecticut (town and city permits only), Delaware, District of Columbia, Georgia, Hawaii, Indiana, Kentucky, Louisiana, Maine, Massachusetts (local license issued by town you reside in, with separate permits needed to auction in other towns), Minnesota, Missouri, New Hampshire, North Carolina, North Dakota, Ohio, Pennsylvania, Rhode Island, South Carolina, Tennessee, Texas, Vermont, Virginia, Washington, and West Virginia.

The following states do not require an auctioneer be accredited (remember this in evaluating the auctioneer for honesty in the auctions you attend in these states): Alaska, Arizona, Arkansas, Colorado, Florida (some local restrictions), Idaho (tax must be paid to county tax collector on new merchandise sold), Illinois, Iowa (local restrictions), Kansas, Maryland (local restrictions, especially in the city of Baltimore), Michigan, Montana, Nebraska, Nevada, New Jersey (local restrictions), New Mexico (but state laws on puffing and the amount of fees that can be charged), New York (local restrictions), Oklahoma, Oregon, South Dakota, Utah, and Wisconsin.

The real shocker of course, is the inclusion of New York in the list of states that do not require auctioneers to be accredited. The auction capital of the world is not governed by state regulations. Anything can and probably does happen. To be sure, New York City, in the tail-wagging-the-dog manner that afflicts the entire state, does exercise some control. Basically in New York, however, you must depend on the professionalism of the individual auctioneer. In such cases, no matter what the locality, caveat emptor (Latin for "hang on to your pocketbook").

To be fair to the Big Crabapple, such lofty auction houses as Christie's and Sotheby's by tradition put far higher restrictions on themselves than any state regulatory agency ever would. As to "Honest Abe" Crinklewinklestein, that wild-and-crazy auctioneer appearing for one night only in the decrepit store over to Flatbush Avenue, tell him to keep his ever-loving, doggone, pea-picking run-up bids to himself and hold tight to your wallet, because otherwise that good ol' northern boy is going to lay it to you, grinning like the hog in the rutabaga patch.

Fig. 8-2. Colonels Terry and Sherry Hester of Traveler's Rest, S.C.—here selling off a one-handled jug—are a husband-and-wife auctioneering team, both having their license.

Fig. 8-3. Colonel Gilbert Hollifield has been a star in the game for years. Here he does an estate sale from the porch of a house.

LEARNING THE PROFESSION

In the states that regulate auctioneers, obviously you will need to acquire the necessary amount of information to pass the required examinations. Even if you live in an unregulated state, however, the necessity of mastering the techniques and tools of the auctioneer remains.

How do you learn how to do the auctioneer's chant? What is the best method of bookkeeping and sale-tracking during an auction? How do the different types of auctions differ? How the heck do you get the assignments to do them in the first place? How do you advertise and promote an auction? You need all these and many more pieces of information to become a successful auctioneer.

The best way to get this is information is to go to an auction school. Typically these schools provide two weeks of intensive training, preparing you to become a beginning auctioneer or pass the licensing examination of your home state.

There are a number of good schools across the country; Mendenhall's in High Point, North Carolina is one, and quite a few of the auctions in my area that I cover on a regular basis for the various antique tabloids are run by Mendenhall graduates, including nice people like Colonel Johnny Penland and Colonel Jerry King.

The top school in the nation, however, is located in the Midwest: the Missouri Auction School. You'll find graduates from this school all over the country, even in the North Carolina mountains where Colonel Lee Long and his son Cameron, also a licensed auctioneer, have gained a very good reputation for fair dealing and for putting on good antiques and collectibles auctions. The Missouri Auction School is the oldest in the field, having been established in 1905. It is often called the "Harvard" of auction schools. To get a free catalog, call the school at 1-816-421-7117.

Like most auction schools, Mendenhall and the Missouri Auction School both offer a two week course—a very intensive two-week course, I might add. So, if you really want to be an auctioneer, take a two week vacation from your present dead-end job and attend an auction school. Go prepared to work, though, because no one is going to give you anything; you must earn it.

Other auction schools around the country include the Florida Auctioneer Academy in Orlando, Florida; the Associated Auction School in Hurst, Texas; Mason City College of Auctioneering in Mason City, Iowa; the International Auction School in South Deerfield, Massachusetts; Reisch World Wide College of Auctioneering, also in Mason City, Iowa; River Basin Auction School (which also features rodeo announcing) in Bismark, North Dakota; Reppert School of Auctioneering in Decatur, Indiana; and the Fort Smith Auction School, Fort Smith, Arkansas.

Costs of courses vary. The Mendenhall School of Auctioneering has been charging $395 for the two-week course. To this price, you would need to add the costs of lodging and meals (although the school can get you a discount on those). Considering that all the money you spend to become a licensed auctioneer can be easily gained back on your first good sale, these auction schools are offering really good deals indeed.

Additionally there are various correspondence courses available, such as those from the National Institute of Real Estate Auctioneers in Newport Beach, California; Victor McDonald Company, Auctioneer Division in Victoria, Texas; and the American Academy of Auctioneers in Broken Arrow, Oklahoma. This last school, to give an example of costs, offers the course, including cassette tapes, for $49.95.

WHAT DO I LEARN?

Two weeks, even two intensive weeks doesn't sound like much, but you will be surprised what gets crammed into that short length of time! Remember that many of these schools have had years to perfect their courses—again since 1905 in the case of the Missouri Auction School.

Let's take an example from the Mendenhall School of Auctioneering promotional booklet that was previously mentioned. In two weeks you learn about automobile auctions, antique sales, auction houses, livestock sales, farm sales, merchandise sales, household sales, sales management, machinery sales, real estate sales, tobacco sales (a very big and extremely important industry in North Carolina), estate liquidations, the way to get in business, ring work (assisting an auctioneer), business liquidations, liquidation auctions of other types, salesmanship, ethics, clerking and cashiering, pony and horse auctions, bankruptcy auctions, advertising and promotion, public speaking and voice, self-confidence, values and other special auctions, and promotion of your own career.

Here is the way some of the times break down. Forty hours is spent on drill—that's the auction chant, rhythm, speed, clarity, and so forth. Law gets 2 hours and is a coverage of the auctioneer's legal responsibilities. Antiques takes up 6 hours, and the values, woods, and advertising of antiques are

Fig. 8-4. Colonel Jerry King, in conjunction with the Mendenhall auction school, helps to train many new auctioneers, often letting them serve as his assistants in auctions to gain experience.

some of the specifics discussed. Farm sales and real estate auctions both come in for 6 hours each, with auto auctions getting another 6. The running of an auction house, advertising, and managing takes 4 hours, and business liquidations also gets 4. Various miscellaneous subjects, including field trips, night classes, student auctions, ring work at actual auctions, contracts, public speaking, and contracts take up 21 hours. With the other subjects presented, the total in the two-week period is 110 hours of instruction. Mendenhall, like several of the other schools, is approved for veterans' training—your chance to jump overnight from retired private last class to colonel.

It sounds like a lot for two weeks and it is! It is a real and worthwhile challenge and test of yourself. (I am planning on taking the course myself, just as soon as I can break away from book deadlines and can spare the two weeks.)

However, don't think that surviving such a course guarantees you instant fame, success, and riches in the auction game. None of these schools claim that your learning period is over the day they hand out the graduation certificates. In fact, no school of any sort should claim that. It simply isn't true. Only when you enter the crucible of experience and someone turns up the heat do you really begin to learn.

Yet, we all have to start somewhere, and that first step is usually the biggest. This is where, if you want to become a colonel, an auction school is invaluable.

Mendenhall will accept students as young as 16, or even younger by special permission. The school also accepts and trains foreign students. A young person wanting to become an auctioneer should realize that most states require a practicing auctioneer to be 18 years of age. However, in the unregulated states, a young man or young woman, with a little guidance from parents and adults familiar with the auction business, could rather easily earn the money for college or a very good start in life. The American free enterprise system really works for those who are willing to acquire and use knowledge, with a lavish application of good old elbow grease.

One more quote from the Mendenhall catalog on learning to be an auctioneer: "You should realize now that a proper knowledge of auctioneering can mean greater income for you and a brighter future. Don't put off your decision. Do something for the person you see in the mirror. Education is the least expensive item you will ever purchase. It will grow and increase in value as the years go on. No one can take away your education. Benjamin Franklin once said, 'Empty the coins in your purse into your mind and your mind will fill your purse.' "

SUMMATION

Becoming an auctioneer offers a good career opportunity. Auctions are obviously in a period of boom right now, and the need for auctioneers has never been greater. The profession has never been more respectable either, even if you do call yourself "Colonel" and wear a stetson—which most auctioneer supply firms will give you a real deal on. Get yourself a silver belt buckle and a pair of cowboy boots, too; you've earned the right, and that includes all you lovely lady colonels, as well. I salute you, sir or madam.

Now if one of you budding auctioneers will just cry off the next chapter—that's the one on selling instead of buying at auction—I just know that good-looking reader down front is going to come up with the winning bid. So just launch into that chant you learned at auction school. Now's your moment to shine!

"Gimme a eight, a eight, a eight, gimme a eight . . . I gotta eight a eight . . . a nine . . . a nine . . . I see a nine. Sold to the good-looking reader, a Chapter Nine . . . Carry that over to 'im, would-ya Marve?"

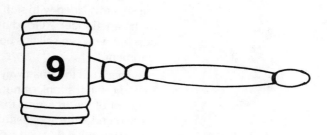

Selling Instead of Buying

Most of what we've covered so far, with the exception of the material just presented on how to become an auctioneer, has been oriented toward buying at auction. However, there is another way to make money in this lively and fascinating marketplace, and that's to sell things.

Your reasons for selling vary, of course, depending on what it is you want to move. Perhaps it's that stamp collection you have amassed over the past 30 years. Maybe you have inherited a large amount of jewelry or antiques and other household furnishings that you have no sentimental attachment to but believe are valuable. Maybe you just want to sell the items you bought at a steal at a previous auction. (In the trade this is called *racking up a profit*.) Maybe you're just plain tired of that old lamp, the oak dining room chairs, or the big gilt-framed mirror in the hallway and have decided to sell them.

Another valid reason, in these days of widespread burglaries and other rip-off crimes, is that you might not want to take chances on continuing to hold silver, jewelry, and other valuables in your home. So, you might decide to sell them and stash the money in the bank, or put it toward junior's college education.

There are times in our lives, too, when selling by auction provides a welcome solution to crisis. A death in the family, divorce, moving from one part of the country to another, or from a larger house to a smaller one or to an apartment—all these can saddle us with the problem of having to get rid of large amounts of items in a very short time.

On the other hand, you might be associated with a church or civic group and want to use the auction as a means of fund-raising. Fund-raisers work exceptionally well. I recently attended one such annual sale held for a local orphanage, the Eliada Home. Tons of stuff were donated and several auctioneers offered their services free. Because it was for a worthy cause, bidders would cheerfully run up outrageous prices for sheer junk, laughing and competing with each other to see who could pay the most ridiculous price for something totally worthless. This type of fund-raiser is

Fig. 9-1. You can sell anything at auction, even this pinball machine, which brought over $200.

fun and very effective.

Regardless of whether you are selling for your own profit, handling surplus for the company you work for, or raising funds, the auction can work quite well. Again, the hallmark of the auction is its ability to move large amounts of merchandise in a very short period. No other form of selling is as efficient as the auction in accomplishing this desired result.

For your own personal property, no matter how desperate the circumstances that have forced the sale on you, it is not necessary to give it away. Here pops up again our recurrent theme of knowledge. You don't just call up the first auctioneer in the telephone book and tell him to grab his ham-

mer and come on over. Instead, you first do your homework, just like you do before going to an auction to bid.

We'll look at large estate and other household sales shortly, as well as the fund-raising variety, but first are some considerations in selling single items at auction.

KNOWING THE MARKET

You don't just go traipsing into the nearest auction house, arms laden with stuff, plop it down, and say to the auctioneer, "Good morning, colonel. I understand you can sell this here junk for me on consignment."

That's not the smart way to do it. You first need to find out if it's junk or not. Most people have no concept of the treasures that lurk in their houses, hidden under the appellation of "just stuff." Again, I recommended that you read Emyl Jenkins' *You're Richer Than You Think* (Rawson, Wade 1982). This book is a terrific starting place if you are unfamiliar with antiques and collectibles. Boy, are you going to be surprised! Most people throw away a for-

Fig. 9-2. Bill Hagan does an auction in an antiques store in Black Mountain, North Carolina. The auction mode of selling is especially strong in its ability to move large quantities of merchandise in a very short time.

Fig. 9-3. Still got the train set you got for Christmas in 1952? Toy trains are always on track to get high prices at auctions.

tune during their lifetimes simply because they haven't bothered to find out some of the things that have value. As Oscar Wilde said, "The true mystery of the world is the visible, not the invisible."

What you need to do is check a number of sources to find out the approximate market value of the piece or pieces that you want to sell. The sources that you check will, of course, depend on what it is that you are going to offer. There are several general ways in which to find the market value of items.

Retail stores are always a good place to find information. Visit several stores and make a note of the current prices on the types of items that you are selling. You can correlate this information with the age and condition of your pieces to come up with a good ballpark figure of what you should be able to get. A solid mahogany table, for example, that your Aunt May paid $100 for in 1926 and left to you in her will years ago is obviously worth more than $100 in today's market. If a similar table in the furniture stores around town (assuming

you can find solid mahogany anymore; more likely it'll be veneered chipboard) is selling for $1500, someone will most likely be happy to pay $500 to $800 for your table at auction, and be in sheer ecstasy over having saved almost half the cost of a new one.

In other words, and this is important, don't let some shady auctioneer or dealer condescendingly take it off your hands for $15, as do so many people, especially elderly people, who are prey for these reprehensible shysters. You find out what you have, and you take the several-hundred-dollar profit.

However, there is another side to the coin. A treasured family heirloom might turn out to be worthless after all. A rude shock might await you upon taking in a piece that has been in your family for generations. From generation to generation, the word has come down that this item is worth a lot. You learned this as just a tiny little bopper, and the lessons we acquire then remain the strongest with us. Alas, great grandpa might not

Fig. 9-4. Bookkeeping is all important in holding an auction, even when it must be done on the fly, as this young lady is doing in a tobacco auction.

have known his sterling from cheap silver plate, or his great great grandma might have just taken the peddler's word that the jewelry she was buying was indeed solid gold and not gilded pot metal, as in truth it was.

The real truth of the matter, and once again I refer you to Emyl Jenkins' book, is that often the revered heirlooms are practically worthless and the family crud—the junk that nobody in the last six generations thankfully got around to throwing out—is worth bunches. Knowledge is the key to unlocking the riches sleeping in cobwebbed corners of your attic or under that pile of old *National Geographic*'s in the back bedroom closet.

By the way, this is not to say that those heirlooms which are not worth a lot monetarily still do not have value. They do. They are a part of your family's history, to be handed down to the next generation. Even on the ones with value, you should perhaps think long and hard before selling. Some things really are more valuable than money, the accumulated love and goodwill of generations

of your family being one.

Continuing on market research, another base to be touched in your research on older pieces is to visit the local antique shops. Again, find out what similar pieces to yours are going for. Solicit quotes from the dealers on what they would pay for the item and especially, if they would accept it on commission, what price they suggest it be tagged at.

Also send away for catalogs of upcoming auctions that have items like the ones you want to sell. You can get addresses for these through the many fine antiques and collectibles publications such as those listed in the Appendix A. Consider any charge you might have to pay for these catalogs as a necessary investment. Prices run anywhere from free up to $50 or more. (Obviously, only more expensive pieces like sterling silver, jewelry, or fine art justifies a $50 expenditure.)

The descriptions and estimated bid prices on the items similar to yours are what you want from these catalogs. Follow up by requesting that the auction firm send you the list of prices realized after the auction is held. In fact, as a general reference, you should collect as many of these catalogs and their associated prices realized lists as possible. Having the material stuffed into your overflowing bookcases will stand you in good stead many times over the years. I always grab up catalogs or price lists if I run across them in a used book exchange or flea market. Usually they are incredibly cheap because of low demand. Even if you can think of no possible use for it at the time, squirrel it away. There is no such thing as having too much knowledge. If it overflows your house, chances are that by that time you can afford to move to a larger one anyway because you have put all your knowledge to good work.

If an auction featuring pieces like the ones you want to sell is being held nearby, go to the preview period and talk to the auction house personnel about what they think the items will bring and why. Also examine the offerings carefully so that you can correlate their condition with that of your own. Condition, to a collector especially, is usually all important. Then attend the actual auction itself and make a note of what the pieces bring.

Many auction houses offer free appraisal days, during which you can take your smaller items and get an estimate from various experts of what the pieces might sell for. Also, on larger pieces like furniture, you can hire the auctioneer to come out and appraise the item on your premises. If you pay for this service, be sure to insist that the results be in writing. Not only will doing so cause the appraiser to take more pains because his professional reputation will be backing the appraisal, but such documents are also excellent for homeowner's insurance claims in case a break-in or other rip-off occurs before you can sell the stuff.

By combining and weighing data from all these sources, you can begin to get a pretty good idea of what your pieces will bring at auction. The next step is to decide which auction to take them to.

THE RIGHT AUCTION HOUSE

An auction house with regularly scheduled auctions is the best bet for selling your items. Again, though, check around and get estimates on what the pieces will go for. If you are selling jewelry, for example, find out which houses have jewelry auctions coming up. It might be better to wait a few weeks for a sale specific to your type of offering since more qualified buyers will be attracted to such an auction. The selling price will thereby be enhanced.

Many auction houses require you to sign a contract before they'll accept your consignment. This practice is good; it protects both you and the house. Just be sure you know what it is you're signing. Read the whole thing, paying special attention to those whereases, by the party of the first parts, and so on. Following are some points that you should check.

Find out what commission you must pay. In New York City and some of the larger California auctions, a buyer's premium of 10 percent or so is charged. This means that you, as the seller, should only be charged a 10 percent seller's commission. In other parts of the country where no buyer's premium is charged, you should expect to live with 20 to 30 percent as a commission. If the auction house asks for anything higher than that, pick up your stuff and hit the trail. You can get a better deal down the street.

Above all, remember that rates are negotiable and that contracts can always be changed. If what you have is especially valuable, or if your name has some public recognition that would be prestigious for the auction house, then it's pretty easy to get the rate lowered a bit, hence raising your profit. Regardless, it's always worth a shot. Maybe business is slow and the house will accede to your demands just to get the sale. The worse they can say is "no" to your request. However, just getting the lowest commission rate should not be the only criterion you employ for choosing an auctioneer.

You should also check to see what sort of insurance is offered on your property (auction houses get broken into also, y'know), and how much this insurance is costing you, since you can bet most auction firms add it to the commission, rather than foot the bill themselves.

Next, on important items, look to see if the auction house will charge you for featuring it in its catalog. If you want a picture of it to appear (therefore creating more interest and a higher price), then you sometimes have to pay for it. This is one of the hidden costs of selling that you must look closely for in contracts.

Look also for packing and freight charges if the auction house sends a truck to pick up bulkier items or large collections. See how much this charge is. It might pay you to insist on crossing out this clause and hiring your own truck.

If you want to place a reserve on your consignments, look to see if you will be assessed a fee for this service or a commission for having one of the auction house's employees "buy in" the item during the actual auction to protect it from going under the reserve price. Since auctioneers normally prefer to have unreserved auctions, they often structure their contracts so that it is a real hassle for you to put a reserve on a piece. Remember, you are free to hassle back and ask for a change in the contract.

Also, do not agree to pay money up front nor sign a contract that requires you to advance money. Auction fees are typically deducted from the price received by the auction house from the winning bidder, with the balance going to you (and your cut should be the larger one or you're being had).

Selling on consignment is, you will find, quick and easy to get the hang of, and a tool you can use to stack up profits for many years to come. Moving an entire estate, however, is a little more complicated.

ESTATE SALES

In the scheme of things, reality considered, there will probably come a time in your life when you are faced with the problem of disposing of your own or someone else's estate.

An *estate* is simply the possessions owned by an individual. Most estate sales are held to close out the affairs of a deceased person, most likely one of your relatives. This doesn't have to be the case, however. You might want to sell a good part of your estate because you are: taking a job in another state or moving to a smaller house or an apartment, because you need to raise cash for some major project or satisfy the IRS on back taxes, or for other reasons, such as divorce.

In general, your estate sale can run all the way from the smaller items of everyday living such as soap dishes and kitchen utensils, to the house and grounds themselves. An estate sale is often a massive undertaking—just walk around your house counting things; we all have a lot of stuff.

There are four options you can exercise to move an estate quickly. Briefly, they are: a tag sale, an outright sale to a dealer or auctioneer, a professionally run auction on the site of the estate or an auction where the contents of the estate are transferred to an auction house and sold there (except for the house and lot, of course). Each option has its advantages and disadvantages.

Tag Sale. A *tag sale* is one in which you tag all the items to be sold with the price you want for them and then advertise the sale for such and such a date. The problems with this type of sale include how to determine the value of each item, how to figure out how to control the crowd, and how to make sure all the money gets collected. There are companies in some areas who will run a tag sale for you, charging a fee of course.

The advantages of a tag sale are obvious. You get the money quickly (at least on those things that were priced to sell). Also, the possibility, at least, exists of selling out, especially if you are willing to cut tagged prices when asked (and you will be deluged out of your senses by people demanding that you do that very thing). Which brings us to the disadvantages. It is most unlikely that a tag sale will accomplish what you want; that is, to move everything. You are going to be left with a bunch of junk laying around.

Sale to a Dealer. The next option you might choose is that of selling the whole kit and caboodle outright to a dealer. Should this choice be made, you still must do the proper homework to have an idea of what the estate as a whole is worth. Also, you certainly aren't going to get that much from a dealer, who must consider getting a good wholesale price so that he can afford to warehouse the stuff for the months or years it may take him to sell it piece by piece.

A dealer is under no obligation to tell you the true market worth of your goods and will be trying to get everything as cheaply as possible. If you haven't done your homework and have no idea of what is in the estate, you are going to make the dealer very happy indeed. Still, you do get the money immediately, and one of your conditions can be that the place is cleaned out entirely, alleviating you of that sometimes painful and tiresome task.

On-site Auction. The best of the four choices is to sell at an on-site estate auction. There is something about going to someone's house that makes bidders think they are really taking advantage and getting good buys. This perception can work to your favor, really running up the prices realized. The key to a successful on-site auction is to procure the services of a good auction company who will help you properly evaluate items and who will push the more expensive ones during the auction. If the auctioneer doesn't want to be bothered to do this, insisting instead on just lumping small items together in box lots, tell the sucker to take a hike and find a more competent, professional auctioneer. The auctioneer's job is to get the most he can for you.

Auction at an Auction House. The last choice, moving everything to an auction house, is good if you must vacate the premises too quickly to properly advertise an on-site auction. There is obviously more cost involved in this option, as well as the possibility of damage to various items while they are in transit. However, this choice could work to your advantage in that the auction house would have both its regular crowd there and the ones attracted by the advertisements for your estate sale.

The overall disadvantage of taking the auction route is also its advantage. Not even the most competent expert of a single item's worth can hit what it will bring at auction. Your estate might sell for next to nothing, or it might bring far more than you had ever dared dream about. You are at the mercy of a host of factors such as the weather, the current economic conditions, and competing auctions. "You pays your money and you takes your choice," as the old cliche goes. Careful homework on what you have in the estate and choosing the best, most professional auctioneer possible is of utmost importance because they can be used to at least stack the odds slightly in your favor.

FUND RAISERS

The grandest, absolutely most fun way a civic, church, or other nonprofit group can raise money is to stage an auction. People will come, be entertained, pay outrageous prices for the junk donated (although you need some good stuff, too), and go away happy and contented that they've helped out in a worthy cause. If you've kept costs down and managed it right, there'll be a nice chunk of change left to put in the kitty of your group.

Donations of both pieces or services to be auctioned off and of such services to your group as those of an auctioneer and the various means of publicizing the auction are the keys. Get these and you can hardly fail to turn a profit. Acquire the knowledge and spend the time to do it properly, though. Visit as many businesses as you and the others helping out can. Many of them will donate items which they will write off on their taxes, to help out your group.

Get the word out that you want donations from private individuals and the junk will roll in. A children's home in my area, the Eliada Orphanage, has been holding auctions for the past 7 or 8 years to tremendous success. There is no reason at all why your nonprofit organization could not benefit from using the auction as a fund-raiser as well.

CONCLUDING THOUGHTS

As we have just seen, auctions work both ways. You can buy or sell at them, and the advantages of the auction can be applied to your own needs. The answer, should you ever be faced with having to sell off a lot of stuff in a very short time, is the auction.

Now, we have completed Section One and

move on to Section Two, information on specific types of auctions. Yes, yes, reader, I see your bidder card being waved. I'm going to give you a quick knockdown on this one so we can get on with the book. Sold! To that mighty fine looking reader there.

Section 2:

Specific Auctions

PUBLIC AUCTION

🖐 Pu

AN EXCITING SIX DA'

Davis Auction Service is pleased to announce they have
auction the contents of a three story building full of fine an
that has been in storage for eight years along with persor

Auction will be held in seven (7) sessions as follows:

Tuesday, January 21, at 7:00 p.m.
Wednesday, January 22, at 7:00 p.m.
Thursday, January 23, at 7:00 p.m.

Auction will be held at Main Street & Coffee Street
are as follows:

Furniture
Teak & Ivory Coromundel Screens (3)
Marble Top Tables in Oak, Walnut, Etc.
16 Dining Tables in Oak, Walnut, Etc.
Desks, All Sorts of Buffetts
China Closets, Console Tables
Court Cupboard, Heavily Carved
Carved Bookcases
3 Pump Organs

Gilbert J. Hollifield Auction & Realty Co.
Hwy. 70 W., P.O. Box 939
Marion, N. C. 28752

Unreserved Auction

Personal property from five local estates,
private collections, and other consignments
Saturday, March 22, 1986, 10 A.M.
Preview Friday, March 21, 7-9 p.m., 2 hours prior to sale
Asheville Country Day School,
1345 Hendersonville Rd., Asheville, North Carolina

Partial Listing

Furniture and accessories: Federal (Southern) 2 drawer
server with scroll cut skirt, pair 19th century William and
Mary style wing chairs, French Art Deco armoire, English
Hepplewhite chest, 6 drawer chest with overmantle,
mahogany breakfront, pair Louis XVI style loveseats,
butler tray on stand, 5 drawer walnut chest with marble
top, English Art Deco dining room suite, drop leaf
Sheraton style dining table, set 6 shield back chairs, carved oak sideboards, 18th century style bedroom suite with
queen size bed, lingerie chest, chest of drawers, stand,
drop leaf dining table, 6 chairs, Chippendale style camel
back sofa, Queen Anne style leather wing chair, French
style bookcase, 2 stack lighted bookcase, early Bible box, 3
drawer sewing stand, many other chests and tables,
rosewood barometer, early 19th century rosewood melo-
dion, copper lavabo (dolphin), brass spy glasses, compass,
nautical protractor, nautical sign, brass accessories including candlestands, fender, sconce, over 20 clocks including wooden works (unrestored) by Seth Thomas,
Thomas Barnes, O. Hopkins, 8 day mantle clocks, many
paintings and prints including works signed R. H. Collins,
C. P. Dietsch, W. McClean, B. de Blois, R. Nippress, W.
T. Richards, W. Towne

Glass, porcelain, and related: Large Stuben vase, 106 pieces
(service for 12) English china, Limoges tea service, custard
set, 33 piece set pattern glass (pleat and panel), Venetian
glass, Cambridge, figurines, stemware, Art glass vase, Art
Deco compote, cut glass, much more.

Silver gold, and related: $5,$10,$20 gold pieces, fine cameo
tiara with fitted case owned by Gen. Johnson Pettigrew,
Sterling holloware including 3 piece tea service, bowl,
basket, dresser pieces, water pitcher, purses, over 200
pieces Sterling flatware including 47 piece set in fitted
case, 14K Tiffany earrings, 14K, 18K rings, stickpin, gold
thimble, Sterling cigar cutter, misc. jewelry, ornate plated
ware, Kirk Repousse berry spoon, much more.

Other: 18th century style upholstered chairs, child's pull
wagon, down comforters, Planisphere (1871), frames,
chandaliers, meerschaum pipe, lamps, mirrors of many
styles, child's Chippendale style slant front desk, marble
bench, tribal artifacts (Africa, New Guinea) weapons,
held, drum, early Coleman lantern, old telephone, post
rds, fans, daguerreotypes, set 5 ice cream chairs, boxes
ens, books including art and antiques, leather bound
ks, penny slot machine, furniture of all descriptions,
erprise Coffee grinder, much more.

ms of Sale: Cash or approved check Buyers unknown
to us, must present proof of credit All items sold by
program without reserve

Plan for a full day Over 500 lots will be sold Food
vailable Preview will not open before 7:00 p m Delivery
service available

ctions: 2 5 miles South of Intersection of I-40 and
25 south on U S 25 South (Hendersonville Rd)

Auction Schedule
4 Asheville Country Day School
1 30 year private collection antiques (contents of home)
Johnson City, Tenn

vices, Inc.
s
olina 28787

254-6846
and Tennessee

ABSOLUTE AUCTIO'
April 5, 1986

PUBLIC ESTATE AUCTION

Saturday, April 12, 1986
10:00 a.m.

Estate of the late Mr. Robert J. MConaty
12 Conway Drive, Greenville, S.C.
Conway Drive is behind Hidden Lake Apartments
off Pleasantburg Drive, Rt. 291

Auction Will Be Held Absolute At The Above Conway Address
TERMS: Cash or Good Check
PREVIEW: Friday, April 11th from 12:00 p.m. till 5:00 p.m.

CHINA, GLASS DECORATIVE & COLLECTIBLE ITEMS: Royal Doulton Toby & Oliver
Twist Mug, 4 Planters Peanut 75th Anniversary Jars, 2 Large Size Beswick Tobys, Delft
Planter, Signed Hawkes Etched Glass with Sterling Lid, Sterling Compote, Sterling
Flatware, Lots of Costume Jewelry, Musical Figurines, Venetian Glass Pieces, Majolica
Cat, Paperweights, Ruby Pinch Bottle & Stopper, Black Iron Fire Insurance Marker, Seth
Thomas Steeple Chime Clock, Service for 12 and Serving Pieces Noritake China,
Assorted Pen Knives, Lenox Swans, Nut Dishes and Vase and Leaf Server, Group of
Miscellaneous Foreign Coins.

PICTURES AND LAMPS: "Common Wild Duck" Framed Print: Curier/Ives "Clipper-
ship" Sweepstakes Print, Black/White Framed Theatre Poster, String Art Framed
Piece, Limited Edition Signed Print R.J. McDonald #887 of 1776, Pr. Duck Decoy
Prints, Several Wall Barometers, Many Other Oils and Prints, Brass Electric Oil Lamp,
Pr. China Based Table Lamps, Brass Double Student Lamp, Brass Floor Lamp, Brass
Double Student Floor Lamp, Pr. Satin Glass Lamps, Other Lamps.

FURNITURE: Pine Two Door Cabinet, Rush Bottom Pegged Ladder Back Chair,
Handmade Large Round Table with Lazy Susan, Upholstered Lounge Chairs, Small
Desk and Chair, Library Table, Maple Entrance Hall Cupboard/Table, Pr. Oak End
Tables, Oak Coffee Table, Rocker Recliner, Tweed 3 Cushion Sleep Sofa and Matching
Chair, Birch Student Desk and Chair, Tweed 2 Cushion Sleep Sofa, Maple Captains
Chair, 6 Drawer Cherry Chest, Twin 7 Drawer Cherry Dressers with Mirrors, Bedside
Tables, Double Bed, Metal Office Desk, Wooden Desk, Painted Chest of Drawers and
Small Table.

OTHER MISCELLANEOUS: Quasar Microwave, Old Perfection Oil Heater, Morse
Portable Sewing Machine, Bell and Howell Floor Model TV, Stereo AM/FM, Admiral
Stereo in Maple Cabinet with Freestanding Speaker, Fireplace Tools, Portable Motorola
TV, 12" Penncrest TV, Fisher Stereo/Radio Record Player, Sylvania Portable TV,
Projector, Screen, Tripods, Minolta Camera and Accessories, Air Rifle, Binoculars,
Many Pots, Pans, Kitchen Accessories, Linen, etc.

Many Telephones, Calculators, File Cabinets, Typewriter, and Miscellaneous Office
Equipment.

AUCTION

LEE LONG
REAL ESTATE AND AUCTION COMPANY
Candler, North Carolina 28715

ESTATE AUCTION

Saturday, October 5, 1985 at 10AM
(preview: Friday, October 4th 3-6 pm)

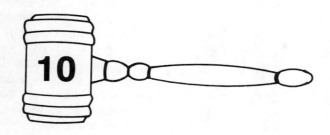

Antiques and Collectibles

The field of antiques and collectibles in general, and this type of auction in particular; offers the greatest consistent potential for profit than any other. However; in order for you to profit at you need knowledge. There are gems in with the dreck, gold down in the dirt, buried treasure and hidden wealth—but you must be able to recognize it when you stumble across it.

Knowledge consists of three phases. You must first realize that what might superficially appear to be junk is indeed valuable. Next, you must read articles and books, examine authenticated examples in shops and museums, and become thoroughly familiar with the areas you choose to specialize in to enable yourself to recognize the valuable. Thirdly, you must know the current market value, using this data to formulate your bidding strategy.

However, there is no way that you can learn it all. The wisest thing is to specialize in just one, two, or maybe three major categories. Let's consider several areas.

FURNITURE

Much modern furniture is crassly designed and crassly made. It is of cheap plastic and gaudy chrome, devised for almost instant obsolescence. People of taste have always preferred antique furniture for its elegance of form and its proven durability—after all, it has been about for a 100 years or more. Young professionals, as a class, seem to get interested in antiques early and begin furnishing their home with these fine pieces, perhaps not realizing the tremendous nest egg they are building up for later years when their investment in antiques has increased three or more times in value.

Hence, furniture is the star at most auctions, especially those wonderful country auctions, but you usually have to stay awhile to see the dressers, chests, and bookcases get trotted out. Because furniture is in such high demand, most auctioneers structure their sales so that these pieces come in the later portion of the auction thus enssuring that the crowd stays around.

Fig. 10-1. All sorts of glassware and pottery are offered at antiques and collectibles auctions. It is up to you to sort the valuable from the trash.

The most popular styles of antique furniture today are the various eighteenth-century ones, their designs created by such master English cabinet-makers as Chippendale, Hepplewhite, and Sheraton. The Queen Anne style also dates from eighteenth-century English fashion, and the Regency style comes from France. Also popular, but somewhat later in the nineteenth century, is the French Empire period design.

Note that I have been careful to write *design*

or *style* and not *pieces*, which would indicate authenticity—i.e., meaning actually made in the period that the design evolved. So here's your first and most important major lesson in antique furniture. You will seldom find real Hepplewhite or real Chippendale in an antique sale, unless you're at Sotheby's, Christie's, or one of the other big New York or London auction houses.

If you do find an authentic piece that no one else seems to know about, by all means buy it. Your dream has come true, you have just made a killing! Take it to New York and mop up at Christie's. You had better be right, though, because their in-house experts are going to go over your big find with a fine-toothed comb, and be skeptical as heck since significant eighteenth-century desirables seldom come out of the American hinterland without someone knowing the exact antecedents of the piece.

More likely, and it should legally be described as such by the auctioneer in his catalog and verbal introductions, the piece will be *in the style of* Chippendale, Hepplewhite, Queen Anne, Regency, Empire, or whatever, which means that the item was made after the period. Since these designs were and still are immensely popular, reproductions were made from the early nineteenth century on, and are still being made. You can buy brand new Chippendale-style chairs, or a Hepplewhite-style chest of drawers off the showroom floor of almost any fancy furniture store today.

The fact that someone did so in 1966, was divorced in 1975, and sold the piece at that time, after which it went through about eight owners, doesn't mean all that much except that here is another nice piece of 20-year-old furniture that's worth a moderate decent amount. However, it is worth nothing like it would be if it were a nineteenth-century reproduction, or an authentic of-the-period piece. So don't be fooled as so many are, all excited by the auctioneer's hype.

"She's a beaut, ain't she, Marve? Push that there chest of drawers around so the folks can see it better. She's Hepplewhite style, ain't she Marve?"

Poor old Marve, nursing a hangover and just wanting the sale to be over with, would agree if the auctioneer told him the piece was made on Mars.

"Yessuh, Colonel," he'll mutter in long practiced reply, "it's old all right, old as the hills."

The auctioneer will then roll on hot and heavy with the bidding, and it'll quickly pass your maximum bidding level as less-knowledgeable bidders go wild. You, you canny person you, just wanted it for the back bedroom, they think they're getting rich.

Wait a minute, though, this doesn't mean that reproductions—as will be well over 90 percent of eighteenth-century style pieces in country auctions—are worthless. Not by a long shot. A well-crafted nineteenth-century style piece can still easily be worth several hundred or thousand dollars. If you wish to specialize in furniture, these will probably be your main stock in trade—the ones you lust after and stalk from auction to auction.

As a sort of aside here, some modern pieces can be had quite reasonably because of their size. Sofas and couches, for example, are big and bulky to move; so many people will dump theirs off at the local auction house and buy another when they get to their new home. Usually a fancy couch that cost $1500 or so new can be got for only at $100 or $200 at auction, a considerable savings for you on something of utilitarian value. The same goes for large library tables or any other bulky furnishing. Smaller items that can be more easily moved, however, will be in greater demand and bring proportionally higher prices.

Chairs also seem to be fairly good bargains, probably because there are so many of them. Smaller matched sets of dining room chairs, such as 4, 6, or sometimes 8, usually bring decent prices. However, you can get some very good buys occasionally on sets of 10, 12, or 16 since few people have houses large enough to use them. The secret here is to keep the 6 that you need for your dining room and sell the rest as a matched smaller set, or better yet, as two smaller sets. Keep repeating the process as long as you can find the larger groupings. You'll make money doing it.

In popularity in many areas of the country now is oak. The auctioneer has but to softly breathe the word and bidder cards go up all over the house. As a result, you can obtain good buys in furniture constructed of other types of wood simply because they are not currently fashionable.

Specializing in antique furniture, whether to furnish your house in the most elegant manner possible or for the purposes of resale, can be very rewarding indeed. Buy yourself a truck, however, and develop big muscles because they made those pieces to last and last and last.

RUGS AND OTHER ORIENTALIA

No, not "rugs," *Orientalia*—of or pertaining to the Orient, as in China, India, Japan, and so forth.

The China Trade, as it was called, was especially important to America from colonial days through the early nineteenth-century clipper ship era, and on into the modern period. The Europeans started it by importing tea, pepper, and other spices, and a new-fangled thing to eat off of which came to be called *china* and beat the traditional utensils all hollow for convenience.

"From records of the various East India Companies," writes porcelain historian Anthony Du Boulay, "it is possible to see how the trade grew."

Fig. 10-2. Pisgah Pottery vase and ashtray. Pisgah pieces, from a North Carolina mountain pottery, are fast joining such Ohio lines as Rookwood, Weller, and Roseville as being desirable art pottery to collectors.

Fig. 10-3. Antique toys, especially trains, are always highly sought after by collectors, hence their value stays high. Here Ed Hyers of Looking Back Antiques shows off some of his trains.

Examples mentioned include the *Catherine* in 1637, with 53 tubs of china; the *Macciesfield* in 1724, bringing 150 chests; and ten years later the *Howard Grafton*, making port with 240,000 pieces in 240 chests. However, the English were not alone; the Danes are reported to have brought in like amounts. Obviously this new kind of tableware was very popular compared to the older wooden trenchers and pewter platters.

The Chinese are, as anyone with experience in the East can tell you, the world's craftiest merchants. They had absolutely no intention of losing their profitable monopoly; so it was a considerable triumph for the Germans when, around 1710, they worked out the method for making porcelain. The Europeans immediately put this new technology to work and trade with China dropped off. However, it never completely died. Chinese and Japanese tableware is of such high quality that it has always retained a stable market share.

Plates were not all that was being brought in, though, especially during the glorious days of the early nineteenth century when clipper ships skimmed around the Horn and across the Pacific

to China. All sorts of wondrous items came; jewelry boxes, exquisite lacquered screens, clever nested tables, wall hangings, huge urns, and much more. It was all popular, desirable to have, and used as decoration in the homes of the rich and influential—which is one reason why there is so much Orientalia in auctions today.

Luckily for those who might like this field, the supply of antiques in it will never dwindle, thanks to the factories in the Far East that are still busily churning them out by the gross lots weekly. These are fakes of course, but they also are a staple of import houses in places like New York, who turn around and sell them to country auctions, import showrooms, and the like all over the United States and Canada.

If you specialize in Orientalia, you had better know exactly what you are doing. Those bustling factories over there have fakery down to a science; it takes real knowledge to detect the true from the fraudulent.

Oriental rugs are an extension of this same topic, although about 97 percent of what is called Oriental in auctions is really Persian, Caucasian,

Turkoman, etc.—from the Middle East, not the Orient. Too much room for deception exists here. In fact, Orientalia in general is the most dangerous field in antiques, and hence most rewarding for the truly knowledgeable. Put in many long hours of study before you jump in and start bidding, especially when the bidding level, as it so often does, sails past the $1,000 mark on an "Oriental" carpet.

GLASSWARE, ART POTTERY, CHINA

When I first got into the antiques and collectibles field, furniture was my thing. It's big, it's beautiful, it's valuable. Alas, however, it is also heavy and bulky to store, and the old back screams after a day of trying to properly polish and clean it. So smaller items beckoned.

Collectors abound in art pottery, china, and glassware; this huge, very broad field has incredible scope and absolutely something for everyone. *Depression glass*—(wares made during the Great Depression era following the stock market crash of 1929)—has been popular for many years, and still is readily traded. There are a number of famous art potteries whose work is much in demand, among them Rookwood, Weller, Roseville, and Pisgah. Blue Willow china and other patterns are highly sought after.

What's more, in this field, you can put a whole day's auction buying into that one carton and easily carry it out by yourself. Lest you think this is penny ante stuff, wait until you see some stunning little piece like a Royal Daulton vase go for $1,000 or more. There are killings to be made in this area by the truly knowledgeable, just like in furniture and Orientalia.

FOLK ART

Folk art is a candidate for the hottest growth area in antiques, the one where getting in now will give the knowledgeable investor the greatest chance for profit. Besides, folk art has a magic about it that can become quite addictive.

There is currently a strong expansion of interest in antique folk art. Because of scarcity and, if there is justice at all in the world, the love expended in the creation of these pieces, this is now one of the fastest growing areas of collectibles. On the average, prices on the older pieces have increased something like tenfold in just the past 5 years.

Most of us, though, are not in the category of being able to spend hundreds of dollars per item to amass a collection of eighteenth- and nineteenth-century pieces, no matter how wonderful they are.

Fortunately there is one general classification of folk art that is readily available at reasonable prices and that, aside from just the sheer joy of collecting, is a good investment.

Folk art can be divided into three broad periods. The first is the pioneer days, from the first settlements up until the late nineteenth century in many areas, (like the North Carolina and Tennessee mountains). Second was the great revival in folk art beginning around 1900 and continuing through the depression era. Lastly is the current upsurge in contemporary crafts work. The middle period is the one that concerns us here.

Fig. 10-4. Carolyn Walsh of Train Tracks Ltd in Erwin, Tennessee shows off an old railroad lantern. Look for things like this at country auctions. If you buy them right you can easily make a profit.

87

Fig. 10-5. These beautiful chairs were offered at an antiques and fine art auction.

In the first decades of this century, a movement to revive handicrafts gained widespread impetus, especially in the West Carolinas and adjacent areas. The Biltmore Industries in Asheville, the Hindman Settlement School in Eastern Kentucky, Tallulah Falls Industrial School in North Georgia, the John C. Campbell Folk School, the Penland weavers and potters, and the Tryon toy makers and wood-carvers are just a few of the groups that started people working with their hands again. The Depression era reinforced this trend, bringing again the necessity encountered in pioneer days of making what you needed instead of buying it.

The Penland group, named after a locality in Mitchell County North Carolina, is a good example of how these organizations and institutions encouraged, nurtured, and spread the making of folk art during this period. Begun in 1923, this was more of a community effort than an attempt to become any sort of formal school. (This situation later changed.) At first, it was merely a support group of mountain ladies who did weaving to teach each other and find markets for the products of their looms. This excellent project of self-help came to the attention of the state, and money to provide vocational training during the depression was provided under the Smith-Hughes Act. With this influx of cash, training programs were added in pottery- and pewter-making.

Each of these groups or schools trained and inspired hundreds of people to turn out folk art pieces. During the very depth of the depression, the Penland weavers and potters built a "travel-log," a log cabin on the back of a truck, and sent it off with a load of their handicrafts to the 1933 Century Of Progress Exposition in Chicago. The sales and orders from this collective endeavor helped a lot of mountain folk through two very hard seasons.

During the four or five decades of this century, thousands upon thousands of folk art pieces of all descriptions were turned out and are now available in antique shops, junk shops, flea markets, yard sales, and almost everywhere you care to look anywhere in the country. Quilts, wood carvings, pottery, pewter, furniture, musical instruments, rugs, candles, needlework, feather fans, walking sticks and canes, and an almost infinite variety of other items are there for our finding. The prices, at least for now, are still affordable; the fun of collecting, immense.

Naturally, like any type of collectible, you have to specialize to get anywhere. One interesting idea I had, when I was visiting various antique shops in researching this material, was souvenirs. Before the Cherokee Indians evidently dispersed to Japan, Korea, and Taiwan, souvenirs from the major tourist attractions in my area were all made locally. Before World War II, there were all sorts of them. Souvenirs are small, meaning you can accumulate and display a large number in a limited space, and are still relatively inexpensive. One fine example is the small wooden cut I found at Yesterday's Child in Asheville. It resembles a small hollowed out stump with the name *Lookout Mountain* carved in the side. Lookout Mountain is, of course, a long-time tourist attraction in Chattanooga, Tennessee. A collection representing the major tourist attractions of your area with folk art souvenirs made during this middle period of folk art would be fascinating. The collection would also steadily gain in value.

Another interesting basis for a collection might be dolls. I was surprised to find that many, such

as cornhusk dolls from the forties and fifties, can be had for a $1 or less. Certainly for under $10 apiece you could build an impressive group of these. Again, they take little space to display, but afford a lot of collecting pleasure.

Folk art from this middle period of around 1900 to 1950 or thereabouts seems to be one of the most wide-open opportunities available in collecting today. Obviously prices will continue to rise for them as well as for pieces from other periods. Folk art continues to grow in popularity at a rapid rate. Now is the time to acquire what you want.

OTHER AREAS

I could go on forever about the other areas of the antiques and collectibles fields, but suffice it to say that there is money to be made in the ones that interest you. Antiquarian books are nice to dabble in, as is antique jewelry. Silverware always has high value. Art deco items, Tiffany pieces, Americana, and many other wondrous things await the intrepid hunter of the speckle-tailed bargain out

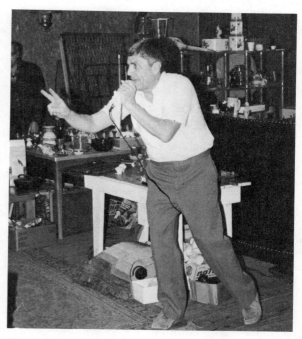

Fig. 10-6. Colonel Johnny Penland runs a warm and friendly country auction.

there in the auction barns of America. With a little knowledge on your part, you can amass a very respectable and valuable collection with far less expenditure of time and money than you might think.

The really nice thing about buying at auction and collecting a certain category is that, should you become tired of it, you have the skills to sell at a profit and reinvest in yet another field. In this manner antiques will never grow old on you. (Sorry, couldn't resist that one.)

PROVENANCE

Provenance, documentation validating the authenticity of a piece, is very important in the more valuable items. A desk made in Philadelphia in 1760 is worth a lot of money, but if there are letters with it showing that Ben Franklin (or any other famous person) owned and used it, it can easily increase three times or more in worth.

Even if it doesn't add value but merely confirms that the item is from the period in which it is claimed to be, such provenance can still provide an extra dimension to owning the piece. Knowing who originally owned it, even if the person is not famous, gives it a delicious spice, an aliveness in excess of the object by itself. So, always look for documentation wherever possible.

AUCTION REPORTS & INTERVIEWS WITH EXPERTS

Reports of antique auctions in the various newspapers devoted to the field are very useful to you in seeing what items are going for, or just what is currently hot in a particular locality. I am including two of these that I did because they are informative and illustrate the various points we have been discussing.

The first is an auction in which a lot of elegant items were offered with provenance, including many pieces of fine furniture and legitimate Orientalia. The second is a typical weekly country auction that happened in the Blue Ridge Mountains of North Carolina, but is repeated every weekend all over the United States and Canada.

After these reports is an interview I conducted with the dean of Southern auctioneers and antiques dealers, 86-year-old Robert Bunn of Asheville, North Carolina. I include this interview not only because it is interesting and informative, but also to show that New York is not quite the auction capital it is always asserting itself to be. Mr. Bunn holds the world's record for price realized on a Tiffany floor lamp: $210,000! Sotheby's and Christie's have yet to even come close to this sale at a backwoods mountain auction. More about this in a moment; first the two auction reports.

The Estate of Miss Claudia Lea Phelps

"We are not responsible," Colonel Ronald D. Long said, in making the usual disclaimers, "for the spellings in the brochure." So began, despite a rather imaginative assault on the word *mahogany* by the author of the brochure, an excellent auction that was elegant in both content and setting.

Your intrepid reporter had to get up at 4:30 A.M. on May 18th, 1985, in order to make the drive down to Columbia but, in the never-ending quest to bring you the very best in auction reports, was rewarded with a beautiful drive. The auction site was just three blocks from the South Carolina state capitol building on Gervais Street, and near the USC campus as well. The facilities, used on a regular basis by Charlton Hall Galleries Inc., are large and well lighted. The crowd attending the auction was comfortably accommodated, and the refreshment concession provided tasty food throughout. Their coffee, I must say, was better than the diesel oil you usually get at auctions.

Colonel Long ably presided over the selling of over 400 items, mostly from the estate of Miss Claudia Lea Phelps II of Rose Hill, Aiken, South Carolina. Miss Phelps' family was historically prominent for many years, and Rose Hill, the family mansion, was filled with fine pieces garnered by the family for over a 100 years. During the early part of the nineteenth century, they had engaged in the China Tea Trade, and many of the lots in the auction dated from that time. To me, knowing the story behind the sale makes such significant auctions as this one even more exciting. It was like peering through a tiny window into the last century and getting to actually touch things that had made the long voyage on a clipper ship across the Pacific and around stormy Cape Horn. This is part of the magic in antiques!

The first item up on the block, a mahogany folding table, marked the general overall quality of the offerings. It got a final bid of $100, and the auction was off and away. To give you an idea of the quality: out of the first 200 pieces, the lowest I saw anything go for was $25 for two Chinese tea cups, and the average was considerably higher. There was practically no junk here.

Several classes of pieces brought very good prices indeed. Furniture, of course, was one of the really strong offerings. The star item here was a beautiful example of chinoiserie, art having paint laboriously built up to give a three dimensional effect. It was a Queen Anne style secretary bookcase (circa 1900) with shell carving on crown and a reeded bunn foot. Careful examination of the secretary before the auction by a large number of obviously interested people foreshadowed the spirited bidding war that finally brought in $5,500. This amount was closely followed by $5,000 for an English slant-front secretary bookcase, $2,650 for a mahogany linen press, $2,900 to win a carved Chippendale style loveseat, $1,700 to get a Chippendale style bureau bookcase, $2,600 for an English breakfront bookcase with butler's-style desk, $1,700 for a round dining room table, and $1,000 to take home a butler's-style secretary with fitted interiors (circa 1840). Dozens of other pieces — chairs, tables, chests of drawers, etc.—also went in the $200 to $2,000 range.

Oriental rugs sold well also, probably because Charlton Hall Galleries had made considerable effort to accurately identify the pattern and place of origin. A 9-×-11 (all sizes approximated to save space) Persian kirman lavar sold for $1,300; an 18-×-13 Zigler Mahal took in $1,100, a colorful 11-×-18 Sarouk got $4,000, a 9-×-12 Esphahan held out for $2,200, a 9-×-12 Tabriz got $1,800, an antique Persian Heriz went for $2,000, another Tabriz (also 9-×-12) sold for $2,500, and a 2-×-20 Heriz runner got $650. Later on, a 6-×-9 Kashan

went for $1,000, a 6-×-10 Qum for $2,200, and a 10-×-6 "semi-antique" Qum brought $2,300. Several others also sold within this price area.

Mirrors reflected the same quality and high average prices as the other items, as did oil paintings and other objets d'art. A small, goldleaf, Adams-style mirror (circa 1820) led off for $150, followed by another Adams goldleaf for $450, then a large goldleaf pier mirror that got $1,200. A seascape signed "F.Walters" sold at the $2,100 level, and additional oils sold for $650 and $1,000. A marble bust signed "Cipriani" took in $900, and its onyx pedestal supported it with an additional $450. A bronze, *Wicked Pony* by Fredrick Remington, got in $3,600 before being tamed; an art nouveau girl on a stand by F. LeLuce was sold for $1,700, and a bronze fountain with its accompanying plaster mold got $1,000.

Many pieces of Orientalia, thanks to Miss Phelps' family's China Tea Trade connections of the last century, were also offered, including a large collection of Chinese Export porcelains. A small Chinese lacquered chest went at $160; a pair of covered tea cups for $35, an oriental cream pitcher for $35; a framed silk hunting scene for $160; a porcelain lamp for $170; an oriental metal lantern for $110; a pair of terra cotta garden urns for $850; a porcelain temple urn for $450; a pair of huge cast stone urns $650; and a 19-inch goldfish bowl for $850.

Some other items of note included a pair of Sheffield silverplated wall sconces selling at $775, a beautifully crafted cloisonne and brass clock at $700, a Jeromes and Darrow mantel clock (wooden works) for $650, an eighteenth-century leather water bucket (reputed to have belonged to the last royal governor of Delaware) for $140, a pair of miniature Victorian walnut rocking chairs for $100 each, and two hand held fire screens (circa 1800) also at $100 each.

A very enjoyable and informative auction.

Johnny Penland and His Friendly Auction

The area's first snowfall of the year had mostly melted away when Johnny Penland (NCAL #3611) cranked up his warm and homey weekly auction on the evening of December 6, 1985.

Penland's spacious building, located at 155 Craven Street, is on Asheville, North Carolina's long time Auction Row. Next door is a regular auto auction, and livestock sales were held for many years only a calf's throw away. Directly across the French Broad River, no more than 300 yards away, stands the Big Burley Tobacco Auction, one of several such warehouses in the immediate vicinity. Even the cold mountain wind, echoing down the line of ancient deserted textile mills and dilapidated buildings by the river, seems to come and go in the rhythmic chant of ghostly auctioneers from decades past.

But there is nothing ghostlike about Johnny Penland's enthusiastic and friendly auctioneering style, nor his building, which is cozy warm and well lighted inside. "Glad you could make it, come right in," is the greeting he offered regulars and casual visitors alike as people began arriving for the auction's weekly starting time of 7 P.M.

Attendance was a little down, due to the sudden cold spell, but the crowd made up for it in auction fervor, if not always with high prices.

Events began in a flurry of small collectibles, with Penland keeping the action fast and furious. A toy train set led off, chugging up to the $7 level. It was followed by a box of older Fisher-Price toys for $6, an ancient-appearing meat cleaver at $3, a matching meat saw for $2.50, an iron poker taking $2, a pair of throw rugs for $1, and a nine-piece Dresden china set for $6.

"We don't care where you start," Penland exhorted in getting the bidding started on a cast-iron pot which brought $20. This led an old gas can for $5, a crock marked "HB" at $2, a handpainted china platter also at $2, and a wooden trunk for $20. "What a night," the auctioneer said in mock exasperation, selling a mattock for $3.50, a Fiesta Ware celery dish at $2, and a brass bell for $11.

One of the surprises in this auction was the lack of interest in a set of andirons reputed to have come from Seely's Castle, the mansion built by Fred Seely on a mountainside high above Asheville during the early years of this century. Seely was the son-in-law of E.W. Grove, developer of the famous Grove Park Inn, and it was Seely who supervised the actual construction. Due to his close connection with the Roycrofters, it seems as if someone would have bought these and irons merely on spec—the average auction prices were certainly reasonable enough. Knowledge, folks, is just as important as having money at an auction. But, to relieve those who were there and are now afraid they missed a real find, these andirons did not seem to have the well-known orb and cross trademark. Still, they deserved better than to have to be withdrawn from the sale because of no bids.

Small items continued to dominate during the early part of the auction. More examples include a Roseville pot at $3, a silverplated copper tray for $2, a 1964 Horseman doll at $7, a handcarved Alaska Indian figurine for $4, and a sausage grinder cranking out a $3 bid. One of the better buys during this period was a set of Walt Disney toy metal kitchen appliances—stove, refrigerator, and sink—going for only $10.

A bit of comedic relief was supplied unwittingly by one of the auction assistants, George Tisdale, who "daylights" as a member of the Asheville City Council. "Ut oh," George said, dropping a china plate he was holding up as Penland chanted it off. The plate hit the floor with a resounding clatter. Tisdale quickly bent and retrieved the plate, then grinned hugely—it was undamaged! Such is the luck of the truly competent politician, and let's hope it holds for the downtown revitalization controversy, huh George?

Several items that had been bought years ago in the Orient by a local resident caused quickening of the pulses amid several bidders. The two most important of which were a large, pale yellow ceramic urn, decorated with an oriental painting, and a sizable hand-carved wooden chess set. The urn went at only $32.50, but the chess set held out against spirited bidding for $125.

Furniture set the tone for the latter part of the auction. Some sample prices were $120 for a dining room table and six "arrow back" chairs, a chest of drawers circa 1930 bringing $45, an oak captain's chair getting a mere $9, and a "maple-looking" chest of 6 drawers going at $30. An oak icebox was the star of the auction, although covered in peeling paint and in desperate need of a good stripping and refinishing. It went for $300.

"Let's look in on the tea cart," Penland said, as his assistants rolled up a teak, marble-topped tea cart. This had been featured at the front of the auction hall where everybody could see it as they entered. It was assumed by many that this would be the top money getter of the evening, but the much rattier looking icebox froze it out for that honor, with the cart selling for only $225.

Robert Bunn
Showing New York How It's Done

Five years ago, while still a mere youngster of only 81, Robert D. Bunn once more attracted national attention, this time auctioning off a standing signed Tiffany lamp for $210,000. This price, from the backwoods of North Carolina, set a record for Tiffany floor lamps that easily eclipsed the previous best: $140,000 at Christie's in New York.

This interview took place last year but Mr. Bunn, now approaching 87, still comes into his store every day, ready to do business.

ROBERTS: How long have you been in the antique business?

BUNN: About 35 years.

ROBERTS: Over the years, what pieces have you found that really stand out in your mind?

BUNN: Well, the one most prominent is a Tiffany lamp that I sold for $210,000 . . . (He shifts through a pile of books and catalogs.) Did you read that about the auction? This was in the *Antiques Dealer* magazine. Now this was in the *Southeast Trader* . . .

ROBERTS: Mr. Bunn, do you mind me asking how old you are?

BUNN: This November the 14th I'll be 86 years old.

ROBERTS: Do you do auctioneering any more?

BUNN: I have people call me, wanting me to handle them, but I turn them over to Lee Long. Lee's a good auctioneer . . . but I'm down at the end of the road now, and I'm just preparing this place, upgrading the merchandise. Sometime within the next year or so I'm going to have this place for sale.

ROBERTS: Tell me some more about the fine pieces you've found over the years, because you have the well-deserved reputation of being the dean of antique dealers in this area.

BUNN: Well, I'd have to go back and think a little bit. You know you handle an awful lot of stuff in 35 years and I've handled some very fine pieces both in American pieces and English. Right at present I have out of the old Green River Plantation the large Irish crystal chandelier from the big living room. It's nearly five feet wide. I have that now and the smaller chandelier out of the upstairs hall. That's two of the finest—chandeliers, that is—that I've had. I have a few very good paintings.

ROBERTS: What are the paintings that you just mentioned?

BUNN: I can show them to you. . . . Right here I have George Henry Boughton, American, born in Norwich, England, and died in London. He's in *Chapin's, Dictionary of National Biography*, Fielding's, *Encyclopaedia Britannica*, and a German biography of painters. Now if you'll look at all the things he's in, you'll find very few men had the records that he has. See?

ROBERTS: Yes, sir.

BUNN: Now I'll show you the painting . . . Right here.

ROBERTS: And the price?

BUNN: I'm asking $7,500. But, of course, like all dealers I might take less. In fact more so now that I'm getting close to the end of the line. Now I'll show you a frame over here that's around 350 to 400 years old. You see the Madonna and Child there?

ROBERTS: Is that a significant painting in the frame?

BUNN: No, just to show off the frame. That frame—I would take $1,250 for it.

ROBERTS: Tell me about this desk here.

BUNN: Well, I'll let you read about it . . . I've got the auction catalog here somewhere.

ROBERTS: I see. "Fine Queen Anne burl walnut double bonnet top bureau bookcase with firmly fitted interior, circa 1800." And you're asking—I saw your tag there—$17,500?

BUNN: I could sell that cheaper. That's about the price they sell for in Philadelphia and New York, see—$17,500. Well, you're liable to pay that when you can find them. They're hard as heck to find to start with. You can just put down that I'd listen to $12,500.

ROBERTS: Mr. Bunn, what advice would you give a person who wants to start as an antique dealer today?

BUNN: Well, first before they go into anything they want to know what they're doing. To read and study, that's what you got to do. There's been so much history in everything. Paperweights—there's a heck of a lot of history to paperweights alone. To the various kinds of furniture. Paintings and prints.

Well, the best way is to think about what the big museums do. Take the S. H. Kress Foundation. They have two or three experts on European paintings, on German, on Italian, on English, on French, and all that. See, everything they have specialists on. The same way in furniture. There's a half a dozen different types of American furniture that people specialize in. And English furniture . . . There's a lot to know, just in furniture.

So a young person starting to learn the business, if they've got time and there's a museum around, they should look and decide what they like best. Whether they like furniture, whether they like paintings, or bronzes, or statuary, or rugs, or whatever. They have to first decide what they want to specialize in because, brother, you can't learn it all . . .

ROBERTS: Over the years, again, what are some of the things you've enjoyed most about being in the antique business?

BUNN: Oh, I'm not tied down. I can leave when I want to. Go where I want to. And I used to go on buying trips to New York about every 60 or 90 days and I'd go up through Washington, Philadelphia, New York. And I made trips up as far away as Montreal, Canada, looking for frames and paintings and stuff. The ones I enjoyed more than any other, that is in this country, were up the Hudson River to those fine mansions built by old millionaires, and going to auctions there. And out on Long Island. Of course I enjoyed England when I was going over to buy in London and Manchester and Liverpool and Birmingham. My father was born in Birmingham, England. He left there a young man right after the Civil War and came over to this country.

CONCLUSION

The field of antiques and collectibles in general, and this type of auction in particular, offers the greatest consistent potential for profit than any other. You need knowledge at any auction, especially the fascinating country antiques and collectibles auctions. Yes, a little study will pay off royally in results. On top of this you will have a bodaciously good time at most of these auctions.

Now, let's see. What's next up onto the block? Ah! The chapter on art auctions. Are you in? Why, sure, I knew you would be. Why ruin a perfect string of winning bids? Sold, to my good buddy, the reader!

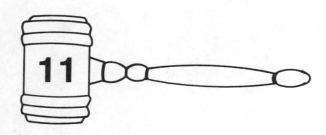

The Art of Buying Art

If you think that fine art is the province of the extremely wealthy auction goer, you are not necessarily correct. Certainly the stories we read in the newspapers about Rembrandts selling for $1,000,000 or so are true, but the majority of art sold at auction goes for less than $1,000. If you care for art, have an eye for the visual, and want to decorate your home with beautiful paintings, sculpture, and other artistic creations, you are going to love art auctions.

New York fancies itself the auction capital of the United States and/or world, and with some, if not complete, justification. (Sorry, folks, but there is auction action going on out here in the boondocks, which sometimes, like with Mr. Bunn from Chapter 10, puts the New York boys and gals to shame!) However, almost all of the really big art auctions on this continent take place in Gotham, that "Baghdad on the Hudson," as O. Henry called it. The major auction firms are located there—houses like Christie's, founded in 1730 in London; and Sotheby's, of similar age and English antecedents but now with branches on five continents.

It is not by accident that the two top fine art and antique auction houses in New York are English. The British tradition of these types of auctions dates back to the eighteenth century, and Britons were in the habit of selecting an auctioneer with the same careful attention to professionalism as they exercised in choosing a solicitor or stockbroker. Sales were conducted with total discretion. If the old duke had to sell off his Chinese snuffbox collection to pay his mistress' annuity (as perhaps might have happened with the Duke of Gloucester), then no one was the wiser. The snuffboxes were simply listed in the catalogs as "property of a gentleman," and His Grace was spared disgrace.

This restrained and elegant British method of running auctions, imported to New York by the two great English auction houses (especially when Sotheby's opened its New York auction room in 1967), did much to improve the image of the auctioneer with the fine art buying elite. Unlike the sometimes boisterous, even crass, American auctioneers—looked upon by the artsy crowd as

Fig. 11-1. Objets d'art require extensive knowledge as to which is authentic and which are merely reproductions. This elegant selection of fine art and antiques was part of a large offering of similar pieces at an auction in Hendersonville, North Carolina, which was presided over by Colonel Jerry King.

little better than bill collectors—the British were decorous and graceful. The old-country charm captivated American anglophiles, and prices realized for paintings soared.

Although English-run auctions do have considerable competition now in New York, and more so in the increasingly prosperous sun belt cities such as Atlanta, Houston, and Miami, it's still "I say! Tally ho, old chap!" when it comes time to decide who gets to sell the original van Gogh that great grandpere brought back from World War I.

Let's look first, more out of curiosity than practical values, at the top of the auction world. Then it will be on to the type of art auction more useful to you and me.

LA CREME DE LA CREME

The topmost spires of the auction universe are to be found at dizzying heights, their bases resting firmly on the continuing record-breaking sales of

fine art and antiques. The worldwide sales of the prestigious international auction houses have passed $500,000,000 per year and are still growing. Movie stars and other celebrities vie with each other to be seen bidding at these much ballyhooed events. The jet set has its subsets of glittering nabobs who follow these stellar auctions.

James Wagenvoord, in his very interesting book *Cashing In On The Auction Boom*, gives an insider's glimpse of this fascinating fairyland of auction high rollers. The top collectors and dealers in, for example, contemporary and impressionist paintings have a definite circuit of scheduled sales that can be followed across the world. They might start out among the marvelous Swiss Alps by going to Zurich in April, then on to New York in May, London in June, and Monte Carlo in July for a prince of a deal. In the fall there's a similar circuit for collectors and dealers in old masters paintings and drawings. Starting with New York in September, October takes them to London, and if it's

November it must be Zurich.

These wealthy collectors and dealers stay in the same hotels, put on the old feed bag at the same posh restaurants, and sometimes develop long-term auction friendships or rivalries. Wagenvoord goes on to report that, in New York, the hotel is the Stanhope and the restaurant is Les Pleiades, and that the real insiders' spot is a Greek-run coffee shop called Three Guys, located on Madison Avenue at 75th Street. He also says that since Sotheby's is now hosting sales in Los Angeles and at Chicago's Drake Hotel, these two locations will probably wind up being added to the auction circuit, as well.

IMPORTANCE OF THE CATALOG

Before we carefully climb back down to art auctions on a less rarefied level, a few words are offered here about auction-house catalogs and how to understand them as regards fine art. Even Christie's and Sotheby's will cater to lower-level buyers by having lots. So, not only might you wander into Christie's at 59th Street and Park Avenue in New York, the new Sotheby's over at 72nd and York, or the old Sotheby's auction room on Madison at 76th Street, but you might actually be able to afford harboring the idea of making a few bids. Even if not, you might want a catalog for your growing reference library. It is worthwhile to learn to read and interpret these top-line catalogs, by the way, because lower-level houses imitate them to varying degrees.

Expect to pay at least $25 or so for the catalog, however, which is why I earlier recommended you be on the lookout for old ones at used book exchanges and flea markets. These you can get for 50¢, $1, or some other reasonable price, and the information authenticating and giving the history of various pieces will still be good.

In the British-run auctions, there is a difference about the atmosphere that hits you as you enter from the street: whispers and echoes of eighteenth century, snuff-sniffing lords and the rustling starched petticoats of their wives or mistresses. However, as long as you look like you might actually let loose with a bid sometime or the other

and don't spit tobacco juice on the floor from the big chaw in your cheek, just about anybody but the Ayatollah Khomeini is welcome—and he could probably get away with a mail-order bid.

Don't get me wrong, I'm an anglophile from way back. However, these top-level, British-run auctions are as different from country auctions as Mars is from Cleveland.

Back to catalogs. Some of the English auction traditions are quaint, to say the least. Christie's, in business since 1730, has the habit of titling its catalogs with ladies' names, much like hurricanes used to be designated. So, you ask for a particular sale catalog by its proper name—something like Gigi or Antoinette. On the other hand, Sotheby's merely assigns a number to its catalogs.

A catalog, no matter its designation, is an important source of data, not only on the pieces specifically described and offered at the sale it covers, but as a continuing reference in case you find similar pieces at other sales, especially lower-level auctions that do not issue catalogs. The fact that you have ready access to this knowledge that others do not can result in tremendous profits for you. This truth cannot be stressed too vigorously. If you get nothing else out of this book but that one single fact, then I have done you a great service.

Just having the catalog and reading it is not all there is to it. You must learn to interpret the shorthand and jargon used by the auction houses. Generally, if you learn one, you can understand the others, as well. They are fairly consistent.

Deciphering the Catalogs

At an auction on the august level of a Christie's or a Sotheby's, everything offered at the sale will go into the catalog. In the cases of significant items—i.e., those that the firm feels will attract a lot of bidding—lengthy, erudite descriptions, along with a photograph of the piece, will be featured.

Usually, at the front of the catalog will be the conditions of sale, the legalese spelling out the terms by which the auction house operates. This is the typical fine print that spells out your liabilities and what the auction firm will or will not do. Caveat emptor is the rule of the day even for the most prestigious houses. You must know and understand these conditions, exceptions, and general stacking of the odds in the house's favor.

Once you have read and digested the conditions for a particular house, it is usually not necessary to reread it in every catalog because they usually remain the same. Just keep an eagle eye peeled for unexpected little changes. However, conditions of sale will vary from house to house; so you must check those for each catalog from a different firm.

Essentially, these conditions of sale are structured to protect the auction house from claims of misrepresentation. Despite the glowing terms of descriptions touting various pieces, everything is sold "as is," and the wording associated with the lot is said to be "in our qualified opinion," which legally means nothing in the way of guaranteeing authenticity. ("Well, hell, boy, we thought it was eighteenth century. You shoulda flipped that sucker over and seen the 'Made in Taiwan' sticker.") The people in the top-line auction houses will couch it a bit more elegantly than a country auctioneer, but the gist of the message will be the same: they aren't responsible, you are. Buyer beware. Another reason why knowledge is so all important.

Let me emphasize this again, because the catalogs from Christie's and Sotheby's and all the auction houses on that heavenly level are such slickly done, impressive, scholarly-appearing tomes that you might be tempted to take them as absolute gospel. It would be a big mistake to do so. Read the conditions of sale carefully and note all the exceptions and backtracking in them. Use this in forming your own opinion of a descriptive passage's veracity and worth.

In spite of all this namby-pamby waffling, catalogs are still one of the most useful reference sources in your auction knowledge library, especially along with their prices realized lists. Just use them as a guide, and not as the final authority.

Attributions

Many catalogs offer a list of descriptive terms. These glossaries vary but are, in general, fairly con-

sistent and logical once you catch on to how the auction house is hedging its bets. Once more, there is no substitute for scrutinizing the piece during the preview period and determining its validity through your own personal knowledge and experience.

For a more detailed description of how the big fancy New York auctions work, I refer you again to James Wagenvoord's *Cashing In On The Auction Boom.* His is the New York scene, while mine is the wonder and magic of country auctions, and I'll not trade it, thank you.

Let's take an example. You go to a large metropolitan art auction and are handed or forced to purchase a catalog. Walking along where the paintings are hung, you see one that strikes your fancy and page through the catalog until you find it listed. How this listing is worded can be of exceptional importance. To be gleefully absurd about the name, we'll say the painting in question is by that famous Spanish artist of the romantic period, Jose Melba Toasteo, painter of such classics as *Afternoon of a Gila Monster* and several houses in downtown Madrid.

Following are some ways that the authorship of the painting might be identified and roughly what each means. Remember that these degrees of attribution will not be exact in all catalogs—much depends on the whim of the person putting together the catalog—but these should still be a useful guide for you. Christie's and others use seven "degrees" of authorship. Christie's definitions, I will say in its defense, are usually quite accurate.

By Jose Melba Toasteo. Use of the painter's full name with no hedges other than the big one all auction firms throw in means that the auction house is saying "This is, in our opinion, a work by the painter named." The "as is," of course, is always implied to leave the house room to slide out from under a mistake in judgment.

Attributed to Jose Melba Toasteo. Here the house is telling you something like, "In our qualified opinion, this is a work from the period of the artist and we think it could be in whole or part by him . . . maybe."

From the Circle of Jose Melba Toasteo. "In our qualified opinion, from the period of the artist and closely related to him."

Workshop of (or Studio of) Jose Melba Toasteo. The house is saying that the painting was "possibly, in our qualified opinion, executed under supervision of the artist."

School of Jose Melba Toasteo. "In our qualified opinion, this work is by a follower or student of the artist."

In the manner of Jose Melba Toasteo. "In our qualified opinion, a work in the style of the artist, but possibly of a later period."

After Jose Melba Toasteo. "In our qualified opinion, a copy of the work of the artist." The fact that it is a copy doesn't tell you much as to age. It could have been painted during the eighteenth century or last Tuesday, and either could theoretically be listed the same way.

Sotheby's uses a somewhat less exact method of attribution, usually having only three general designations of authorship. In our example, the entry in the catalog for this painting might go something like one of the following.

Jose Melba Toasteo. A listing of just the author's name means, "The work is, in our best judgment, by the named artist. This is our highest category of authenticity in the present catalog."

*Jose Melba Toasteo. "While ascribed to the named artist, no unqualified statement as to membership is made or intended, as described in Paragraph 2 under the terms of Guarantee."

Attributed to Jose Melba Toasteo. "In our best judgment, on the basis of style, the work can be ascribed to the named artist, but less certainty exists."

Although Sotheby's attributions are less exact than Christie's, it should again be pointed out that neither house will warrant them as being absolutely true, nor will any other auction house. It is strictly up to you, the buyer, to determine whether or not you think the piece is authentic and to bid accordingly. Remember, attributions and the other descriptive information in auction catalogs are simply general guidelines.

DROPPING ON DOWN THE SCALE

Art auctions are also held at many lower levels than the alpine majesty of the big New York houses. Even country auctions are big on old oil paintings and the like. You should realize that paintings were extremely common in the nineteenth century, and that just because a work happens to be old doesn't mean it's especially valuable. The artist who painted it has much to do with the price. *Whistler's Mother* is worth a lot. *Herman Q. Crudmucker's Mother*, even if she was painted at the same time on the same type of canvass and using the same brand of paints, is worth much less because no one has ever heard of Herman Q. Crudmucker. There were tens of thousands of nineteenth century artists equally obscure.

This doesn't mean that Herman's painting, especially if it's in a nice gilt frame, is not going to bring several hundred dollars. It very well could; there is always strong demand among bidders for art of this time—i.e., "wall fillers."

Anyway, you will find old art mixed in with collectibles in most antiques auctions—not just paintings, but bronzes, small sculptures, figurines of all sorts, and much more. However, there are a lot of auctions that also sell new art—meaning just painted in the last year or so. Some artists' cooperatives will have this sort of sale and exhibition to help their members raise enough money to starve in comfort.

The peddling of amateur art by auction is a proven fund-raiser for various other groups, as well. Under one of my other hats, that of a science-fiction writer, I am a guest at several science-fiction conventions each year. Most of them have an art room where amateur artists can hang their work for display. Marvelously vivid colors hit the eye as you walk into that room—starships, nebulas, unicorns, dragons, Captain James T. Kirk of "Star Trek" fame, and many more themes from speculative fiction. Some of it is good, some atrocious, but much of it is avidly sought by collectors.

A white tag is usually affixed below the pictures on which interested persons can write their bids. At the end of the convention an auction is held—usually with one of the guest authors serving as auctioneer—and the pieces are paraded through the room. If someone wants to bid higher than the highest price written on the tag, bidding is on; otherwise the tag bid takes it. If there is no tag bid and no one present wants the piece of art, it goes back home with its creator. This type of auction helps defray the expenses of the convention, and makes money for the dedicated amateur artists, as well.

SUMMARY

Art auctions exist on all levels, from the sublime to the ridiculous, from Rembrandt and Gauguin to Elvis on black velvet and the paint-by-numbers botches of Bozo's kid brother. You can follow the grand international auction circuit, haunt your lo-cal fund-raising art auctions, or check out the offerings amid the junk so beloved of country auctioneers.

Knowledge, as in any auction-related field, plays a tremendous part in art auctions, since the offerings are very much "buyer beware." You must learn to interpret and accept the waffling that goes with attributions and the other information contained in the catalogs from even the top-line auction houses.

Still, if you think it will look good on your wall . . . While you're trying to decide that, let's auction off Chapter 12, the one coming up on autograph and manuscript auctions. What'm I bid? . . . A bid . . . a bid . . . I gotta winner . . . I gotta good reader over there . . . Sold to the good reader!

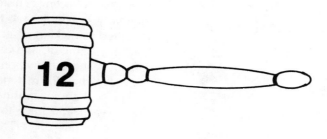

Autographs and Manuscripts

One of the stronger and more exciting growth areas in collecting today is the field of autographs and manuscripts. Prices realized at auction on signatures of famous persons, their letters and papers, and documents of historical significance continue to rise. If you are considering investing for the future, you are well advised to squirrel away autographed material for a few years before putting it back up on the block. This has been one of my personal collecting areas for several years.

Such well-known dealers in this field as Charles Hamilton have held many auctions dedicated to the autograph and manuscript collector where many thousands of dollars worth were gaveled down to delighted bidders. Hamilton has also written a number of important books in this and other collectible fields.

Seldom is an auction devoted totally to one type of collectible. Usually, auctions are mixed, with lots representing several categories. Hence, this section of the book might be a little misleading if you try to think of things in absolutes. In real life, many shades of gray prevail.

So, as you've probably deduced by now, what I am doing is giving you as much "getting started" knowledge as possible on each field, so that you can apply it, and your additional researches, not only, say, at an autograph auction *per se*, but in buying autograph material at a more general country auction, or at an antiques auction, or wherever you might find it.

And do I have some fantastically good data on autograph and manuscript collecting and buying for you. It was my fortune a few months ago to meet George Sanders, a nationally recognized expert on autographs and a long-time collector. Following is part of that interview. It's worth its weight in gold for all the hot tips contained therein.

Being the one answering the questions is a somewhat novel experience for George Sanders. During more than 30 years of interviewing thousands of notable people, Sanders has usually been on the other side of the microphone.

Harry S. Truman, John F. Kennedy, Martin Luther King, Robert Kennedy, Ronald Reagan—these are only a few of the movers and shakers who

Fig. 12-1. George Sanders, one of the world's leading autograph collectors, has an extensive reference library and carefully researches his acquisitions. He buys much of his new pieces at auction.

have given Sanders exclusive interviews on such talk shows as his long-running nationally syndicated radio and television program, "Sanders Meanders."

As a newsman and an actor himself in over 20 motion pictures and on television—he was a regular on "Wild Bill Hickok" with Guy Madison and Andy Devine, and also on "December Bride" with Harry Morgan—it was only natural that Sanders should start collecting the signatures of the hundreds of celebrities he came in constant contact with. His personal collection totals over 17,000 pieces—all kept track of by a personal computer.

Now 62 and enjoying early retirement, Sanders devotes full time to his hobby of autograph and manuscript collecting. He has already earned a well-deserved reputation as a very knowledgeable scholar in the field of autographs and manuscripts.

This interview took place in Mr. Sanders' home February 6, 1986. Enjoy.

INTERVIEW WITH GEORGE SANDERS

SANDERS: I am tremendously interested in what I've been involved in for about 35 years now, which is the collecting of historical documents. I've gotten very heavily into it, to the extent that I'm considered some kind of an authority. I do know what I'm looking at, and have a tremendous interest in it, and a tremendous investment also.

I've watched the material go from where you could pick up choice presidential pieces for $100 to now when you have to pay anywhere from $2,000 to $5,000 for it. That's quite a jump.

I find this hobby fills my time, because I do a lot of research, as you can imagine. I put my collections together so there's a lot of time involved.

ROBERTS: How do you find new pieces now for your collection?

SANDERS: We go all over the world to shop. I was in Europe last year and went to the London Autograph Show. I'm in the UACC[1] and the Manuscript Society[2] as a member. So I went to the UACC show in London.

We were very fortunate on the European trip and picked up a lot of material in London. We shopped around and it was quite exciting because you go into a place like a stamp store, which we did, and ask if they have any covers with signatures on them. The guy pushes across a couple and they're Charles Dickens pieces. He's selling them dirt cheap because the stamps on the envelopes aren't very important and that's all he cares about. And this happens frequently. You get a bargain because stamp people don't care about it.

I bought a James Polk free print from a stamp

[1]Universal Autograph Collector's Club (International), P.O. Box 467, Rockville Center, NY 11571.
[2]Manuscript Society, 1206 N. Stoneman Avenue #15, Alhambra, CA 91801.

auction several years ago. I paid $35. It's a $750 item, but not in stamps. (laughs) It's just not important to them. So there's some real bargains out there.

You know, you sometimes just get lucky. Helen reads everything and it was on a Sunday. We had left London and were in Geneva. We were standing in front of an antique store and she read a poster. Somehow, with her very mediocre French and my none at all, between us we made out that there was going to be a book fair in a nearby town and that this place was going to be closed the following day, which was today.

We decided to go and went over to the train station, got on the train, and used our Eurorail pass. Got to the book fair with nobody there speaking English—they were all speaking German, French, whatever.

I'm telling you I had a picnic because I bought some of the most beautiful pieces. One was a poem, in his hand, by Alexander Dumas *pere*[3]. It's an original, never been published, signed. It is just magnificent. If I told you what I paid for it you wouldn't believe me. Dirt cheap.

That and lots of other things. We found two Freud letters, and they are very expensive. I paid what they thought were dear for them. But remember the American dollar was up last year and the Swiss franc was down. So it's that kind of bargain you can take advantage of.

ROBERTS: You mentioned an upcoming vacation trip to Brazil. Since a number of wealthy Confederates migrated there after the Civil War, are you going to be on the lookout for material related to that?

SANDERS: Lot of Americans went there—fourth generation I guess or fifth generation Southerners from the Carolinas and Georgia. Yes, very good thought. We definitely will be shopping in Rio and in Brazil. You never know what you're going to find. I'm sure you've done it. Go in a used book store and find a letter in a book.

ROBERTS: Do you specialize in anything?

---

[3]The father as opposed to the son, Alexander Dumas *fils*, who wrote successfully also but never equaled his father's more famous works like *The Count of Monte Cristo* and *The Three Musketeers*.

SANDERS: Yes, I have it divided topically. I'd say the number one portion of my collection is U.S. Presidents. That also means association pieces. Like, for example, if the president was assassinated, then I have something by the hand of his assassin. This also includes First Ladies, Cabinet members, and so forth. I have all of the U.S. presidents.

Then I have another division in which I lump together artists, composers, sculptors—the artistic side. Then I have one just for the Civil War, and another of military leaders from all eras, heads of state, and celebrities.

I have a great collection of entertainers because I knew so many. Of course, my collection when I first started was on the basis of all the people I interviewed on the air. I kept guest books, with one page for each person. Over the years, when you do as many as I did—the syndicated show, "Sander's Meanders" was an interview show and I had that on for years—the autographs mount up quickly. So all those people that I interviewed, and all the Hollywood people, all the political people were asked to sign my books. Towards the end of my career I was doing news, talking to people of importance. So I had graduated from entertainment people.

There was so much in the collection of genuine in-person signatures. Like I'll show you this Jack Kennedy that's in here. I have dealers coming to my home and everyone puts a bid on this piece. Because one that you had Kennedy sign for you personally is much more important.

There are 17,000 pieces in the collection. Of course my really good pieces are kept in the vault down at the bank. The important presidential pieces and all that.

Anyway we go to shows all over the world. Washington, Atlanta, New York. We spend a great deal of time with autograph people — people who have more knowledge than I do. I go to them to bask in their knowledge. But when you've collected anything for 40 years you get pretty sharp.

I have a peculiar talent—I don't know why—but I've always been able to read other peoples handwriting. I never realized this was very important until I got deeper and deeper into autographs and found everybody else is complaining. 'George, what does this say?' they would ask, and I'd want to know why bring it to me. They were the experts, but it's hard, it's difficult for them apparently.

I found out what a help this was as I got more and more into the hobby. I realized that this was a rare talent. I can take a whole collection—let's say of Civil War letters—and put them in the right chronological order and then proceed to read and get really involved in this guy's life.

In fact, sometimes I get carried away if I get an entire collection of letters. There was a bunch of letters I picked up in this area of General Swift—F.W Swift, the Civil War general who won the Congressional Medal of Honor. I found about 700 of his letters locally.

I have no difficulty in reading handwriting. Once I find their swing, once I pick out a few keys, I can read right through it as if it was a relative I had always heard from.

I usually go to experts when it comes to language problems. I don't read German that well, I don't French or Spanish that well. So I will turn the material over to specialists and they send me their translations of it. Usually you have to pay for that kind of assistance.

It would be difficult for you to mention—for example in my collection of authors—anybody I don't have. I have just about everybody under the sun. During my years of doing interviews, I did a lot of authors. If an author was coming on the show, I'd always rush to the store and get some of his books. They see me coming in for an interview dragging a big stack of books, new and old. Most authors are happy to do that.

ROBERTS: What about authenticity of a piece, and how do you tell if it's worth the money?

SANDERS: I have probably as fine a library as anyone for private research, where you can check out facsimile material. Plus I have the good fortune to know personally people like Charles Hamilton, Paul Richards, and Mary Benjamin—people who are long-time collectors, dealers, investors in autographs.

My mentor was and has been for years a lady who's now in her late seventies, Mary Benjamin.

She's the daughter of Walter R. Benjamin, founder of the oldest autograph firm in America. Mary's one of our dearest friends and I can always call on her at any time.

There are times when some of the lesser-known dealers in the field will come to me and ask my opinion on material. I've reached that stage, which is rather nice.

But, to answer your question, one way is through personal knowledge of people—because many of the persons I knew and interviewed are now vintage and I have all their handwriting in my own collection. I know what their handwriting is like. I know what their signature is like and have copies of it right here. And I've always made copies of what I have. So there is no chance that you are going to come up with a piece that I can't identify and tell you whether it's valid or not.

It takes years of study to know what's autopen and what is not. What is secretarial and what is not. I can only tell you that it takes 40 years of experience to pick up an item that someone is telling you Clark Gable signed. I had Gable on my show and I can tell immediately as the item is being handed to me that it's secretarial. And people get so mad. But it takes years and years of experience.

This is not a hobby that you can go into and not study. You learn something every day. I'm sure you've seen in antiques that no two hand-crafted pieces are alike. Well, no two letters are alike. If Jack Kennedy wrote a letter in longhand, he didn't write any two the same. Even his handwriting is a little bit different. But you surely know after awhile whether it is definitely his or not. Or whether it is Abraham Lincoln's or not. There's just no question in your mind.

ROBERTS: What about nineteenth century secretarial pieces? I understand that some of those are significant.

SANDERS: Are you aware of who Sir Henry Irving's[4] secretary was? There was so much mate-

---

[4]Henry Irving, 1838-1905, was an extremely successful English actor and theater manager who is credited with raising the social respectability of acting as a profession. He was knighted by Queen Victoria in 1895.

rial written by Henry Irving, signed by him, but the body of the letter was written by Bram Stoker[5] and there was a good deal of that.

It was quite fashionable for, say, prominent Englishmen to work as secretaries to prime ministers and to ultimately become prime minister themselves. I was studying someone yesterday, Malmesbury[6]. I didn't know it, but Malmesbury, who was one of the great diplomats of William Pitt's era, served as a secretary. So his handwriting is on a lot of William Pitt's material. I didn't realize that until, as I say, yesterday, when I received a piece that was sent to me from England.

ROBERTS: This may be a bad way to phrase it, but what is "hot" right now?

SANDERS: It depends on the age of the collector. To the young, teenagers, there's a very good market for rock artists. It's a market that's doing very well. Material's selling well. It's not something I would be interested in because it's faddy. I wouldn't recommend it.

ROBERTS: How do you think it will do over the long term?

SANDERS: I hate to be put on the spot (laughs) because I have friends who sell rock material, but I have no great hopes for it. I feel that the kids will treat it as Andy Warhol said. We'll all be famous for about 15 minutes.

So when you start talking about individual rock-and-roll artists, I can tell you about the big band leaders who were so outstanding when I was a kid. Like let's take Russ Morgan, Music in the Morgan Manner. Who remembers? There are exceptions. Glenn Miller was martyred. That makes him very valuable. Glenn Miller is still a very valuable autograph and very hard to come by. And Tommy Dorsey is still a hard autograph and it's worth something.

In the area of rock artists, I'd say the Beatles will always have a good value because they were the first. The first of anything is usually valuable. Take inventors. Thomas Edison, Eli Whitney, Cyrus McCormick, and all the other great inventors that come to our mind here in a conversation are extremely expensive items. They have never died. I think that you'll find probably that Bruce Springsteen will join people like the Beatles. Elvis Presley is still an expensive item. A good signed photo of Elvis goes for a very good price.

If we're talking about firsts—the first new sound in rock—that kind person will be valuable, but the run of the mill will just be run of the mill. No great appreciation. But I don't see appreciation on movie star autographs either, because they, too, come and go.

ROBERTS: What about World War I autographs? I read that they were high between the world wars, but have dropped now.

SANDERS: Right on. Now the few people who still hold their value—and they don't go for the prices you think they'd go for— are John Pershing, because he was commander of the American Expeditionary Force. Foch and Joffre[7] are still good. Some of the Germans—Ludendorff. But I can only name about ten.

Revolutionary War material—now that's specialists and it has held up in value magnificently. But that's American, and if you're smart and live in America, you'll collect American material. Begin with colonial material only if you have the money.

Presidential material in the United States will never go low. You can specialize in any President and you won't go wrong. There's an appreciation there for any of them. I know a lot of autograph people in a conversation want to steer clear of this. But I'll say that I couldn't be interested in any hobby that doesn't show some appreciation. Autographs are too expensive to fool around with, putting your money into them, if there's not some sort of gain.

Now that's directly opposed to what a lot of autograph dealers want to hear. But why should anyone invest a thousand dollars in a Sigmund Freud letter and learn that it's only worth $600 twenty years from now, or six years, or five years from now.

---

[5]Bram Stoker, 1847-1912, is a British author best known for his now classic tale of a blood-sucking vampire, *Dracula*.
[6]James Harris, Earl of Malmesbury, 1746-1820.

7 French commanders

ROBERTS: Who are the top people in autographs today?

SANDERS: Paul Richards is one. Charles Hamilton, another— he's done more for autographs than any other person I know. When I first got into autographs, I met Mary Benjamin, and I've buying material from her for over 30 years now. I've watched her prices go from $20 for a U.S. President to where you couldn't get one now for under $150. Any President.

ROBERTS: What about association pieces written by people who are not famous?

SANDERS: One of the things that started me on the Civil War was that my wife's great-great grandfather was second-in-command of the 20th Connecticut Volunteers which, since we now live in the South (laughs), we don't talk much about around here. In any case he was a respected officer who managed to live through all of the campaigns.

His letters had been handed down and no one in the Doolittle family had ever done any work on them. Years ago I had time in the broadcasting studio I worked in—time in between programs, time in between station breaks—so I started working on his letters, which we still have. They went through the entire Civil War.

He would be an example of what you were asking. Because what's important in his letters is that he describes in great detail Lincoln's reviewing of his troops, and meeting the president. He didn't like Lincoln. He apparently had never voted for him. He referred to him as "the Great Ape in the White House," which was the first time I had ever seen that expression.

Yes, I find association pieces extremely important. A nice letter that talks about some intimate thing going on in a cabinet by a little known cabinet member—who on his own is not important—but he's writing about something that is. He was there, he was a participant. If he relates standing up and saying something was bunk and they went ahead and did it anyway and out came Teapot Dome, that letter is worth maybe more than any letter I've got of Warren G. Harding himself.

If you've got a letter written by Alfred Fall[8] in which he writes and says "Well I'm an old man now and I don't mind admitting that we did do so and so, but I don't know why Harding was kept so clean, because he knew as much about it as I did," suddenly we're talking about a $2,000 letter and nobody knows who Albert Fall is in this day and age. It's the fact that he's putting the finger on Harding that would make it so valuable.

As well as I know Dick Nixon, if I had a note from some of the people I also knew who were in his cabinet and I got them to say something in an aside where they indicate that Dick knew, just that, and he knew long before it came out, hey, I've got $1,000 letter. So association pieces are important, and no old family letters should be tossed aside until you have read them and read them carefully and understand what they're saying and what they refer to.

Sometimes a letter will pop out of California, for example, and the man will be an old timer writing with very bad grammar, very bad English, but he's in the gold fields. And he's writing in 1849. If you check the date he's maybe there like the day Sutter discovered it. What happens? We come across things like that all the time. The man's name doesn't mean anything but what he's writing about does. He's an eyewitness.

I've got a letter from an American upstairs—I don't know who he was and can't find any record. But it's a three-page letter written about the Russians in 1850. And it is unbelievable because you would think it was written yesterday giving an American's view of how Russians behave. Their secretiveness, their connivances, their mistrust in outsiders, etc. It's all there in this letter. He's writing from Moscow. I don't know who he was, but I tell you one thing, the letter is absolutely fascinating and the envelope with it. So a letter like that, with that kind of description of what's going on inside the czar's group, is not only exciting to read, but it has historic value.

---

[8]Albert Bacon Fall of New Mexico was Secretary of the Interior under Harding. It was later proved that he had accepted bribes while in office in the matter of naval oil reserves.

There are various facets of autograph collecting. That term, itself, is a misnomer. Autograph collecting is what you do when you go up to someone and ask them to sign your autograph book. Or get a menu signed. That's autograph collecting.

But when you start talking about manuscript collecting, you're in a whole different ball game and now its content that means so much more than who signed. It would be lovely, if you could acquire it, to have a beautiful letter from Thomas Jefferson. But if you can get a letter from someone who lived at Monticello at the same time, and happens to be a very good writer, maybe the overseer of the slaves, and if this man is relating how Jefferson is telling him to get the slaves in line by whipping them every day at 3 P.M., that's a fantastic piece because he's saying Thomas Jefferson supports abuse of slaves.

The same thing would apply if you had a letter that showed Abraham Lincoln treated the slavery thing, the 16th Amendment, as an afterthought. He was using it as a means to an end. But he was not that concerned and there are letters of his that prove before he was president of the United States, he did not understand why you shouldn't have property in the form of slaves. So here's the Great Emancipator—and of course that's the reason that a great many well-educated blacks no longer revere the name Lincoln—not really understanding the evil of slavery. Thanks to collectors, those letters have become available to all of us, and we are no longer in the dark as to what he really thought.

Yes, that's the exciting part—to find letters with significant content. But you've got to do your homework and, as I say, if I didn't force myself to go out and walk every day, I would hibernate until I died, spending 8 to 12 hours a day and never leaving my desk. It's that exciting. I care that much about it.

CONCLUSION

Autographs, manuscripts, and historical documents offer wide scope for interesting collecting and for buying and selling at auction. Like antiques and art, this is another field where a little knowledge gives you a tremendous advantage when you are bidding on that old bundle of letters that everyone else thinks is worthless.

But, for now, let's move from autographs to automobiles Come now, we have Chapter 13 up on the block. Do I have to launch into an auctioneering chant this late in the book? . . . Ah, I thought not. There's goes the reader's hand up. Sold!

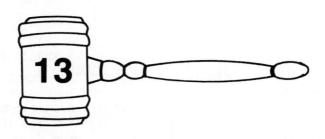

Getting It In Gear, Auto Auctions

America's 80-year-plus love affair with the automobile extends over into the auction arena. Sedans, sports cars, vans, motorcycles, trucks, go carts—you name it, they can all be bought at auction and at considerable savings. Since cars are so widespread, they turn up quite often at all types of auctions. If you really look, you'll find whatever you want and at a good price.

Estate sales frequently include a vehicle or two. Even such snooty auction houses as those on the Christie's/Sotheby's plateau will upon occasion include a car—if you can be so crass as to call a mint-condition Dusenberg or something on the order of Hitler's limousines by the pedestrian term of *cars*. The Hitler vehicle sale is an interesting one, showing the fascination we all still have with one of the most evil men in history almost 40 years after his death and the fall of Nazi Germany.

The Hitler automotive sale was held, not in New York but in Scottsdale, Arizona, in 1973. Old Adolph the Ugly's personal parade vehicle, a 1940 770K Mercedes-Benz touring car with bulletproof doors, armor plating, and windshield glass 2 inches thick was won by a $153,000 bid. The car itself was a hummer. Although it weighed over five tons, it had a 230-horsepower engine that could zoom it along at 135 miles per hour. Since perhaps the only one good thing that Hitler did was to have the autobahns constructed (the German equivalent of our much-later interstates and far ahead of their time), no doubt his driver got to do a little hot rodding in real style out on those long, flat stretches of concrete.

Another car of Hitler's in the same sale brought $93,000. However, it was a domestically made car—a battered and cheap 1934 Ford—that brought the most. This little vehicle was not exactly in pristine shape either, being riddled with over 200 bullet holes. Because of our fascination with crime here in America, though, this car- which the notorious Bonnie and Clyde were ambushed in and gunned down by the Feds—sold for an incredible $175,000! Someone really believed in buying American.

The greatest price ever paid for a used car, according to the *Guinness Book of World Records*,

Fig. 13-1. Cars such as this 1957 Mercedes are not vintage but they are fast becoming classic automobiles and are highly sought after at automobile auctions.

was also at an auction, this one in 1979. A telephone bidder in Princess Grace's Monaco placed the offer during a Christie's sale in the Los Angeles Convention Center on February 25th, 1979. The winning bid was $421,040 for a 1936 Mercedes-Benz roadster from the M.L. Cohn collection. Judging from this and the Hitler limousine sales, perhaps what the Mercedes salesman told me once about their high resale value is correct, but it was the high new sale value that kept me away. I'll just keep driving my faithful old Volvo; you purely just can't wear them suckers out!

Most automobile auctions, however, are of two categories: the common, everyday, exhaust emitters we drive down to the 7-11 for another six pack of milk, and the more affordable classic cars favored by collectors. Let's take a look at the classics first and close out the chapter with the more practical automobile auctions, the ones where you can save money whenever you need to replace or add a vehicle to your mighty fleet of one or two.

CLASSIC AUTOMOBILE AUCTIONS

Classic /or vintage automobiles are normally those made before 1950, but several in the fifties have already achieved, or are in the process of achieving the classic designation. These two terms, classic and vintage, are often used interchangeably, but actually they have slightly different meanings. *Vintage* refers to an older vehicle, while *classic* can be applied to one that made a large impact on the car loving public, such as the 1957 Chevrolet or the 1955 Thunderbird. The terms can also be used together; i.e., as in a classic vintage Bugatti Type 41 "Royale," of which only six were made. This Bugatti, by the way, is the largest production car in the world, being 22 feet long with a 7-foot hood. Some still survive and how auctioneers must dream of handling the sale on one of those!

Classic sales are big business indeed. Both of our haughty international auction giants, Christie's and Sotheby's, have automotive sales divisions. One large firm, with the especially appropriate

Fig. 13-2. You can buy everything at auction from this toy double decker bus to . . .

name of Kruse Auctioneers (headquartered in Auburn, Indiana), specializes in this type of automobile auction, and there are similar firms as well.

Auctions featuring classic or vintage automobiles are held regularly all over the United States and Canada. These sales star the rare and unusual collector's items that have been lovingly cared for or painstakingly restored by wealthy owners. However, cars for daily, if somewhat elegant, usage are also offered. Such cars meant to actually be driven out on the dirty old highway include Bentleys, Daimlers, Mercedes-Benzes, and Rolls Royces that are pushing at but have not achieved classic status. I have suggested to my friends for years that a Rolls for Christmas would be a quite nice present for me, especially since there already is an *RR* on the front. It would save them a fortune in monogramming! They give me ties instead, I don't wear ties. A Rolls Royce, I would wear (out, probably).

You can find out about classic car auctions being held in your area by consulting the local newspaper's classified advertisement pages under both "Automobiles" and "Auctions." There are a number of specialty publications as well. *Old Cars Weekly*, published in Iola, Wisconsin, is one of the leading tabloids devoted to this field. Many of the newsstand automotive magazines carry advertisements for classic sales, and catalogs or sales notices are available from the three auction firms mentioned earlier.

PRACTICAL CAR AUCTIONS

There are several good sources for some very excellent buys at automobile auctions. *Repossessions*, cars on which people have defaulted on payments, are one. Often, because the lender has already received part of the purchase price, he is not overly concerned about getting full book value for the car and you can move in for the kill.

Repossessed cars, like most items at auction, are sold "as is," but quite often the new car warranty will still be in effect. Also, because the lender

Fig. 13-3. this real one!

exercised his lien on the car, the title will be clear. Normally, also, the mechanical condition of these cars will be good, because they are relatively new. Your inspection can consist of starting up the car and the old classic (and rather pointless) maneuver of kicking the tires. Test driving is usually not allowed, and payment consists of something like 25% by cash or certified check at the auction and the balance in 3 to 5 days. Any arrangements for financing the car are left up to you.

Another place to get cars is from an auction conducted by a law enforcement agency that has confiscated them from various lawbreakers. Despite the fact that the law is selling them, title is not always completely clear. Still, you can get some extremely good bargains there because the police, sheriffs, or whatever just want to get shut of the vehicles, and are not concerned with making a profit.

Other sources include bankruptcy and liquidation sales of car dealerships and government surplus sales such as those run regularly by the postal service in some areas (those little left- handed steering jeeps are neat, huh?). Watch your newspaper for the announcement of these sales and the ones mentioned previously.

CAR AUCTION DEALERSHIPS

There are now a growing number of regular car auctions. These are basically divided into two groups: those that sell only to dealers and those that will lay a car or truck on anyone with the jack to pay for it.

Cars at these auctions come from all sorts of places: repossessions, other auctions, surplused fleet cars from corporate or government sources, retired Highway Patrol cars, and everywhere in between. (Remember, *caveat emptor*!)

This type of sale is normally held on a weekly basis. Inspection is almost always limited to crawling over the vehicle and starting it up. Test drives are prohibited. A deposit is required if you win the bid, with the balance by cash or certified check due within a week, or the car goes back in the next auction and they get to keep your deposit with considerable glee.

The regular car auction, whether you're buying as a dealer or as a private individual, does require a good foundation in mechanical knowledge and careful inspection and checking. The CBS News program, "60 Minutes," ran a segment a couple of years ago on some of the prevailing abuses in the auto auction business. One of the most odious consisted of running the odometer back in huge increments, thus raising the prices realized on the vehicle.

One of the things documented during this report was a Tennessee-Pennsylvania connection. Auto auction firms in the North would buy cars out of Tennessee that had been odometers run back and minor cosmetic body work done to make them look in much better shape than they really were. The titles also sometimes came up for a little judicious "fender straightening." One small Tennessee town, with hardly more than one stoplight in the whole place, had over 100 registered automobile dealers, showing what a huge business this fraud was (and no doubt still is).

Buyer beware! You can get some amazing bargains at automobile or any other type of auction, but you can also lose your tail and your bus ticket home, just like in Las Vegas. Yes, I am going to say it again: knowledge is the key! This fact cannot be emphasized often enough.

TURNING OFF THE IGNITION

Okay, we can shut down the automobile auction chapter now. In summary, you can get some really good buys at auction on both classic or vintage cars, and also on the good transportation that we need from day to day. Since most of us buy cars from time to time, it'll pay you to learn about the automobile auction route.

Now, let me have a bid on Chapter 14, Bankruptcy Auctions . . . Yes, I see your hand, reader. My, but you're getting quick on the trigger. Thanks and sold! To the reader.

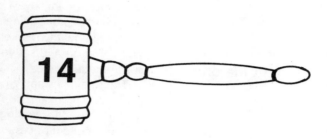

Bankruptcy/Going-Out-of-Business Auctions

Auctions that feature fine art, antiques, and vintage or classic automobiles get all the glamour in the press. Yet, if the totals of prices realized were added up from all the auctions held in the United States and Canada each year, the proceeds from bankruptcies and other legally forced sales would be shown to dwarf those of these other auctions the same way like Wilt Chamberlain would dwarf Mickey Rooney.

Legally forced sales come in all sizes and shapes, and are to be found at every level of the auction game imaginable, from the break up of a large international corporation to the dissolution of the mom and pop grocery down on the corner because pop passed away. Most auctioneers will gladly handle a bankruptcy or going-out-of-business sale; some specialize in them. The standard method of paying for their services is a negotiated commission percentage on each item sold.

On the very high end of the spectrum of auctioneers who handle such sales are the specialist firms that handle huge industrial plant liquidations.

Anyone who has ever worked in, or even just walked through, a factory realizes the thousands upon thousands of objects that cram every nook and cranny. Especially in an older factory—generally those that get closed out anyway— does this proliferation of items abound. The auction is, as we've already seen, particularly well suited to quickly and profitably clear all this mess out.

However, an auction for a huge factory requires more than your friendly local auctioneer, who probably only has five or six people working for him. Sure, he'll gladly and enthusiastically take on the task, while refusing to admit how far out of his league it is. The specialist firms, on the other hand, have an army of workers who flow through the plant tagging, cataloging, and organizing what at first seems absolutely unmanageable into a finely orchestrated movement of pieces across the block come auction day. Such an auction company costs more, but gets more.

GOOD BUYS FOR YOU

Skim over the auction advertisements in the clas-

Fig. 14-1. Advertisement for a going-out-of-business auction.

sified section of your local newspaper, especially in the Sunday edition, and you will find more than one of this type of auction almost every week. Car dealerships, paint stores, farms, wholesale supply houses of all kinds—no matter what you may be interested in, sooner or later there's going to be a bankruptcy or foreclosure auction that offers exactly what you need.

Obviously you, as a private buyer, do not want nor need to purchase the entire inventory of a defunct textile factory. Not even 1,000 gross pair of orange and purple knee-high socks would be all that attractive at any price—it would take every garage in the neighborhood to store them. Such deals are better left to people in the salvage selling business with the warehouse space to take advantage of big deals like this.

However, there are several categories in which you can buy at this type of auction and in quantities that will be of use to you. The savings over buying such merchandise at a retail store can be considerable or, frankly, you can lose your belt and suspenders by not having done your homework. You must know the market value of the items you want to bid on and set your bidding limit lower than the retail price.

The sale of a small grocery store—such as the hypothetical mom and pop's mentioned earlier—is especially good for getting such things as canned foods at excellent prices, while not saddling yourself with a garage full of case lots. A sale of a wholesale food distributor, on the other hand, might run to entire pallets stacked high with cases of baked beans and the like. That is quite possibly more baked beans than you would use in three centuries.

A good buy is not a good buy if you can't use it or if you do not have the warehousing space to store it until it can be resold at a profit. You should exercise a bit of prior thought not only regarding bidding limits, but also concerning what happens if you actually win the bid.

There are some items, even at an auction of a wholesale distributor, that you can use. Take toilet paper. Whether we care to talk about it or not, it's a necessary convenience to have. When I was in the First Air Cavalry in Vietnam, those little mini rolls that came in C rations took on an incredible importance when we were out in the jungles, occasionally for weeks at a time. Having two or three rolls stuck in the elastic band that held the camouflage cover on your helmet was the difference between civilization and savagery. They were a badge of honor, and worn proudly by officers and enlisted men alike. Those of you who were also there can understand what this meant. You can never have too much.

Here in America, a case or two of such paper out in the garage is not going to hurt anything either if you get it at a super price. It isn't going to rot and you know it will be used up eventually.

Paper towels, napkins, anything else that your household uses a lot of, all can be bought in this manner at sometimes a very small percentage of what you'd have to pay in a retail store. Besides, you can also trade partial lots with your auction-going buddies for something that they have too much of and you need.

The auction of a wholesale distributor, or a even a factory, also means that a lot of incidental items common to all businesses will be offered—things that you might want and need, Office furnishings is one of the obvious categories. Desks, chairs, file cabinets, typewriters, adding machines, typewriters, office supplies such as paper and ribbons, pencils, pens, and much more are to be found in all offices.

These days, also, many firms have personal computers that can be picked up reasonably if the business falls under the auctioneer's hammer. The computer has become a status symbol now, one sitting on an executive's desk or on the sideboard as a turf-defining necessity just like the electric pencil sharpener used to be. Needless to say, many of these computers still in pristine condition. Having been used about as much as the pencil sharpener in this day of cheap ballpoints.

Which sort of slides us into the final category in which you can benefit by buying at a bankruptcy or other type of going-out-of-business auction: secialized supplies or equipment. If you are a paint contractor, for example, obviously you would gladly bid on large quantities of paint. Getting paint at a distressed sale price—i.e., below wholesale—would enable you to underbid your competitors and still make a greater margin of profit.

This type of buying can help any small business be more competitive in today's dog-eat-dog business environment. Here's a lesson in business that I learned the hard way—by having a stereo shop of five years. Large corporations increase their profits by increasing sales, small businesses increase profit by decreasing overhead.

Even, when you have a small store, throwing a sale doesn't necessarily help. You take in more money, but the cost of selling is higher because you are giving a discount and the amount of over-all profit is not always that high. Decreasing overhead is the only real answer—so crystal clear, yet seemingly so hard to grasp since those thousands of businesses fail across the United States and Canada everyday. Like I say, this lesson was learned the hard way.

So, to lower overheads, the owner of a small business can make good use of auctions. Store fixtures like counters and display racks, calculators, cash registers, office furniture, and all the rest being bought low auction prices means that much more money to be invested in merchandise and day-to-day expenses.

Just as importantly, much of the merchandise itself can be obtained at auction. Many clothing stores do this quite often, but any shop selling dry goods, hardware, or just about anything can eke out their stock with good buys at auctions, hence increasing the overall profit margins. It could spell the difference between life and death for your small business.

TYPES OF FORCED SALES

A sizable portion of this type of auction is legally mandated sales, or *lien sales*, a person or business owes creditors more money than can be paid except by the turning of property into money. Using the various chapters of bankruptcy, the courts can force an owner to sell out in order to pay up, or the court itself can run the sale. The IRS also gets into this type of forced sale.

Whether such insensitivity and lack of understanding as the courts and the IRS show is right or wrong, you might as well take advantage of this fact of life. A court- or IRS-ordered sale is stacked in favor of the auction buyer because the property must go and the officials handling the sale usually have little idea of what the stuff is really worth. So there are many opportunities to use your own knowledge and make a killing.

An actual *bankruptcy proceeding*, as opposed to a lien sale in order to satisfy the IRS or courts, has some peculiarities. First of all, the sale is usually to satisfy a specific amount owed to creditors, with the balance of money received from the sale, if any, going to the bankrupt party. Therefore, the creditors have no rights to the debtor's property above this discrete sum.

Here's where this can get you. Because creditors only get the amount owed them, if the bankrupt person or company can scrape up enough money to satisfy the creditors' combined claims before the auction, he is in effect buying back his property at the auction itself for the amount of the money owed, no matter how high other bidders are willing to go). This is called the *right of precedence*. Even if you do lose a good buy this way occasionally, you must admit that this right is fair. Lord knows things are hard enough in business as it is without having to start completely over by buying all new store fixtures and the like.

The courts and the IRS also muddy the auction waters by offering everything to a *bulk* bidder. This practice means that even if you won a a lot or particular group of lots, you really might not have. Here's how this odious bit of business works. As each piece is sold, its price is recorded and added to the sum of all that has been sold before. At the end of the auction, the grand total is announced and bids are solicited from anyone who wants to top it and thus buy everything in the auction, canceling all your winning bids! This is done, so say the lawyers and judges, to forestall future litigation because they can say that every path was taken to get the maximum return. Me, I think it's what we used to call "Indian giving" when we were kids!

Continuing onward, *foreclosure sales* differ from bankruptcy sales in that a creditor actually takes over the property in question, repossessing it and taking actual title. A bank foreclosure on a mortgage is an example. Usually good buys can be gained at these auctions, as well, because the lender usually know beans about the business or other property.

Voluntary liquidations are sales in which a business person or private individual holds an auction of his own free will to raise money or just to clear out excess property. Sometimes a store will hold a liquidation as a means of getting rid of merchandise that is not selling and raising the money to invest in more attractive inventory.

FARM SALES

Okay, here's one sort of distressed sale that you folks in New York City might want to ignore. Of course, when the "taters and turnips" quit coming and you have to start eating asphalt, some changing of the mind might occur.

The South and the Midwest are literally the breadbaskets of the nation. In many areas of these two great geographical regions, the farm auction is the main way in which young farmers acquire their first farm and older ones add more land in an increasingly desperate attempt to make ends meet.

People such as country music superstar Willie Nelson and the Farm Aid concerts he supports have done much to emphasize and make public the plight of the small family farm. High interest rates and low prices for crops have combined to cause more foreclosures than at any time since the bad old days of the Great Depression. Sure, the prices you pay for food are high in the supermarket, but it's the middlemen who are getting those profits, not the farmer.

On to practicalities. As regrettable and sad as the death of a farm may be, there are incredible opportunities for the bidder to pick up machinery and implements at bargain prices, as well as the land and buildings themselves. As in any form of buying at auctions, your own knowledge is all important. You must weigh a piece of equipment's utility to your own operation, judge its condition, examine its current market value, and form your bidding limits from that data.

Again, alas, taking advantage in this manner of someone else's misfortune might mean the difference between success and failure on your own farm. Auction buying can be your salvation if handled with knowledge and care.

SUMMING UP

Bankruptcies and other types of distressed sales offer the knowledgeable buyer considerable chance for profit and for obtaining materials and supplies for his own use at exceptionally good prices. Court- and IRS-forced sales, in which the items are to be moved at any cost, can give you the best buys of all.

Now . . . Uh huh! I see your hand going up already. Anticipating the auctioneer already, are you? . . . Oh, all right, I'll accept your advance bid. Chapter 15 coming up is sold to the bidder. Get their number, will ya Marve, and take it on over to them.

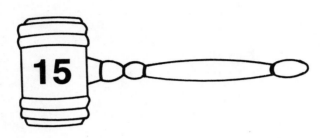

Commodity Auctions

The commodity auction has traditionally been, and still is in wide usage worldwide. In the United States and Canada it is still the primary method of selling large amounts of such things as tea, coffee, sugar, jute, hides, and tobacco at the justly world-famous southern tobacco auctions! Grains and other agricultural products are also sold at auction by various boards of trade, such as the famous ones in Chicago. Yes, pork belly futures get to market this way, as does wheat, corn, soybeans, cotton, and a good many other things.

Commodity auctions such as these are really the province of specialized traders, and regular auction goers are well advised to stay away unless you just happen to need a hundred tons of soybeans or whatever—with the exception of going to tobacco auctions, as we shall see shortly.

There are, however, other types of auctions that you might even be participating in already without realizing it. Stocks bought through a stock exchange is one good example. If you tell your broker to buy 100 shares of Amalgamated Buggy Whip, he'll tender the offer on up the line until a broker with a "seat" on one of the exchanges such as the New York Stock Exchange, will bid on (and in this case, there not being much demand for buggy whips) buy the stock for you at your stated price.

Even those boards of trade sales and stock exchanges are auctions, although they are run by specially trained business people instead of the cowboy-hatted, silver-buckled "colonel" of more conventional auctions. If, however, you do trade in one of these, the same principles of bidding limits and obtaining knowledge still apply. In the big leagues of commodity trading where you can literally lose $100,000 in 10 minutes or less, it applies with a vengeance that our friend, old Bozo T. Clown in the country auctions, would never cotton onto.

TOBACCO AUCTIONS: THE ULTIMATE ENTERTAINMENT

There is absolutely nothing so entertaining as the southern tobacco auctions held all across such

Fig. 15-1. In the world-famous southern tobacco auctions, the buyers move along with the auctioneer along the rows of stacked tobacco.

states as Tennessee, North and South Carolina, Kentucky, and Georgia every year—in the summer for flue-cured and in the winter for burley tobacco. You'll find it's the cheapest and best fun you can flat out all fired have and you don't even have to chew, spit, smoke, or dip "sooze" (old folks term for snuff) to all-out enjoy yourself! Just don't stand too close to someone that does, or you'll get your brogans splattered.

Tobacco-raising and the free and independent life it supported for the small farmer is fast disappearing. The current bias against smoking is killing the tobacco industry, and farmers are desperately seeking other cash crops. Even now only government subsidy and price supports really keep the tobacco farmer in business. It is an especially irony of politics that, on one hand, the fed-

eral government is trying to stamp out smoking through the Surgeon General's office and allied health agencies, and on the other hand, is keeping the business alive by buying up surplus tobacco so that farmers are guaranteed a minimum price for their crop. Perhaps all this is by design, since both sides have powerful blocks of voters.

Yet, no doubt in a few years the tobacco industry will be gone. No one, anymore, is going to argue that smoking is the best thing you could possibly do for your health.

All this aside, there yet remains that glorious way of life. I was raised up in it and hate to see it go. The tobacco auction is one of the last outposts of this, so go and enjoy it while you can. And, years from now, when it is but a dim memory, tell your grandchildren. Tell them that progress is good, but it sometimes has a terrible price.

Yes, I grew up on a tobacco farm. I pulled suckers in the hot summer sun until my arms were sticky messes. I helped strip the leaves from the stalks in the fall and bundled them together after they had *cured*, (or turned golden brown by being hung in the barns. Having those huge baskets of tied "hands" selling at auction in the tobacco warehouse was always the result.

I had the privilege of knowing a lot more about the tobacco auction business than did most people. My uncle, G.G. Ball, is a legend in the game, having been associated with it for more years than most of us have been alive. Now 86, he still works the floor for one of the local tobacco warehouses. He'll probably never quit, and is typical of the very thing of all about this way of life: its people. The farmers from all the mountain counties around Asheville, North Carolina, appreciate him. Many would not think of having any other house sell their tobacco but the one that he's working for.

Born in Madison County, North Carolina, Garland Ball came up the hard way—farming, raising tobacco himself, driving an old truck over the minimal roads of the Great Depression era to haul hogs back from over in Tennessee. Trading in livestock—buying them and reselling them often at livestock auction—is how my Uncle Garland and Aunt Minnie raised their children and got where they are today.

I just wanted to mention this in a national book while they were still around to get a kick out of it, and to make my point again that progress has its price. So, enjoy the tobacco auction while you can. It won't be around for much longer!

CONCLUSION

Commodities of many sorts are sold at auctions; grains, hides, tea, coffee, sugar, and much more come to market in this manner. Stocks and bonds are also sold at auction on the various stock exchanges. The world-famous southern tobacco auctions are a final bastion in a dying yet still much-to-be-admired, way of life. Any sort of com-

modity trading takes scads of specialized knowledge and a goodly amount of capital. Yet, I recommend attending tobacco auctions as an unparalleled form of diversion.

Now, the next chapter up on the block concerns something as new as last week: computerized on-line auctions, another example of the wonders of the Space Age. So gimme a bid . . . a bid . . . a bid . . . I gotta bid . . . I gotta reader bidding. . . . Going once, going twice, it's done cotton pickin' gone to mah fine buddy out there, the reader!

Fig. 15-2. G.G. Ball checking tobacco before it's sold. Now 86, he still moves faster than many people half his age.

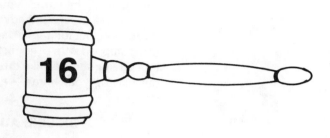

Welcome to the Future: Computer Network Auctions

The Delphi Computer Network, a division of General Videotex Corporation, and Interactive Office Systems of Boston combined the week of June 1, 1986, to present the first on-line computerized auction open to the public. It is a new and exciting facet of the space age, adding the age-old auction marketing method to the dazzling in-home buying services already offered by Delphi and the two other major computer networks for individual users, CompuServe and the Source. The best of all that's old and new!

In Chapter 6 we discussed the Antiques Special Interest Group on Delphi and how this could be used to extend your knowledge. The on-line auction gives you a chance to use that knowledge in a most fun manner.

Okay, I'm getting a few blank stares from out there, so a few definition of terms first. A *computer network* is simply a huge, multimillion dollar complex of mainframe computers that can accommodate simultaneous communications with hundreds of personal computers at any one time. The three just mentioned and a fast-growing list of others exist to allow personal computer users access to an

almost unbelievably wide range of services. "Talking" to one of these gigantic computer systems, or using it to send messages back and forth to other users, is referred in computer jargon as being *on-line*.

To accomplish this communication, you must purchase a device for your personal computer called a *modem*, which hooks the computer to your telephone. The modem then allows your computer to dial up one of the computer networks and exchange information. Many local electronic bulletin boards exist that are completely free, but the major national networks charge a modest subscriber fee per hour of use. Because you are exchanging data at computer speeds, an hour can go a very long way indeed. Delphi, for example, charges $6 an hour during the evening hours, including all telephone charges. Generally, networking is cheaper than voice long distance because you can exchange a lot more information.

Networking is simple, easy, and an incredible amount of fun. It is like having access to the New York Public Library on your dining room table (that's where my computer lives), and an excep-

Fig. 16-1. The personal computer has opened up the world to us through data networks and the extension of our personal ability to do work.

tionally sophisticated form of CB radio. The other night with Delphi I "talked" to a high school teacher in Japan by typing on my computer screen. His English was better than mine (alas, no great accomplishment).

Aside from the vast array of other advantages that owning your own computer offers, networking alone is worth it, especially for the auction goer who is constantly in need of good, usable, profitable knowledge. A personal computer can quickly pay for itself. With the prices now down under $1,000 for good, IBM-compatible systems, there's little excuse not to join the space age. You can even "talk" to me on-line in the Delphi Antiques Special Interest Group and ask questions (some of which I may even be able to answer).

Following is some information on how the Delphi on-line auction works. I had my computer record it and drop it into my word processing software (FinalWord II by Mark of the Unicorn), where I condensed it into a more readable format, such as putting the menus into one sentence instead of showing them in rows and columns as they actually appear on your computer screen.

This introduction to the on-line auction is

reproduced here by kind permission of General Videotex Corporation and Interactive Office Services, Inc. The auction itself was to benefit the public television station in Boston.

From a practical standpoint, although the Delphi network allows you to bid from literally almost anywhere in the world, you needed to be in the Boston area to take full advantage of this particular auction, but for a small charge, you could have items shipped. We're going to be seeing more online buying services like this. Auction going without leaving your home—what will they think of next, eh?

ON-LINE AUCTION

Welcome to the Channel 2 Auction On-Line brought to you by DELPHI/Boston. DELPHI/Boston is a product of Interactive Office Services, Inc. and General Videotex Corporation.

For those of you who are not members of DELPHI/Boston, when you exit the auction you will be given an opportunity to join DELPHI/Boston; $10 of your $29.95 membership fee will be donated to WGBH TV Channel 2.

WGBH Auction Menu: About the Auction, Items Available (for bidding), The two Collection (view only), Wine Catalogue (view only), Donate Item to the Auction, Auction Cookbook, Exit to DELPHI/Boston. *Type first few letters of your choice:*

Here I typed **AB** to get the system to choose "About the Auction." That menu then appeared.

About the Auction Menu: Speed Bidder Cards, Hotline, Submitting a Bid, Dates & Times, Bid Confirmation, Reserve Bidding, Pick-Up, Exit to Main Auction Menu.

After this menu was displayed, I was asked to make a choice like this, *"ABOUT AUCTION > (Type first few letters of choice):"* I entered **sp** to learn about Speed Bidding.

Speed Bidder Cards, (+) bid, Bid, BID! and often. But if you find the process of reciting your name and your address and your telephone number time consuming—and a bore—each time you place a bid, then SPEED BIDDING is just for you. For just $10, you will receive a SPEED BIDDER number to use instead of your name, etc. Saves so much time and, we guess, your patience.

Now when you call to place a bid, give your SPEED BIDDER number, in addition to the telephone number from which you are calling, and of course information on the item on which you are placing a bid.

Better yet, become a SPEED BIDDER PLUS, for just $25.00. Additional privileges include making an appointment to pick up and pay for your purchases. No more waiting for your items to be gathered as you stand in line. Another PLUS is no after 11 P.M. confirmation calls. We'll check with you in the morning.

Would you like to become a SPEED BIDDER?

I answered **no** and asked instead for information about submitting a bid, and here's what the system told me.

Submitting a Bid: You can bid for any of the items listed in the area entitled "Items Available (for bidding)." All you have to do is select a category of items to view. Scan the contents—each entry is numbered. The Scan listing will include the current high bid for each item listed in that category. You can elect to read the details about the item being offered, or elect to bid directly without viewing this information at all.

You may bid any time of day or night. However, bids are only posted on the auction floor between 1 P.M. and 1 A.M. New high bids are updated on-line as quickly as possible after they are posted on the auction floor.

You may bid as many times as you wish. We do ask, however, that you help contribute to the auction by becoming a DELPHI/Boston subscriber and using your new account for subsequent bids. WGBH receives a charitable donation based on your sign-up and your usage of the Auction menu in DELPHI/Boston.

Be sure to see also the listings in this area for details and sign up for Speed Bidding and Speed Bidding +, as well as for Reserve Bidding.

DELPHI/Boston and the Channel 2 Auction (WGBH TV) cannot be held responsible for correctness of any on-line listing.

(Yeah, just like any auction. Remember that,

whether you are bidding by computer or popping your hand up and down at a country auction).

Bid Confirmation: No confirmations are made on-line. Once your electronic bid has been entered, it is transmitted to auction headquarters where it is printed and entered in the same manner as all other bids.

You can check on-line to see if your bid has been accepted. Just locate the item on-line in the area entitled "Items Available (for bidding)" and you will be shown the current high bid. To guard against the possibility of someone else's bid of an equal amount being accepted before your own bid is entered, it is advisable to avoid bidding in even amounts which are multiples of 5. Thus, bid $61—rather than $60—and the likelihood is that any high bid for an item posted for that amount is yours, and not someone else's.

Once an item is sold on the auction floor, expect a call within 2 hours if you are the high bidder. Only that confirming call indicates that you are the high bidder.

Calls to verify your bid may precede any confirming call.

Then I inquired about "Pick up."

Pick Up and Shipping

Pick-Up: Lucky you. You have been confirmed as the successful high bidder on one or more items presented on the Auction. Now what?

Pick up and pay—in an effortless way, by giving us overnight to process your confirmed bids and then: come early in the day, come weekdays if possible, know your item numbers, pay by cash, credit card (MasterCard or Visa) or check (not more than $1,000 total purchases) and certified check.

Pick Up and Pay is located at the Loading Dock of WGBH, 125 Western Avenue, Boston. Pick Up and Pay Days and Hours: (given here for specific dates. You would need to inquire on-line for current dates and times).

Shipping Information: Most items—cars excluded—in our on-line version of the auction can be shipped for a shipping charge of $5.00.

Be sure to tell the confirming operator that you want the item shipped.

If you are the successful high bidder for a travel item, you will receive a gift certificate in the mail.

The Auction Hotline

The auction "Hotline" on the night I was on research for this chapter had 11 articles available for bids. They were (to give you an idea of the diversity): an 18-carat diamond and emerald brooch, a Bang & Olufsen audio system, a blister pearl and gold neckpiece, four jungle end swing sets, a Jacuzzi Caressa portable spa, a Kloss Novabeam Model 100 projection color television, a marquis cut diamond, a necklace, one bottle of 1899 Gruard Larose, a Super Pro swing set with gym, and a Grand Cru L'humiditemp. Additional information about each of these was available on-line.

Reserve Bidding

Reserve Bidding: Going to be out of town for a day or two? Can't watch every day? Working late? And you really want to place a bid on that trip . . . that business machine . . . the new auto . . . the Time Sharing? You can place a reserve bid on items valued at $2,000 or more. The auction will bid for you, according to your instructions. Tell us your top and final bid and we'll place bids in increments of $50.

I now exited the "About the Auction Menu" and returned to the main WGBH Auction Menu, where I asked about specific items available for bidding.

Items Available for Bidding

Items Menu: Travel, Computers & Business Equipment, Automobiles, Home & Personal, Rugs, Exit to Main Auction Menu.

I chose automobiles. There were 10 cars available, all donated by various New England automobile dealers. These included 1986 models of Volkswagen, Buick Skyhawk, a Mitsubishi Mighty Max sports truck, a Toyota MR 2, and a Pontiac Grand Am. Not needing a car at the moment, I declined to enter a bid and exited.

Conditions of Sale

Regardless of whether you attend an auction in person or through the medium of a computer network, you should know the conditions of sale in order to avoid nasty little surprises, so I selected "Information" to find these out. Here's what the system responded with. These, by the way, are instructive as to Conditions of Sale at in-person auctions, as well.

FIRST ARTICLE: Lot numbers are for purposes of identification and indicate order of sale.

Measurements are given in inches; height is stated first, then width, then depth, if applicable. In the case of framed works of art, measurements refer to the framed size if so indicated.

"Signed" signifies hand-signed by the artist, unless otherwise indicated.

The price represents the donor's estimated value of the item. This is furnished as a guide to prospective bidders.

SECOND ARTICLE: Proceeds will benefit WGBH/Channel 2, 125 Western Avenue, Boston, Massachusetts 02134. Telephone: (617) 492-2777. WGBH/Channel 2 assumes no risk, liability, or responsibility for the authenticity of the authorship of any property identified in this catalogue (that is, the identity of the creator or the period, culture, source or origin, as the case may be with which the creation of any property is identified herein).

All property is sold "as is." WGBH/Channel 2 does not make any warranties or representations of any kind or nature with respect to the property, and in no event will be responsible for the correctness, or deemed to have made any representation or warranty of description, genuineness, attribution, provenance, historical period, or condition of the property. No statement in the catalogue, or made at the sale, in the bill of sale or invoice, or in the script or elsewhere shall be deemed such a warranty, representation, or an assumption of liability.

WGBH/Channel 2 makes no representations or warranties, expressed or implied, as to whether the purchaser acquires any reproduction rights in the property. WGBH/Channel 2 reserves the right to withdraw any property at any time before actual sale.

Lots will be sold to the highest bidder at the full amount of the successful sealed or telephoned bid. In the case of duplicate bids, the earliest bid received will be the one accepted.

WGBH/Channel 2 reserves the right to reject a bid from any bidder. The highest bidder acknowledged by WGBH/Channel 2 shall be the purchaser. In the event of any doubt on the part of WGBH/Channel 2 as to the validity of any bid, WGBH/Channel 2 shall have the sole and final discretion to determine the successful bidder. If any dispute arises after the sale, WGBH/Channel 2 sales record shall be conclusive in all respects.

Successful bids will be confirmed by telephone shortly after the on-air announcement of sale. WGBH/Channel 2 reserves the right to dispose of the property in any manner it deems appropriate if the successful bidder or his authorized representative cannot be reached by telephone within a reasonable period of the announcement of sale on air. WGBH/Channel 2 reserves the right to dispose of the property in any manner it deems appropriate if the successful bidder does not remove the property within the agreed-upon period of time. WGBH/Channel 2 is a tax-exempt organization.

THIRD ARTICLE: Bidding is done by phone during the on-air sale on Channel 2, June 1, from 6:30 P.M. on. The auctioneer will describe each item being offered and will give its item number and on-air title.

If you see something you wish to bid on . . . dial 492-1111. One of our volunteer operators will answer your call. To make a bid, give the item number and the on-air title. Bidding increases must be in multiples of $5.

Your operator will tell you the highest bid posted so far. Remember, you will be more likely to succeed if you place your highest bid the first time you call.

Once you place your bid, you must hang up. If at any point you wish to increase your bid, please call again and place another bid.

Most of the items in The Two Collection are presented just once. Items that are of greater value or of unusual interest may be shown more than once.

If yours is the high bid, a confirming operator will call you within one hour of the on-air announcement. The operator will also give you instructions for picking up your item. If the confirming operator is unable to reach you or your authorized representative within that time, the item may have to be offered to the next highest bidder.

FOURTH ARTICLE: Successful bidders must arrange for payment and removal of purchases within 48 hours of telephone confirmation. WGBH/Channel 2 reserves the right to dispose of the property in any manner it deems appropriate if the successful bidder does not remove the property within the agreed-upon period of time. Items should be approved by buyer before removal from WGBH/Channel 2 Pick Up and Pay counter. 1) Payment may be made by Visa or MasterCard. Personal checks for $250 or more must be certified. 2) Packing will be done by WGBH/Channel 2 at the sole risk of the buyer. 3) The purchaser shall be responsible for transporting his purchases at his own expense. 4) Items are to be paid for and picked up at 125 Western Avenue, Boston.

CONCLUSION

I then exited Delphi and went back to work on this book. Total elapsed time to get all of this information plus as much again that I did not include because of space limitations was just seven minutes! Total cost from Asheville, North Carolina to Boston, Massachusetts was right at 70¢. Not bad. Computer networking offers fantastic benefits, not just in auctions, but in all fields. I hope you will take advantage of it.

Now, let's get back to our little on-going auction, and get some bids rolling on Chapter 17, Estate Auctions. Oh ho, reader! I see your bid coming up on my computer screen. You catch on fast! Sold, to my friend, the good-looking reader.

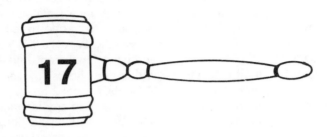

Estate Auctions

It is a fact of life that people die. Sadly, the collecting passion of a person while alive is not always shared by his relatives. After the collector is gone, relatives just want to get rid of "that junk," unknowingly robbing themselves blind in some cases.

Regardless, estate auctions offer boundless possibilities. They are akin to country antique auctions in that there is about 99 percent junk mixed in with the good stuff. We all accumulate a lot of trash during our lives, and an estate auctioneer has to move it all, usually with a lawyer breathing down his neck to make sure he does.

Estate auctions are often held in the yard of the late lamented's house. During the preview period you are allowed to tramp through the house and explore all the tagged items in every nook and cranny. I admit to enough sensitivity to feel a little embarrassed at the inherent disrespect of all this, but it is the way things are done and the most efficient method for the surviving relatives to quickly close out and divide up the estate.

The word *estate* also refers to the property of a living person; you and I and Bozo all have estates. There are many reasons why a living person would want to hold an estate sale. Some of these include being transferred out of town to a new job and wanting to make a clean start of it; for an elderly person, being forced to enter a nursing home; or having overwhelming debts.

In previous chapters we have discussed going to estate and other types of auctions and how to profit thereby. Basically, the same rules apply. Do your homework, know the market value of the pieces you are interested in, and set you bidding limits, sticking to them with all the ferocity of the world's most ambitious super glue.

ON-SITE INSIGHT

Some dishonest auctioneers, as we discussed in Chapter 5, have a habit of "salting" estate auctions, especially those held in the home of the person whose estate is being sold. You need to be aware of this practice and cast a suspicious eye on what appear to be unusual furnishings in a house sale of any sort.

ESTATE AUCTION
MONDAY, APRIL 21, 1986 at 7:00 PM
(Preview: One hour prior to sale)
REALTOR
at
INNSBRUCK MALL SHOPPING CENTER
TUNNEL ROAD/ASHEVILLE, NC

Complete household furnishings of the late Ms. Norma A. Cummiford of 528 North Griffing Boulevard, Asheville, N.C. will be sold at public auction on the above date.

PARTIAL LISTING: Mahogany Secretary bookcase; Dropleaf dining room table; Six Windsor type dining chairs; Buffet; Serving cart; Ethan Allen commode; Corner dropleaf table; Bedroom suite; Love seat; Wurlitzer Piano; Bookshelves; Kitchen table and two chairs; Sears wringer washing machine; Foot stools; Televsions; Cedar chests; Miscellaneous tables and chairs; Pictures; Postcards; Linens; Bookends; Pewter duck-on-nest dish; Flatware; Glassware; Sterling spoons and forks; Porcelain including Wedgwood coffee and tea pot; Heisey pitcher and small bowl; Bronze figurines; Pottery; Large collection of birds carved by Walter Powell of Tennessee; Lead glass birds; Costume jewelry; Pocket watch 14K, 21 jewel; Kitchen utensils, pots and pan, samll appliances; Box lots; More...

MONEY: 1878 Trade Dollar; 1853 Liberty seated Half Dollar; 1860 Half Dime; 1865 Two Cent Piece; Silver dollars, Half dollars, Indian Head pennies; 1915 Silver Certificates; 1915 Cuba coin.

Sale conducted by:

LEE LONG REAL ESTATE & AUCTION
Lee Long, Auctioneer, NCAL 705 • Cameron Lee Long, Auctioneer, NCAL 2513
Telephone (704) 667-0333
Candler, NC
Not Responsible for Accidents Refreshments Available

Fig. 17-1. Advertisement for an estate auction.

An auction of household furnishings is typically held on the site; i.e., in and around the house itself. If, upon attending one of these auctions, you note that many of the furnishings do not seem to fit the house, you can also begin have reservations about the auctioneer.

GOOD BUYS AT ESTATE SALES

There are some good buys in antiques at estates sales, but these are in the minority. Most people simple do not collect antiques as such; if there is something there most likely it's by accident. This is not to deny that there are some very excellent antiques and collectibles estate sales, but these are usually heavily publicized as such.

However, if the auctioneer doesn't know beans about antiques, you are going to have a field day. Many times the lawyer handling the estate will get the cheapest auctioneer available, and often gets his money's worth, hiring someone, perhaps, who normally specializes in automobile auctions or livestock auctions.

Still, the obvious stuff will probably go to the big antiques auction houses, and you'll be limited to making the occasional killing in small collectibles. However, estates sales are always worth checking out to at least the extent of drifting by the preview. There is absolutely no telling what your knowledgeable eye might light upon.

Obviously you will find some things at estate auctions more often than other items. If you need furniture—since everybody's estate contains furniture—going to a few estate auctions with a pick up truck should net you some very nice furnishings at a fraction of the cost you would pay at a retail furniture store. The same goes for kitchen utensils and all the other little odds and ends that make up our household inventories. So, it's very worthwhile to constantly check the classifieds for estate sales near you and pop over to the preview period.

What can you expect at an on-site estate auction sale? Here are a couple of examples from estate auctions that I covered for *Carolina Antique News*. The first was held in North Carolina, the second in Greenville, South Carolina.

TURN-OF-THE-CENTURY CABIN AUCTIONED

For Bessie Jamison, 77, the auction on Main Street in Marion on November 24th, 1984 was a bittersweet event; she was bidding farewell to treasured possessions. Bessie has spent the last quarter of a century living in the rough log cabin built by her father around 1900 near Old Fort, North Carolina. The cabin, with no running water or electricity, was still furnished with many of the items that her parents brought to it over 80 years ago. A post Civil War era pie safe that had belonged to her grandmother, two hand-carved oak beds, oil lamps, a nineteenth-century pendulum clock, and dozens of other pieces handed down from pioneer life graced her home.

With the death of her brother last July (who had been eking out a living farming with a horse and no farm machinery), Bessie reluctantly decided to sell the cabin, land, and furnishings—no longer wanting to fight the cold mountain winters in her drafty homestead. It's the end of era for Bessie and, in a smaller sense, for all of us. The treasures she passed along in this auction were more than just things, they are part of a vanishing way of life.

The auction was ably conducted by Gilbert J. Hollifield (NCAL #2116), who combined the pieces from Bessie's cabin with another estate and other selected items. The site was a sizable frame house in Marion. Inspection was on the Friday eve-

ning preceding the sale, and from 9:00 to 10:00 A.M. on Saturday the 24th. Because of the size of the crowd, the auction was held outside, which turned out very pleasantly with a sunny day and temperatures in the mid-sixties. Approximately 350 people attended with, according to the registration information, representation from 10 states and 61 different cities. Buyers from as far away as Texas, New York, Maryland, and Massachusetts were present, reflecting some of the excitement over this unique offering.

Having seen Gilbert Hollifield in action before, I expected a friendly, smoothly running auction and such was the case. The auction started promptly at 10—or at least as close to the exact starting time as any auctioneer ever gets. The first item on the block was a cow bell from Bessie's consignment. The clangor of the bell being demon-

Fig. 17-2. Some of the contents from Bessie Jamison's cabinet.

strated got everybody awake and the event in gear. (It went for an $8 winning bid.)

Significant pieces in the early going included several pieces of pottery and other vessels. A pewter pitcher went for $22.50; a fine example of North Carolina Penland pottery (marked) sold for $35; a buttermold (Bessie's) caused spirited bidding and got $70; two churns were auctioned, one for $45; the other for $60; several baskets were in the $20 range; a basketwork woodcarrier attracted $35; a glass demijohn pulled down $14; and an English-made china set (current patterns) was won by a $575 bid. But the most excitement was caused by the 5-gallon crock from Bessie's cabin, marked "DS." This piece, from one of the earliest potters in Catawba County, North Carolina, was actively sought by several knowledgeable collectors in the crowd and was finally taken for $410.

Furniture seemed to sell well, also. Bessie's pie safe—alas, not in all that great a shape—still brought $575. A three-drawer chestnut chest was sold for $200, a dropleaf table brought $290; a dresser circa 1820 got a winning bid of $600; another chest of drawers auctioned off for $270; an oak china cabinet attracted $450; and a walnut end table was won for $105. There were some good bargains achieved by buyers in all this bidding. A morticed and pegged wardrobe sold for only $200, prompting Gilbert to congratulate the winner by saying, "That was worth coming up here for, wasn't it?" The buyer, nodding vigorously, obviously agreed. Other notable pieces of furniture included a drop-front desk at $500, a walnut dropleaf table for $350, a trundle bed for $90, and Bessie's linen press, which brought $100.

Several Persian rugs were also offered. These were part of the second estate contained in the auction, that of Mrs S.G. Page of Lake Takoma, North Carolina. The rugs caused interested bidding, with the lowest selling for $400. The largest, room-sized and even having a small hole, was actively bid on with $1,600 taking it.

Some interesting miscellaneous items were also sold. An old brass-bound telescope got $90; a zitherlike musical instrument went for $140; a "corn squeezin'" jug from Bessie's stuff brought $27.50; a pair of homemade crutches (that her father had used) sold for $17.50; and the old cabin clock, a late-1800s pendulum model with a broken spring, was taken for $170.

A mixture of pathos and humor accompanied the sale of some commonplace things that Bessie Jamison had used every day for the last 25 years. Her broom sold for $18, an old flatiron for $17, her rolling pin for $15. Holding up her bucket and dipper, Gilbert described how she had walked a quarter of a mile each day to fetch water. "A lot of miles on this old bucket," he said, auctioning it off for $20.

How Bessie must have felt, seeing these parts of her life go. It truly must have been a bittersweet time for her as—unknown to either myself or Gilbert as he auctioned—she stood there in the crowd, watching and listening. "I carried water from way down in the holler," she said in a recent newspaper interview. "I fell and broke my rib carrying water one time." Speaking of the life she and her brother had led; "It's rough farming, plowing a horse and having no machinery." And on the good times as a little girl some 70 years ago: "There were plenty of old log houses here then. We loved it. We'd go pick grapes, pick up hickory nuts, or we'd go hunt brown field mice nests. We had more fun living in a place like this than children do in town."

RAIN FAILS TO DAMPEN AUCTION

These are the times, wrote Thomas Paine, that try men's souls. An invasion of redcoats wielding Brown Bess muskets was one of the few things that auctioneer W. Angus Davis, SCAL #565, wasn't beset with during his auction of November 16th in this beautiful "upstate" South Carolina city of Greenville. Some men melt in the crucible of combat and others go on to achieve great heights of bravery. Angus Davis is one of the latter, calmly standing his ground, microphone grasped firmly, facing and defeating adversity.

Rain is something any auction held outside must contend with from time to time. The tidal deluge of the early morning hours had dwindled to sporadic showers and a nearly constant drizzle by the 10 A.M. kick off time. But, from time to time, the rain would intensify. Davis and his crew were prepared for this with loaner umbrellas, but it was sheer auctioneering ability that kept the crowd happily standing in that soggy yard and bidding enthusiastically during the course of the auction.

At no time was Davis' leadership and calmness under fire more apparent than when a lady collapsed in what appeared to be an epileptic fit. He kept the crowd from venting their curiosity and rushing to the scene, marshaled medical personal from the audience, and made sure the paramedics were summoned. Most importantly, he kept the auction moving. It turned out well, with the lady recovering and the ambulance call being canceled.

The auction itself was in a worthy, albeit sad, cause. The household furnishings of Mrs. Lemma Ashmore, now confined to a nursing home, were being sold to help offset the high costs these places demand. Mrs. Ashmore had lived in the house since the late thirties. Lemma Ashmore's daughter, Mrs. Elizabeth Akers of Madison, Indiana, was on hand to accept the well wishes of those attending and to provide history on the pieces, many of which had been bought as she grew up in the house prior to and during World War II.

Assisting Angus Davis was his lovely wife, Dorothy—who holds SCAL #749—and Colonel Terry Howe, SCAL #1092.

The auction began as disappointingly as the weather, with two rocking chairs bringing only $10 apiece. A flurry of small items followed. A green shaded lamp brought $25, two small octagonal framed pictures $3 each, a finger lamp (converted from kerosene) only $15, a 6-gallon crock for $12.50, and a ceramic teapot at $10—these being representative prices for many other articles of like nature.

In auctioning off two brass horsehead bookends, Davis showed the humor and warmth that helped him hold the crowd. "No ma'am," he said to the winning bidder, "you don't have to take fifteen and a half. You got it at fifteen. You don't have to bid against yourself." This got a good laugh, even from the lady whose fervor was such that she wasn't going to be beat by anyone for the bookends.

This was followed by a box of assorted glassware selling for $12.50, a set of five Japanese blue and white china rice bowls for $5, and two green glass candleholders for $4. Then came an old wooden golf club up onto the block.

"Bob Hope probably started with this one," Angus Davis said; and the crowd twittered, not noticing that it was starting to rain again. The club, in rather poor shape—maybe Hope did start with it—sold for $12.50 and was followed by a sewing basket at $7.50, a folding hatrack for $3, a beaded purse bringing $17.50, and a Royal Staffordshire dish at $9.

"When you get it, it's yours," Davis announced. "Take care of it like you do your wife." He then proceeded to sell an 11-piece set of Heisey glass plates (unmarked) for $3 each. This was the turning point in the auction as the crowd became more intense. The good stuff was coming!

Furniture seemed to be what most knowledgeable buyers had come out for on this rainy Saturday. A Windsor rocker set hearts to pounding, selling for $140. Two cane-bottomed side chairs got $55 each; a "fat man's chair" (low and wide) brought $25; and another rocker $75 as more buyers got out their bidder's cards and stood ready to flip them up.

A Southern Clock Co. "ogee" clock—once sold door to door before the last world war—struck a responsive chime in one bidder's heart, being taken for $220. A Martha Washington chair sold for $60, a ladies writing desk at $270, and a converted (from kerosene) Gone With The Wind lamp for $70. Other furniture items of note included a burl walnut, marble-topped table getting $475, a mahogany drop leaf dining room table for $150, and a china buffet at $425.

"Get their addresses," Davis admonished his assistants in mock alarm over the low prices. "We're going to have to get the law. They're stealing everything."

The furniture-selling continued, with the pieces being left in place in the house due to rain but interested bidders allowed to go in whenever they wanted to refresh their memories (or just get dry). A mahogany server was bid up to $200, a recliner went at $70; an open arm rocker was sold for $55; and an antique black iron plant stand held up for $60.

The two real stars of this auction were a bed and a couch—both attributed to E.H. Henly, a Greenville furniture craftsman, and circa 1939. At least this is the year that Mrs. Akers, then 13, remembers her mother buying them. Considerable interest was voiced before the auction by various persons familiar with Henly's work. The couch, camel-backed with carved wooden legs, came up first. One bidder was on the telephone inside the house during this, signaling his assistant who was outside under the auctioneer's eye, but they dropped out before the winning bid of $600. The bed was a four-poster "rice carved," which caused a flood of bidding that, like the precipitation, came in spurts. Finally, $1,050 took the bed.

CONCLUSION

Estate sales are common. You can most likely find several in your area every month. They offer good buys in household furnishings, utensils, and all those other little odds and ends we use from day to day. Plus, there is always the change of making a killing by spotting something of value that others fail to note. However, be sure to watch for dishonest auctioneers who "salt" houses.

Now, go get your tax returns for the last 5 years before we get to the next chapter. It's on government surplus auctions, and although there are some absolutely fantastic bargains, guess who pays for it in the end? Right. The person whose name appears on those tax returns: thee and me.

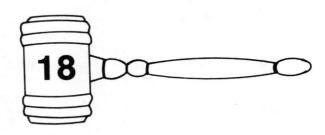

Government Surplus

The world's largest continuous auction is run year round by the federal government's General Services Administration (GSA). Almost anything you can think of that the government owns eventually gets "surplused out" and sold at auction. Boats, planes, land, typewriters, two-way radios, computers, office furniture, cameras—you name it, they sell it, all totally subsidized by tax dollars. These auctions run the whole gamut, from the bids by mail type to the more conventional ones where a brave crowd staunchly stands its ground in front of a raging auctioneer.

We've all seen the classified advertisements in the back of magazines for years, "jeeps $15, trucks $50, airplanes $100 . . ." These are correct in that the items named have been sold at government auction for the stated prices. However, you might not be able to get them for any such, although you can certainly get them far cheaper than the government did. Nor should you bother sending in the money the advertisements ask for. I will give you the same information free that they do

for money. You can also get it from any public library.

The information is simply how to get on the GSA mailing list. So you can submit bids on what strikes your fancy in the mail auctions and receive notification of the in-person auctions. I once bought the complete electronic equipment for an entire airport, albeit a small one, by GSA mail bid. What a load! The fender wells on my station wagon were scraping the tires as I came up the mountain back home. I had a moving trailer clanging along behind, too. However, it was very profitable, and I tripled my money, even counting the burst radiator hose.

Anyway, I will also include not only GSA auctions, but state and local government ones as well. You can get some fantastic bargains in this manner. Many times the government knoweth not what it does, selling off stuff it still needs and has to buy back. Once I bought a small crate of surplus silver-plated ultra-high frequency radio connectors, called N connectors, for 10 cents a pound! Another agency of the government gladly bought several orders from me over a couple of years time, paying for each connector what I had paid for all of them.

This situation is by no means uncommon in the surplus business, and the bill for all this mismanagement is ultimately footed by us, the taxpayers. (Perhaps it is simply too big for anyone to effectively run.) Regardless, if you are a staunch auction goer and willing to acquire the knowledge necessary to deal with the various GSA and Defense Department auctions, you can make good money at it. You'll seldom get jeeps for $50, however.

GENERAL SERVICES ADMINISTRATION

The GSA is a federal agency created by the Federal Property and Administrative Services of 1949. Its purpose was, and still is, to act as the government's office manager. The GSA keeps track of and manages literally billions of dollars worth of property, machines, supplies, materials, and more— all belonging to Uncle Sam, with the exception of what the military has. That's's handled by the Department of Defense.

The GSA does it all, from buying paper clips to leasing, operating, maintaining, and even constructing government buildings all over the country. The department also oversees the National Archives and the other important government filing operations. Therefore, there is hardly anything at all you can think of that the GSA doesn't buy and use, or not use and decide to surplus out.

Of most concern to auction goers is a branch of the GSA called the Federal Supply Service. These are the boys and gals who decide what brand of car the government buys this year, how many pencils Congress is going to need, and so on, and so on. Obviously they can't always get it right and a lot of overbuying or stupid buying occurs. We've all heard the stories of the $400 hammer and the $600 toilet seat, but that's just the tip of the iceberg.

Forget all that for the moment, though. The nice part of this game is that when the government decides it wants new cars for the various motor pools, fancy new computers instead of last year's models, or any of a zillion other items, the people in that particular agency declare the stuff obsolete and gleefully order new items.

It's then up to the GSA to get rid of the old at whatever price it can, and this is usually abysmally low. Auction goers are taxpayers too, and at least we can get a little of our own back from the government in this way. No, I don't like paying taxes, and such monumental waste as the federal government seems to glory in is the reason why. Meanwhile, I buy what I can at GSA auction and, in the no doubt forlorn hope the government will eventually wise up, urge you to do the same.

Mistaken Legends of the Game

There are some things that everyone seems to assume about government auctions and other types of surplus sales that generally just aren't true. Let me qualify what I've said. Although you can get very good prices buying from the GSA, most of the time the government is not going to completely give the items away. While they are not out to make much of a profit, there is growing pressure on these bureaucrats to adopt a stance more in keeping with true market values.

From the viewpoint of taxpayers, it's hard to complain about this, luckily, however, they don't always adhere to this policy, and it's nice to be there when something juicy does slip through. Still, don't be surprised if your ridiculous bid for a piece, even though it is the high one, is refused. The GSA does have the option by law to pull an item from the sale if the price is too low in its opinion.

Then there are those classified advertisements in the back of the magazines that I've mentioned already. All that happens with these is that the mail order firm cashes your check and, if you are lucky, forwards your name to the central GSA mail list office in Boulder, Colorado, who then puts you on its specific-category mailing lists just like it would have if you had written it free to begin with. This is an old mail-order scam that was being played when I was just a kid (and that wasn't yesterday, I can tell you). I blew two very hard-earned bucks back in the late fifties to find this out the hard way.

Write the GSA for free. The addresses for your particular region are in the back of this book.

There are also persistent stories that the government has thousands of vehicles like never-used jeeps stashed away and occasionally sells off a warehouse full for $50 apiece or so. This is hogwash. The government sells a lot of jeeps all right, but they have always been pretty much driven into the ground and still go for several hundred dollars each.

How the GSA Sells

The General Services Administration uses four basic methods to dispose of surplus property. The agency doesn't' like to use the word *auction*, referring to them instead as *public sales*. They are, however, auctions—no two ways about it.

The first way is the *conventional auction*. You come to the place of the sale, register, and are assigned a bidder number. The auction then proceeds as any in the private sector might, and you are under the same constraints of "as is" and using the preview period to best advantage. By all means, scrutinize each lot carefully, apply all your knowledge, and set a bidding limit. You'll be glad you did.

Sealed bid sales are the most common, and desirable, method because you can really widen your area of operation since they are handled mostly by mail. You write out your bid on a special form and mail it in to the appropriate GSA office. This is the way I got all the airport electronic equipment mentioned previously. Many times you'll find yourself breaking the preview rule by bidding on something a couple of hundred miles away without having seen it.

The simple secret to bidding by mail is to bid very low so that even if it is junk, you'll still come out. Even though you will do a lot of bidding and get few items, the ones you do get are almost always well worth it. Also, if you win a bid, you do have to go and pick it up and pay for it, whether you want it or not. Otherwise the GSA gets ill with you and puts you on its nasty list.

There is also an on site method of auctioning called the *spot-bid sale*. In this method, you sit down with other bidders in a room and fill out bid cards on the various items desired. Then the cards are collected and the winner of each announced.

The fourth method is the *negotiated sale* and is usually only employed for very large scale items, like a million dollars worth of surplus oil or something. In this type of sale, the GSA negotiates with a small group of buyers until one meets the required price.

How to Find GSA Sales

The GSA must move somewhere between $50,000,000 and $100,000,000 worth of surplus property and materials every year; so it wants your business. Therefore, all you have to do is to get on the mailing lists appropriate to the types of items you are interested in, and you will get a flood of mail announcing items for sale and auction in your area.

To be included on these computerized mailing lists, you must write to separate offices—one for all property excluding real estate, and the other for real estate offerings. For materials, which most of us are interested in, you write to the General Services Administration, Director of Personal Property Division at the GSA Regional office for your area. Addresses for all ten regions are included in Appendix A.

The GSA does sell real estate now and then: old Air Force bases, various government buildings, land, all sorts of real property. If you want to be notified of these sales, you should address a request to the General Services Administration, Director of Real Property at the same regional address as you would write the personal property director.

DEPARTMENT OF DEFENSE AUCTIONS

Military surplus is handled by the Department of Defense and is a bit harder to get to than the GSA's surplus. First of all, the material has to filter down through a series of steps in which it is offered to various organizations. If the Army surpluses some jeeps, for example, they might first be offered to another branch of service, like the Marines, or to the National Guard or Reserves. The State Department might also get in on it, working a deal to give or sell them to one of our poorer allies overseas.

We are dealing with the government here, remember. Expect to do some paperwork. You'll receive a "Surplus Personal Property Mailing List Application" in return. Choose the geographic areas listed that you are interested in, and check off which of the 55 categories of items you want to receive auction and sale notices on.

When your mail box does start echoing to the plop of surplus auction notices, you will note that they all have one little phrase on them telling you that the lots are offered "as is, where is," which means exactly what you might think it means. Watch out. Buyer beware. Just like in any auction.

If none of these many possibilities are met, then the vehicles might be offered to a nongovernment agency like the Red Cross or the Boy Scouts. Only if no one wants it does it finally reach anything resembling public sale.

Generally, if you are 18 years of age and not in any of the armed forces or associated with a Department of Defense Property Disposal Office, you are eligible to bid on military surplus. Once this level is finally reached, the system is very similar to that of the GSA. To get on the national mailing list, write to the address given in Appendix A. Request a copy of the Department of Defense Surplus Property Bidders Application.

This list, however, is for national sales, which tend to be for the big money folk who can afford to buy a fleet of 2 1/2-ton trucks. Local sales are probably more your speed. You can find out about local sales by writing one of the three regional Department of Defense Property Disposal Offices.

(See Appendix A for these addresses.)

OTHER GOVERNMENT AUCTIONS

The Internal Revenue Service, the United States Customs Service, and the Postal Service also hold periodic auctions. These auctions will often be advertised locally in your classified adsvertisements, or you can check with the agencies involved and find out when they have auctions coming up.

In addition to federal auctions, many state and city governments also dispose of property by auction. Usually a little judicious scanning of the governmental listings in the telephone directory will help you find someone who can tell you who to contact about getting on the mailing list for these.

Law enforcement agencies on all levels also resort to the auction to dispose of confiscated materials no longer needed for evidence. Again, reading the advertisements in the local newspaper and making the telephone calls will keep you on top of these sales.

CONCLUSION

The GSA is indisputably the largest auction house in the world. It is worthwhile to get on the GSA's mailing lists for each of the 55 categories that you have an interest in. Department of Defense auctions are more complicated and less easy to utilize unless you have a lot of money and can buy in large quantities. IRS, Customs, and Postal Service auctions are worth checking on. State and local governments, and various law enforcement agencies also hold auctions from time to time.

Since the government gives us so much bull, I guess that is as good a lead in as any to the next chapter: livestock auctions.

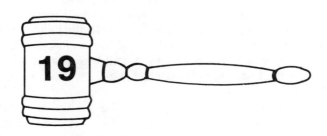

Livestock Auctions

Livestock auctions are important in many areas, and not just rural, either. The rural angle, of course, is obvious. Farmers raise cattle, hogs, and other animals, selling them at auction as a continuing source of income. However, everything from riding stock up to race horses also is sold for millions of dollars. Horse auctions are to be found all over and at a number of levels, even in New York City.

James Wagenvoord in his book *Cashing In On The Auction Boom* relates how the Fish & Wildlife service in New York not too long ago sold a 12-year-old Morgan horse at auction. The horse had been used to patrol one of the beaches out on Long Island. The winning bid was just $50, no doubt because a horse is rather hard to apartment-break. In a more horse-oriented part of the country, that same animal would have easily brought several hundred dollars. However, this story still has a happy ending, because the GSA official selling the Morgan took the low price to make sure it got a good home, and to protect it from being turned into dog food.

WHY ATTEND A LIVESTOCK AUCTION

If you are a farmer, the reason for attending animal auctions is obvious—it's one means by which you obtain your livelihood. I was born and raised on a farm and lived the tradition of loading a cow or calf into a flatbed stake truck and sending them off to the "Thursday" or the "Friday" market. After the sale, we'd go stand in line in the tiny, hot office, flies buzzing through the open screen door, to pick up the check. And the farm would survive a while longer.

Even if you have no interest in farms or farming, attending livestock auctions is still as much fun as going to a country auction because, at the lower and most common levels, these auctions are a specialized form of the country auction.

The magic, the hoopla, the auctioneers in the cowboy hats are there (and a lot of other people in stetsons, as well). These auctions usually have rows of tiered seats ringing a sawdust-filled pit where the animals are paraded through by the auctioneer's assistants with varying degrees of ease.

Fig. 19-1. Colonel Joe Silvers readies this "iron mule," which he sold at an auction that featured horses, as well.

In fact, a good part of the entertainment value of these functions is the hilarious antics of assistants trying to keep balky animals moving.

You've never seen funny until you've seen one of these assistants twisting a reluctant-to-move cow's tail, with her looking back in disdain as if to say, "oh yeah, big deal" and then venting her disgust in that direct and uninhibited bovine way—which is why livestock auctioneer's assistants never wear their best Sunday-go-to-meeting cowboy boots into the ring.

Even if you don't intentionally attend a livestock auction, you may wind up at one anyway. Many general country auctions will occasionally include animals, sometimes as a joke, sometimes seriously. There is nothing like parading a live chicken through an auction to wake people up, and our old buddy Bozo can always be counted on to give a fair imitation of a rooster crowing or, if he's been doing a little drinking, stand up and flap his arms in a most leg-slapping manner.

However, there are many legitimate offerings at these auctions as well. I went to one where several saddle horses were offered and sold in with the lawn mowers, garden tractors, furniture, and all the rest. Having horses or other animals tied up outside does add to the carnival atmosphere of a country auction, whether you care to bid on them or not.

BUYING AND SELLING LIVESTOCK

The buying and selling of livestock is a highly complex business that we certainly don't have the room to cover here. However, if you are engaged in it, the same basic principles governing any auction apply: make good use of the preview period, know how to recognize unhealthy or poorly developed animals, have a good grasp of current market values, form your bidding limits, and stick to them like flies to a candy apple.

Be aware of state and federal regulations as to disease, weight, display, and so forth. Have the proper transportation, i.e., at least a truck with high sides and a layer of sawdust on the floor to serve as a cushion. Treat the animals with some kindness. A panicked animal (and I've seen it happen) can kick the heck out of you and your truck both, not to mention injuring itself and costing you money.

With all these commonsense things in place, there is no reason why those who enjoy dealing in livestock still can't make a very good living doing it by buying and selling them at auctions. Again, knowledge is the key. My Uncle Garland, now 86, has had a long and respectable career for more years than most of us have been alive, and it has been based primarily on heads-up use of livestock and commodity auctions. Knowledge pays. He has proved that over and over, and is still proving it. I just hope I'm half that canny and competent when I reach his age.

HORSES

The trading of horses, especially as we drift up through the fox-hunting and racing levels, becomes more and more of a rich person's game. The fiery blood of an Arabian will cost you an oil well or two, but the selfsame principles that govern the tobacco chewing and spitting working stock auctions apply in like manner to the fancy horse auctions. Knowledge, use of the preview period, firm grasp of market value—these always should guide your steps through any kind of auction, much less ones having livestock.

At a livestock auction, by the way, it does pay to watch your step. Cattlemen seldom carry such things as pooper scoopers. Again, a thorough description of horse auctions is outside the province of this book.

ROUNDING UP

Livestock auctions are, like more general country auctions, fun and entertaining to attend, even if you just go to watch. The same principles that guide other auctions apply in these auctions as well. "That all sounds fine," you say, with visions of retiring to the country dancing in your head, "but you gotta have a place to keep horses."

Okay, glad you brought up that point. It brings us to the chapter on real estates auctions. So step right up, what'm I bid for this here fine little chapter and lot coming right up here? I gotta bid, I gotta bid . . . Sold! To the reader. Take that there deed over to him, would ya Marve?

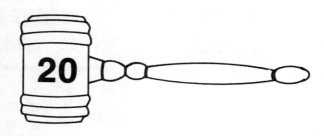

Real Estate Auctions

If you have money to invest, the buying of houses and land at real estate auctions can be financially rewarding. If, on the other hand, you are strapped for money or need to sell your home or property expediently, then the auction is indeed your answer.

Experts in the real estate field sometimes downplay both how important and just how widespread real estate auctions have become. For many years it has been the traditional method of selling agricultural land. In the vacation home boom of the seventies, tracts of land in resort areas were divided up and auctioned off. This practice, which never completely went away, is returning in force as the prime rate again comes back down to a reasonable level.

This chapter covers the methods of payment, title searches and deeds, the benefits of buying real estate this way, and much more.

WHY AUCTION YOUR REAL ESTATE?

Browsing through the Yellow Pages of your tele-

phone directory will quickly show you that there is a veritable plethora of real estate agents hanging out signs all over the place. The current trend is for more and more of these people to pop up. In my part of the country at least, it seems that everybody I know is studying toward getting his real estate license. So who needs to auction it?

If you are selling, very possibly you do. First of all, the real estate auction is usually the most expedient method of moving houses, other buildings, or tracts of land quickly. Many experts claim that it is also the best way to sell—being fast, clean, and fair. They go on to say that it is likely to bring the highest price and stimulate the most competition for a particular piece of real property, pushing buyers much quicker to the moment of decision making.

Selling in this manner is also easier for you. The auctioneer will do all the little details—such as advertising and all those horrendous legalities—that might otherwise soak up your time. He will also do it much better, since he has a good deal more experience in real estate sales than you do.

Fig. 20-1. Colonel Harold DeBruhl, in addition to auctioning real estate, also owns one of the most respected real estate appraising firms in the southeast.

The quickness of selling land or other real property by this method needs to be emphasized again. A real estate agent will list your property and might or might not sell it. The process could drag out for months or even years. An auction, however, assuming you have no reserve, is pretty much guaranteed to move the property for you, and usually at a decent price—although, as with selling anything at auction, you take your chances on that.

You can have an appraisal done on your property to assess its current market value, but real estate appraisals are just educated guesses at best. The only true measure of what some house or parcel of land is worth is what someone will pay you for it. You should take this into account when figuring your reserve price or what you feel the auction should net you.

The auction firm will advertise your property to be sold and in 60 or 90 days, or whatever you and the auctioneer decide is a reasonable amount of time, the sale will be held. If the auctioneer has properly done his job, a sizable number of interested bidders will show up and eat the free hot dogs provided by the auction firm and, again assuming no reserve or at least a low one, the real estate will be sold and you will be shut of it.

SERVICES OF A REAL ESTATE AUCTIONEER

The real stock in trade of the auctioneer who specializes in real estate sales are his business contacts and his promotional ability. He has clients who regularly follow his sales, buying for investment and a variety of other reasons. By engaging the services of such an auctioneer, you can tap all this expertise and favorably increase the odds that

Fig. 20-2. Real estate auction advertisement.

you will get a good price for the property.

He can also maximize the amount of money you can receive for the property by methods that you may be unaware of, or unsure of how to implement. For example, the general trend in recent years (and one that I feel is a crying shame and one that we are going to pay for drastically down the road) is to break up farm land into subdivisions. The sale of a large tract of land, such as one comprising some 2,000 or 3,000 acres, is beyond the means of most people reading this book (and the hard-working guy writing it). However, when an auctioneer breaks it down into many smaller parcels, the number of potential buyers is greatly increased, as is the overall price received for the land. One of the first things a neophyte colonel is taught in auction school is to sell it by the unit and the return will be higher.

Also, the auction firm will handle all the paperwork associated with real property sales. The title searches to make sure the deed is free and clear (i.e., that you really can sell the property), tax assessments, zoning provisions, water table testing, inquiries into existing right of way, inspections of buildings for structural soundness and termite damage, and all the many other things that have to be certified for the buyer's and your protection.

The auction firm can also provide the buyer financing so you can increase the potential purchaser pool drastically. After all, who has cash these days to plop down for something this big? Sometimes it is very much to your benefit taxwise to finance the property yourself. The auctioneer can advise you on how to secure the services of an attorney to draw up a proper contract and so forth.

All these services equally apply if you're the buyer instead of the seller. It is to the auctioneer's benefit to make sure you have complete knowledge of the property and are happy with the sale so you'll buy more from him and recommend his firm.

CONCLUSION

The real estate auction is a fast and profitable way to dispose of real property. An auctioneer specializing in real estate can make the selling of such easier, quicker, and more profitable than can a conventional real estate agent. If you are buying instead of selling, there are a number of benefits as well, and it is worth finding the real estate auctioneers in your area and following their sales.

Okay, now it's time for my least favorite type of auction, the retail auctions. Coming right up, get your bid card up where I can read it, going to sell this one cheap. Sold to the fine-looking reader.

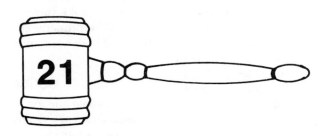

Retail Auctions

In many areas retail, or *gift*, auctions are growing in attendance. Why buy something here that you can buy at K-Mart or one of the other big chain stores? The answers include variety of merchandise, cheaper price (again, if you apply knowledge), and the outright fun of shopping in this manner.

However, there are pitfalls too; so this chapter covers more of the down side about auctions than all the previous ones. There is more abuse of the auction system present in this type of auction than in any of the others.

The travelling tool auction can be good or bad, depending on the operator. So can any other auction where an auctioneer buzzes into town with a truck full of stuff, throws together a single-shot auction, and departs town quickly thereafter. Your recourse in the case of defective or misrepresented merchandise bought in this type of auction is as nonexistent as an ice cube in we-all-know-where.

Frankly, the retail auction is my least favorite of them all. There is just too much room for chicanery and misrepresentation. This is not to say you can't get good buys, but your knowledge is much more necessary in this type of auction, yet returns you a lot less potential for profit than in an antique or a country junk auction.

People who sell at retail auctions, in order to maximize their profits, normally buy crates of really cheap imports from the big companies specializing precisely in supplying to them and flea market dealers. This stuff is generally crap, and this is not just an opinion. Back in the seventies, I was in the business of buying this junk, especially CB sets during that craze, and selling it in wholesale lots to retail auction people. The stuff breaks like crazy, but we sold it (like the auction and flea market people do) "as is," i.e., meaning if it breaks you not only get to keep all the pieces, but the dealer will help you sweep them up and put them back into the box. Still, probably being too honest for my own good in getting rich (something I still haven't managed), I never felt right about the business and soon got out of it.

Admittedly, this experience probably has a lot to do with my distrust of and disgust at retail auctions. Attend a few and make up your own mind. Just apply the principles we discussed in the chapter on chicanery and keep your gloves up at all times.

FINAL THOUGHTS

Auctions are without a doubt the most fun, the most lively method of buying and selling so far developed. Auctions offer a unique opportunity for the knowledgeable buyer to make money. Of all types of auctions, the antiques/collectibles and the country junk auction together provide the most consistent opportunities for profit.

No matter what type of auction you attend, you should take full advantage of the preview period to prod and poke each nook and cranny of the merchandise, checking it closely as to condition, serviceability, current market value, and the like. From all this and your own knowledge and experience, you should set your bidding limit for each piece and stick to it unwaveringly. Even if you don't go to buy, though, auctions are a lot of entertainment.

Appendix A:

Sources

PUBLICATIONS

AMERICAN BOOK COLLECTOR
274 Madison Ave.
New York, NY 10016

AMERICAN CLAY EXCHANGE
P.O. Box 2674
La Mesa, CA 92041

ANTIQUE WEEK/TRI-STATE TRADER
P.O. Box 90
Knightstown, IN 46148

ANTIQUES DEALER
1115 Clifton Ave.
Clifton, NJ 07013

THE AUCTIONEER
8880 Ballentine
Overland Park, KS 66214

CAROLINA ANTIQUE NEWS
P.O. Box 241114
Charlotte, NC 24224

Mr Bill Haglund, Editor
COLLECTOR'S JOURNAL
P.O. Box 601
Vinton, IA 52349

NATIONAL KNIFE MAGAZINE
P.O. Box 21070
Chattanooga, TN 37421

NUMISMATIC NEWS
700 E. State St.
Iola, WI 54990

OLD CARS PRICE GUIDE
700 E. State St.
Iola, WI 54990

JOEL SATER'S ANTIQUES & AUCTION NEWS
P.O. Box 500
Mount Joy, PA 17552

Mr Michael Jacobi, Editor
YESTERYEAR
Box 2
Princeton, WI 54968

AUCTION SCHOOLS

American Academy of Auctioneers
1222 N. Kenwood
Broken Arrow, OK 74012

Associated Auction School
753 Toni Dr.
Hurst, Texas 76054

Florida Auctioneer Academy
1212 East Colonial Dr.
Orlando, FL 32803
(305) 896-9797

International School Auction School
Route 5
South Deerfield, MA
(413) 665-2877

Mason City College of
Auctioneering
P.O. Box 1463
Mason City, IA 50401

Mendenhall School of Auctioneering
P.O. Box 7344
High Point, NC 27263
(919) 887-1165

Missouri Auction School
1600 Genesee
Kansas City, MO 64102

Nashville Auction School
P.O. Box 190
Lawrenceburg, TN 38464

National Institute of
Real Estate Auctioneers
3961 MacArthur Blvd, #212
Newport Beach, CA 92660

Reisch World Wide College of Auctioneering
P.O. Box 949
Mason City, IA 50401
(515) 423-5242

Reppert School of Auctioneering
P.O. Box 189
Decatur, IN 46733
(219) 724-3804

River Basin Auction School
RR 2,
Bismark, ND 58501
(701) 258-1920

GSA MAILING LISTS

Remember to address to the appropriate director
of personal or real property for your region.

REGION 1: Connecticut, Maine, Massachusetts,
New Hampshire, RhodeIsland, Vermont:
John W. McCormack Post Office and Courthouse
Boston, MA 02109

REGION 2: New York, New Jersey, Puerto Rico,
Virgin Islands:
26 Federal Plaza
New York, NY 10007

REGION 3: District of Columbia, Delaware, Maryland, Pennsylvania,Virginia, West Virginia:
7th and D Streets SW
Washington, DC 20407

REGION 4: Alabama, Florida, Georgia, Kentucky,
Mississippi, North Carolina, South Carolina, Tennessee:
1776 Peachtree St. NW
Atlanta, GA 30309

REGION 5: Illinois, Indiana, Michigan, Minnesota, Ohio, Wisconsin:
230 South Dearborn St.
Chicago, IL 60604

REGION 6: Iowa, Kansas, Missouri, Nebraska:
1500 East Bannister Rd.
Kansas City, MO 64131

REGION 7: Arkansas, Louisiana, New Mexico, Oklahoma, Texas:
819 Taylor St
Fort Worth, TX 76102

REGION 8: Colorado, Montana, North Dakota, South Dakota, Utah, Wyoming:
Denver Federal Center Bldg 41
Denver, CO 80225

REGION 9: American Samoa, Arizona, California, Guam, Hawaii, Nevada, the Trust Territory of the Pacific Islands:
525 Market St
San Francisco, CA 94105

REGION 10: Alaska, Idaho, Oregon, Washington:
GSA
Auburn, WA 98002

DEPARTMENT OF DEFENSE

Property Disposal Offices

REGION 1:
DPDR-Columbus
Att: DPDR-CMB
3900 E. Broad St.
Columbus, OH 43215

REGION 2:
DPDR-Memphis
Att: DPDR-MMB
2163 Airways Blvd
Memphis, TN 38114

REGION 3:
DPDR-Ogden
Att: DPDR-OMB
500 W. 12th Street
Ogden, UT 84401

Real Estate

Department of Defense
Surplus Property Sales
P.O. Box 1370
Battle Creek, MI 49016

Appendix B
Recommended Reading

Following are some good books that will give you additional and more in-depth information on auctions:

Auerbach, Sylvia, *An Insider's Guide To Auctions*, Addison-Wesley,1981.

DeForrest, Michael, *How To Buy At Auction*, Simon and Schuster, 1972.

Hamilton, Charles, *Auction Madness*, Everest House, 1981.

Jenkins, Emyl, *Why You're Richer Than You Think*, Rawson Wade, 1982.

Towner, Wesley, *The Elegant Auctioneers*, Hill & Wang, 1970.

Wagenvoord, James, *Cashing In On The Auction Boom*, Rawson Wade, New York, 1980.

Wasserstein, Susan, *Collector's Guide to U.S Auctions & Flea Markets*, Penguin, 1981.

Index

A

A Princess of Mars, 6
absentee bid, 42
Amerada Hess-Getty Oil, 13
*American Book Auction Cata-
    logues (1713-1934)*, 17
American Art Association, 22
*American Art Auction Catalogues
    (1785-1942)*, 17
Americana furniture, 17
Anchorage, Alaska, 13
Anderson, John, 18
antiauction movement, 20
Antique Week/Tri-State Trader, 31
antiques auctions, 83
Apponius, 14
art auctions, 95
art deco, 7
art pottery, 87
attribution, 98
auctio sub hasta, 13
auction, 11
Auction Madness, 36
Auction!, 14
auctions
    antiques, 83
    art, 95
    autograph, 101
    bankruptcy, 113

classic automobile, 109
collectibles, 83
commodity, 118
computer network, 121
conventional, 134
Dutch, 16
estate, 126
gift, 142
going out of business, 113
government surplus, 132
history of, 13
livestock, 136
manuscript, 101
other government, 134
practical car, 110
rea estate, 139
retail, 142
tobacco, 118
types of, 11
auctions with reserve, 33
auctions without reserve, 33
autograph auctions, 101
Avery, Samuel P., 22

B

Babylon, 13
Bangs, Thomas, 18
bankruptcy auctions, 113
bankruptcy proceeding, 115

Benjamin, Mary, 104
bid
    absentee, 42
    off-the-wall, 50
    opening, 37
    shutout, 42
bidder
    bulk, 116
bidder's number, 32
bidding
    candlestick, 16
    dumb, 16
bidding process, 33
bidding signals, 35
bidding strategies, 35
bidding tactics, 40
Biltmore Industries, 88
Birch, Thomas, 18
Bird, Lewis J., 18
Blithedale Romance, 19
Blue Willow, 10
Blue Willow china, 45
Blue Willow toaster, 38
books, 55
Bough, James, 14
box lot, 40
Bridge pitcher, 47
Brook Farm, 19
Brooklyn Bridge, 22

Brown Coffee House, 17
Brunk, Robert, 25
bulk bidder, 116
bumbershoot, 63
Bunn, Col. Robert, 90, 93
Burroughs, Edgar Rice, 6
buying horses, 138
buying livestock, 137

C

Caligula, 14
candlestick bidding, 16
Carolina Antique News, 31
Carter, Maybelle, 28
Cashing In On The Auction Boom, 96
catalogs, 97
Catherine, 86
Century of Progress Exposition, 89
Charles I, 16
Charlton Hall Galleries, 91
china, 85, 87
China Tea Trade, 90
Chippendale style, 84
Chippendale table, 30
Christie's, 16
classic, 109
classic automobile auctions, 109
Cohn, M.L., 109
collectibles auctions, 83
Collectors Journal, 31
commodity auctions, 118
computer network, 121
computer network auctions, 121
conventional auctions, 134
Corpus Juris Civilis, 14
correspondence courses, 71
Crisis In Industry, 25

D

Dana, Charles A., 18
Davis, W. Angus, 129
dealers, 57
DeBruhl, Col. Harold, 140
Delphi Computer Network, 58, 121
Department of Defense, 134
Depression glass, 87
Devine, Andy, 102
Dickens, Charles, 102
Didius Julianus, 15
Dorsey, Tommy, 105
Du Boulay, Anthony, 85
dumb bidding, 16
Dutch auction, 16
Dwight, John Sullivan, 19

E

East Aurora, New York, 39
Edison, Thomas, 105
Eggers, Bryan, 58
Ellenborough, Lord, 19
Empire style, 84
estate, 78

estate auctions, 126
estate sale, 78
Evening In The Hamlet, 23
exposition
    Century of Progress, 89

F

farm sales, 116
Fertile Crescent, 13
First World War, 21
folk art, 87
forced sales
    types of, 115
foreclosure, 116
Freeman, T.B., 18
fund raisers, 79
Funny Andy ferry boat, 48
furniture, 83
    Americana, 17

G

Gable, Clark, 104
General Services Administration, 132
General Videotex Corporation, 58, 121
Georgia guarantee, 65
gift auctions, 142
glassware, 87
going out of business auctions, 113
Goldberg, Rube, 36
government auctions
    other, 134
government surplus auctions, 132
Great Depression, 18, 21
group lot, 40
Grove, E.W., 92
Grove Park Inn, 92
GSA, 132
Guinness Book of World Records, 13, 108
Gutelius, Col. J.P., 20

H

Hagan, Col. Bill, 27, 74
Hamilton, Charles, 36, 56, 101, 104
Harding, Warren G., 106
Hawthorne, Nathaniel, 19
Henkels, Stan V., 18
Henly, E.H., 131
Henry, O., 95
Henry VII, 16
Hepplewhite style, 84
Herodotus, 13
High Lights on Auctioneering, 20
Hindman Settlement School, 88
history of auctions, 13
Hitler, Adolph, 108
Hollifield, Col. Gilbert, 70, 128
horses
    buying and selling, 138
Howard Grafton, 86

Hubbard, Elbert, 39
Hyers, Ed, 86

J

Jamison, Bessie, 127
Jenkins, Emyl, 10, 74
Jensen, Elizabeth Barret, 7
Jeromes and Darrow mantel clock, 91
Joel Sater's Antique News, 31
John C. Campbell Folk School, 88

K

Kennedy, John F., 101
Kennedy, Robert, 101
King, Col. Jerry, 64, 70, 71
King, Martin Luther, 101
Kirby, Thomas, 22
Kovel, Ralph, 56
Kovel, Terry, 56

L

Lancour, Harold, 17
Libby, Charles F., 18
lien sales, 115
Lincoln, Abraham, 104
liquidation
    voluntary, 116
livestock
    buying and selling, 137
livestock auctions, 136
Long, Col. Cameron, 6, 15, 68, 70
Long, Col. Lee, 70
Long, Col. Ronald, 29, 90
Looking Back Antiques, 86
lot
    box, 40
    group, 40
    multiple-piece, 40
Louis XIV, 30
Ludlow, E.H., 18
Lunt, Tom, 49

M

Macciesfield, 86
Madison, Guy, 102
Maine Antique Digest, 31
manuscript auctions, 101
McCormick, Cyrus, 105
McKay, George Leslie, 17
Mendenhall School of Auctioneering, 70
Metropolitan Bank, 22
Miller, Glenn, 105
Mills, P.L., 18
Missouri Auction School, 70
modem, 121
Morgan, Harry, 102
Morgan, Russ, 105
multiple-piece lot, 40
museums, 57

N

National Geographic, 76
Nazi Germany, 108
negotiated sales, 134
network
   computer, 121
New York *Sun*, 23

O

off-the-wall bid, 50
Old Cars Weekly, 110
on-line, 121
opening bid, 37
Orientalia, 85
outroper, 16

P

Paine, Thomas, 129
Park-Bernet Galleries, 22
Pemberton, Ebenezer, 17
Penland, Col. Doug, 27
Penland, Col. Johnny, 70, 91
Penny Cyclopedia, 20
Pertinax, 15
pewter, 9
Phelps, Claudia Lea, 90
pieces
   significant, 38
Pisgah Pottery, 85
Pitt, William, 105
practical car auctions, 110
Praetorian Guard, 15
Presley, Elvis, 105
preview period, 29
price guides, 57
Princess Grace, 109
provenance, 90
public sales, 134
publications, 57
puffing, 38
Pullman blanket, 18

Q

Queen Anne style, 84, 91
Queen Victoria, 22

R

Reagan, Ronald, 101
real estate auctions, 139
Regency style, 84

repossessions, 110
reserve
   auctions with, 33
   auctions without, 33
restrictions, 33
retail auctions, 142
Richards, Paul, 104
right of precedence, 116
Ripley, George, 18
Rookwood mug, 49
Rome, 13
Rookwood art pottery, 32
Rookwood vase, 6, 7
Roseville, 10, 11
Roseville Donatello bowl, 56
Roseville pot, 92
Roycroft Shops, 39
running up, 50

S

sales
   farm, 116
   lien, 115
   negotiated, 134
   public, 134
   sealed bid, 134
   spot-bid, 134
Sanders, George, 101, 102
schools
   auctioneering, 70
sealed bid sales, 134
Seely, Fred, 92
selling horses, 138
selling livestock, 137
Seney, George I., 22
Severus, General, 15
shutout bid, 42
signals
   bidding, 35
significant pieces, 38
Silo, James P., 18
Silvers, Col. Joe, 137
sleepers, 41
Sluder, Col. Jerry, 28
Smith-Hughes Act, 88
Sommerville, Robert, 18
Sotheby's, 16
spot-bid sales, 134
strategies

bidding, 35
Stuart family, 16
substitutions, 51

T

tactics
   bidding, 40
tag sale, 78
Tallulah Falls Industrial School, 88
Teapot Dome, 106
The Auctioneer, 69
The Elegant Auctioneers, 20, 21
The New American Cyclopedia, 18
Thomas, M., 18
Thomas, Moses, 22
Tiffany lamp, 90
Tiffany vase, 29
Tisdale, George, 92
tobacco auctions, 118
Towner, Wesley, 20
Train Tracks, 87
Truman, Harry S., 101
Twain, Mark, 29
types of auctions, 11
types of forced sales, 115

V

Vanderbilt, Commodore, 21
vintage, 109
voluntary liquidations, 116

W

Wagenvoord, James, 96, 136
Walsh, Carolyn, 87
Warhol, Andy, 105
Whitney, Eli, 105
Why You're Richer Than You Think,
   10
Wilde, Oscar, 75
William III, 16
Wilson, Mark, 30
Wolfe, Thomas, 25
Woods, Col. Thad, 4
World War I, 21

Y

Yesterday's Child, 89
Yesteryear, 31

Edited by Suzanne L. Cheatle

Other Bestsellers From TAB

☐ **ALL ABOUT LAMPS: CONSTRUCTION, REPAIR AND RESTORATION—Coggins**

You'll find step-by-step directions for making a wall lamp or a hanging lamp from wood, novelty lamps from PVC plumbing pipe, and designer lamps from acrylic or polyester resins. Shade projects range from needlepoint and fabric models to globes, balls, and tubular forms. There are suggestions for advanced projects, using salvaged and low-cost materials, and more! 192 pp., 196 illus. 7 × 10" Hardbound.

Paper $16.95   **Hard $24.95**
Book No. 2658

☐ **HOW TO TROUBLESHOOT AND REPAIR ANY SMALL GAS ENGINE**

Here's a time-, money-, and aggravation-saving sourcebook that covers the full range of two- and four-cycle gas engines from just about every major American manufacturer—from Briggs & Stratton, Clinton Kohler, Onan, OMC, and Tecumeh to West Bend, and others! With the expert advice and step-by-step instructions provided by master mechanic Dempsey, you'll be amazed at how easily you can solve almost any engine problem. 272 pp., 228 illus.

Paper $10.95   **Hard $18.95**
Book No. 1967

☐ **BUILDING WITH SALVAGED LUMBER**

Here are all the work-in-progress photos and step-by-step directions you need to turn lumber that's available FREE—even painted lumber studded with rusty nails—into beautiful, polished wood. Then you can use this wood to build furniture, panel, floor, build a room addition for under $100, or install expensive wood beams for less than $2 each! So find out how someone else's eyesores can become your goldmines. 272 pp., 122 illus. 7" × 10".

Paper $10.25   **Book No. 1597**

☐ **HOW TO REPAIR CLOCKS—Smith**

A complete guide to repairing and overhauling ANY clock—mechanical, electric, or electronic—antique or modern . . . even large pendulum-operated ones and cuckoo clocks. You'll learn how clocks are designed and how they work; get complete instructions on how to clean, repair, adjust, renovate, and dismantle all kinds of clocks, and how to put them back together. You name the problem; this modern handbook shows you how to fix it! 182 pp., 90 illus. Paperback.

Paper $8.95   **Book No. 1168**

☐ **UPHOLSTERY TECHNIQUES ILLUSTRATED—Gheen**

Here's an easy-to-follow, step-by-step guide to modern upholstery techniques that covers everything from stripping off old covers and padding to restoring and installing new foundations, stuffing, cushions, and covers. All the most up-to-date pro techniques are included along with lots of time- and money-saving "tricks-of-the-trade" not usually shared by professional upholsterers. 352 pp., 549 illus. 7" × 10". Hardbound.

Paper $16.95   **Hard $27.95**
Book No. 2602

☐ **FLEA MARKET TREASURE—D'Imperio**

Dan D'Imperio—recognized authority on flea market collectibles—gives you full descriptions of hundreds of different collectibles from depression glass to toys, from golden oak furniture to Tiffany lamps . . . complete with the most current market values. Discover what to look for when you're buying—or selling—a collectible . . . get the know-how you need to bag a bargain . . . even find out what buys to avoid. 336 pp., 299 illus. Hardbound.

Paper $9.95   **Hard $15.95**
Book No. 1738

☐ **SUCCESSFUL FLEA MARKETING SELLING**

Here's your introduction to an exciting new world of buying, selling, and trading flea market style. It's a look at the pleasures, the profits, and the possible pitfalls of flea marketing . . . all the hows, wheres, whens, and whats of successful buying *and* selling. Covers indoor and outdoor shows; antique and collectible markets; yard, garage, and tag sales . . . discusses dealing with new and used merchandise, even antiques and collectibles. 256 pp., 131 illus. Paperback.

Paper $9.95   **Book No. 1207**

☐ **HOW TO REPAIR OLD-TIME RADIOS**

A collector's guide to restoring and repairing antique radios, chock-full of vital data on testing, troubleshooting, and repairing old circuits and finding substitutes for obsolete and irreplaceable parts. Explains all the in's and out's of a bygone technology. Tubes, tube types, tube sockets, numbering systems, TRF receivers, superheterodyne receivers—they're all covered. Shows exactly how to get that old set into like-new working condition! 252 pp., 162 illus. Paperback.

Paper $8.95   **Book No. 1148**

*Prices subject to change without notice.

═══

Look for these and other TAB books at your local bookstore.

TAB BOOKS Inc.
P.O. Box 40
Blue Ridge Summit, PA 17214

Send for FREE TAB catalog describing over 1200 current titles in print.